HARVARD ECONOMIC STUDIES

Volume 157

The studies in this series are published under
the direction of the Department of Economics
of Harvard University. The department does not
assume responsibility for the views expressed.

Housing and Neighborhood Dynamics

A SIMULATION STUDY

John F. Kain and
William C. Apgar, Jr.

HARVARD UNIVERSITY PRESS

Cambridge, Massachusetts, and London, England   1985

Library of Congress Cataloging in Publication Data

Kain, John F.
    Housing and neighborhood dynamics.

    (Harvard economic studies ; v. 157)
    Bibliography: p.
    Includes index.
    1. Community development, Urban — United States.
2. Gentrification — United States.   II. Apgar, William C.
II. Title.   III. Series.
HN90.C6K35   1985   307'.14'0973   84-21725
ISBN 0-674-40930-2   (alk. paper)

Acknowledgments

This book draws on efforts, spanning more than a decade, to design, build, and use an operational computer simulation model of urban housing markets. The duration and extent of the project make it impossible to acknowledge all of those individuals who contributed to the effort.

While the authors designed and executed the particular program evaluations, the HUDS (Harvard Urban Development Simulation) model used for these evaluations is a close descendant of the NBER Urban Simulation Model. J. Royce Ginn, Gregory K. Ingram, and Herman B. Leonard made major contributions to the development of earlier versions of the urban simulation model. The development of the NBER model was made possible by support from the National Bureau of Economic Research. We owe a particular debt to John R. Meyer, former president of NBER, who provided both financial and intellectual assistance for our model-building efforts.

The major financial support for the urban simulation modeling project was provided by four Department of Housing and Urban Development contracts. Charles Haar, formerly Assistant Secretary of Housing and Urban Development, approved HUD's first grant to NBER for development of a prototype Urban Simulation Model. James Hoben, monitor for the contract, maintains his interest in our efforts to this day. Harold Finger, also a former Assistant Secretary of Housing Urban Development, approved the second HUD award to NBER for further model development and research on housing abandonment.

Shifting HUD priorities caused HUD to increase its funding of the project and to ask us to redirect our efforts toward consideration of the market impacts of housing allowance. Jerry Fitts, director of HUDS Experimental Housing Allowance Program, and Terrance Connell, his replacement, exhibited the understanding, flexibility, and firmness that were necessary to ensure completion of this complex modeling task.

Raymond Struyk, Deputy Assistant Secretary of HUD, approved the HUD contract for research on housing and neighborhood improvement programs. He, Howard Sumka, and George Mansfield provided numerous suggestions for improving the design of the model and devising specific housing and neighborhood improvement programs.

Elizabeth Foukal, Gary Anderson, and Mark Roberts worked as research assistants and programers on the project. Their energy and skill is reflected in many modifications that substantially enriched the model and its potential for policy research.

Romaine Adams, Paula Prior, and Lisa Brinkman typed numerous drafts and prepared the tables and charts. Marcia Fernald edited and in many instances extensively rewrote our prose with intellegence, good humor, and tact. Other secretarial services were provided by the Joint Center for Urban Studies from its unrestricted funds.

Contents

CONTENTS

Housing and
Neighborhood Dynamics

1 Introduction

Based on the results of a sophisticated computer simulation model of urban housing markets, this book assesses the likely consequences of spatially concentrated programs for housing and neighborhood improvement. A direct descendant of the Detroit Prototype of the NBER urban simulation model, the Harvard Urban Development Simulation (HUDS) model explicitly represents new construction, housing rehabilitation, the production and consumption of housing services, household moving decisions, and other determinants of neighborhood change. Unlike more aggregate models of urban development, the HUDS model has the capacity to identify how specific housing policies affect individual households as well as particular neighborhoods.

Though not identical to any single existing program, the Concentrated Housing Improvement Programs (CHIPs) evaluated in this book closely resemble numerous federal and locally funded programs that provide grants and below-market loans to low-income property owners in declining neighborhoods. Subsidy programs of this type generally attempt to achieve two somewhat incompatible objectives: to provide direct assistance to individual low-income property owners so that they can occupy better housing or reduce their housing cost burden, and to arrest neighborhood decline or encourage neighborhood revitalization. This broader social goal is often linked to the effort to reverse central-city decline by attracting more prosperous households to the upgraded neighborhoods.

The evaluation of the market impacts of the CHIP subsidies relies on a series of baseline and policy simulations for a housing market closely resembling the Chicago metropolitan area in 1960 to 1970. Since the program evaluations are no better than the model on which they are

1

based, this book explains the assumptions implicit in the HUDS model. The text chapters provide enough detail to permit readers primarily interested in the policy analyses to assess the methodology and to understand how the model represents the policies; a more technical discussion of model structure is presented in a series of appendixes.

Although the simulations focus on policies that induce owners to upgrade their properties and thus encourage revitalization of central-city neighborhoods, many of the findings of this book are relevant to a larger set of urban development issues. For example, the analysis of how housing rehabilitation subsidies affect the investment behavior of property owners in nearby neighborhoods provides valuable insights about the link between the initial subsidies and sustained neighborhood improvement. The results are also revealing about the extent to which CHIP subsidies would lead to the displacement of low-income residents and indirectly affect residents of nearby neighborhoods.

Neighborhood Revitalization and Public Policy

In the face of inadequate and uncertain funding, the politics of local community development programs tends to spread available money for housing rehabilitation and community development rather thinly among competing households and neighborhoods. This practice is most pronounced in communities where city council members are elected from wards or other geographically defined areas rather than at large. Federal officials and most housing market analysts argue that greater geographic concentration of community development funds will produce "spread effects," or improvements in nearby areas, and thus be more effective in combating neighborhood decline.

Policymakers and analysts also disagree about the goals of community development programs. Neighborhood revitalization and the effort to retain or attract middle- and high-income households back to the central city have long been major objectives of both the federal government and most municipal governments, but support for these policies has weakened in recent years as growing numbers of neighborhoods have been improved. Opponents of what has come to be known as "gentrification" fear that continued upgrading of central-city neighborhoods will entail significant social costs: low-income families will be forced to move, and the supply of affordable rental housing will be reduced.

Despite the long-standing debate over the efficacy of spatially targeted housing rehabilitation programs and the more recent intense political controversy about the effects of neighborhood revitalization, many of the beliefs about the proper design and likely impact of such programs remain unexamined. To be sure, there are numerous examples of what appear to be successful concentrated rehabilitation programs, where success is defined in terms of the well-being of the residents of subsidized buildings. On the other side, there are also many commentators who focus on the displacement of low- and moderate-income households from inner-city neighborhoods. In all instances, however, the assessments of specific community development efforts should — and in practice often fail to — identify which neighborhood changes would have occurred even without the policies.

Given the idiosyncratic nature of target neighborhoods and the diversity of local community development programs, it is exceedingly difficult to isolate policy-induced changes. The quantification of such effects requires a theoretically sound and empirically rich model of neighborhood dynamics that explicitly represents the determinants of housing supply and demand. In simplest terms, the analysis must identify and interpret the interactions among households, jobs, housing units, and public services. Although this is a well-accepted way to look at neighborhoods, the implications for neighborhood policy are still being assessed (Ahlbrandt, 1975; Downs, 1981). Because of the difficulty of measuring the quantity of housing supplied or demanded and of determining the price of comparable housing located in different neighborhoods, it is problematic to obtain even simple descriptions of the quantity of housing services consumed by specific groups of households. A recent survey article by Quigley (1979) makes a fine assessment of our current understanding of housing market dynamics.

Understanding the processes of housing investment and neighborhood change is further complicated by the many factors that influence how property owners and tenants adjust to changes in the housing market. Although Americans are highly mobile, many people develop strong attachments to their homes and neighborhoods. Economists often explain this attachment in terms of moving costs, noting that there are substantial expenditures of both money and time associated with selling or buying a home or searching for a suitable apartment. Urban sociologists, in contrast, emphasize the psychological costs of moving and the social ties that bind households to their neighborhoods. Whatever the cause, the high costs of mobility imply that households may be slow to adjust to changes in income, housing prices, or the changing characteristics of their neighborhoods (Quigley and Weinberg, 1977).

Adjustments in the housing stock in response to changing market conditions may be even slower. Changes in income, employment location, transportation costs, or the composition of the population alter the demand for specific types of housing in a neighborhood. Changes in the cost of capital, energy, and other operating inputs will also modify the profitability of maintaining or investing in specific types of structures in particular locations. Housing capital, however, is durable, difficult to modify, and even more difficult to move; as a result, housing investment is a complex process that depends on both short-term cost and demand factors and on longer-term expectations about neighborhood trends (Kain and Quigley, 1975).

Even a simple program of capital grants to low-income homeowners can trigger a complex set of direct and indirect impacts on the housing market. For example, spatially targeted capital grants could induce housing consumers to choose different types of structures and residential locations, cause a change in the production and investment decisions of some housing suppliers, and affect prices and the average quality of the housing in target neighborhoods. Moreover, any program that modifies supply, demand, or residential mobility may have largely unintended effects on the nonsubsidized residents of target neighborhoods or on the residents and property owners in other neighborhoods.

The political controversy over the issue of displacement has exacerbated the analytical difficulties of assessing the outcome of spatially concentrated programs for housing rehabilitation. Although there is little evidence that federal, state, or local community development programs have in themselves triggered the substantial upgrading of inner-city housing or the wave of condominium conversions occurring in many inner-city neighborhoods, the fear is legitimate that government programs could inadvertently reduce the supply of affordable housing or cause the displacement of low- and moderate-income households. A 1978 *Law Project Bulletin* criticizes federal involvement in such displacement; more balanced discussions are provided by Clay (1979) and James (1980). Analyzing the displacement issue requires, of course, a careful assessment of the likely effects of neighborhood revitalization — that is, the benefits and costs directly attributable to the process of upgrading — and of the changes that would have occurred in the absence of specific neighborhood programs. To the extent that concentrated rehabilitation programs have identifiable impacts on target neighborhoods, it must also be determined to what extent the effects of upgrading spill over to other neighborhoods in the metropolitan area.

Modeling Neighborhood Change

The HUDS model represents a variety of urban phenomena including changes in transportation, employment location, and population characteristics, but it is primarily a model of urban housing markets. Each year the model attempts to simulate the behavior of a large sample of households identified by income, race, age of head, number of persons, and employment status of head; dwelling units are distinguished by number of bedrooms, number of units in structure, amount of capital embodied in the structure, and the level of housing services each provides. The model also assigns households and dwelling units to one of two hundred residential neighborhoods in a typical standard metropolitan statistical area (SMSA), with each neighborhood characterized by five levels of average housing quality. To date, the HUDS model and its precursors have been used to investigate the structure and dynamics of metropolitan housing markets and to simulate the consequences of a limited number of housing policies. The model has been calibrated with varying success to the Detroit, Pittsburgh, and Chicago metropolitan areas and used to analyze housing abandonment and the likely effects of a universal housing allowance.

The modeling approach presented in this book differs from other empirical analyses of the effects of government policy on neighborhood dynamics. Numerous case studies seem to provide evidence that specific housing or neighborhood programs have produced various more or less desirable outcomes. The principal weakness of such case studies is the lack of a baseline. Without a baseline and a carefully designed assessment of what would have happened if the policy had not been introduced, case studies provide only limited insights into the extent to which a government program, as opposed to other market forces, actually caused or made a significant contribution to the observed changes.

Efforts to enhance the case study approach frequently involve the analysis of changes occurring in several neighborhoods over time, including both neighborhoods that have participated in particular programs and "control neighborhoods" that have not received governmental assistance. Multiple regression techniques and other quantitative methods have been used in an effort to distinguish program effects from changes in neighborhood conditions that are the result of market forces unrelated to the programs. Though studies of this type in principle could provide useful insights, the complexity of neighborhood and housing market dynamics has generally frustrated attempts to isolate program effects. Moreover, even when statistical studies demonstrate a correlation between various aspects of program design and neighborhood change, it often proves difficult to move from the correlation to an understanding of causal mechanisms or to generalize the findings to fit new situations.

The modeling approach presented in this book is an effort to expand

knowledge of the behavior of individual actors in urban housing markets, of the process of neighborhood change, and of the dynamics of the
metropolitan housing market. Because this effort provides a detailed
microanalytic explanation of how individuals and markets operate in
the absence of policy intervention, it is easier to understand how particular programs and specific program features affect these processes.
Moreover, by modeling in a general way neighborhood change and
housing market dynamics, the approach can be used to analyze specific
neighborhood or housing programs, as well as to make general assessments of how broad market forces affect the well-being of residents of
specific neighborhoods.

Based on data for the Chicago SMSA, the simulations describe the
likely effects of spatially targeted neighborhood and housing improvement programs. Chapter 2 describes the model and its theoretical and
empirical foundations. In chapter 3 the baseline simulations are reviewed and the ability of the model to capture the important elements of
housing market dynamics and neighborhood change is assessed. Chapter 4 describes the simulated neighborhood improvement programs
and discusses how the model represents the rehabilitation process. The
major findings of the simulations appear in chapters 5, 6, and 7. Finally,
chapter 8 summarizes the results and offers some concluding remarks
on future research directions. The appendixes are designed primarily
for readers interested in obtaining a more detailed description of the
design and calibration of the HUDS model.

2 The Harvard Urban Development Simulation Model

The Harvard Urban Development Simulation (HUDS) model is a direct descendant of the Detroit Prototype of the NBER urban simulation model (Ingram, Kain, and Ginn, 1972). The differences between HUDS and the Detroit Prototype are so extensive, however, that it is best to consider HUDS a completely new model. A second and substantially improved version of the NBER model was used to study the market effects of housing allowances as part of the Experimental Housing Allowance Program (EHAP) (Kain, Apgar, and Ginn, 1977; Kain and Apgar, 1977). Although much more similar to the version of the NBER model that was used to study housing allowances, HUDS also embodies major improvements in design and calibration that grew out of the program of research preceding the policy simulations described in this book (Kain and Apgar, 1979, 1980).

HUDS might be thought of as a third-generation computer simulation model of urban housing markets. As such, it is most similar in conception and purpose to the Urban Institute model developed by Frank de Leeuw, Raymond Struyk, and others at the Urban Institute (de Leeuw and Struyk, 1975; Marshall, 1976; Vanski, 1976; Struyk, Marshall and Ozanne, 1978). HUDS also resembles in some respects the Community Analysis Model (CAM) implemented at about the same time as the Urban Institute model and HUDS (Birch et al., 1974, 1977a). Appendix A contains a survey of the Urban Institute model, CAM, and earlier efforts to develop computer simulation models of housing markets and urban development.

This chapter presents a brief discussion of those aspects of HUDS that differentiate it both from other housing market simulation models and analytical models. The following chapter then considers a number of analytic issues related to the representation of concentrated housing improvement programs by HUDS.

Defining Housing Output

HUDS depicts housing as a multidimensional bundle of residential services that households must consume as an indivisible package at a particular location. Several economists have noted the importance of heterogeneity in understanding housing (Lancaster, 1966; Rosen, 1974; Kain and Quigley, 1975), but most analytical models of urban spatial structure nonetheless treat housing as a homogeneous commodity that can be represented by a continuous quantity, usually referred to as housing services (Muth, 1969; Olsen, 1969). An alternative approach used in analytical models is to assume that all housing attributes except land or residential space are separable and to include them as part of the composite good (Alonso, 1964; Solow, 1972, 1973).

Operationally, HUDS defines a bundle of residential services that consists of three types of housing attributes: structure type, neighborhood quality, and the quantity of structure services. The need to describe housing in this way, as shown in equation 2.1, results from particular features of housing, especially the nature of the underlying production relationships.

$$(2.1) \qquad\qquad B = f(S, N, Q)$$

where B = Bundle of housing services;
S = Structure type;
N = Neighborhood quality;
Q = Quantity of structure services.

Structure type embodies physical features of dwelling units that are difficult and expensive to modify and that appear to matter to housing consumers. Analytical models of urban housing markets ignore these characteristics by restricting their analyses to long-run equilibrium states, in which the heterogeneous, physical dimensions of housing adjust completely. We reject this view of housing markets. Indeed, we consider the durability of both residential and nonresidential structures, and of their associated infrastructure, to be one of the important features (if not the most important) of urban housing markets and of the process of urban growth and development (Harrison and Kain, 1977). HUDS fully accommodates this view.

Long-run equilibrium models unquestionably provide many useful insights into housing and urban land markets, yet there are many questions they cannot address meaningfully. Nonetheless, there is an understandable and seemingly irresistible temptation to extrapolate the findings of long-run equilibrium models to situations that do not satisfy their demanding assumptions. Unfortunately, most real-world situations fall into this category, and the answers provided by the model are often wrong, misleading, or irrelevant. We felt it was essential for HUDS, since it would be used to analyze housing and urban development policies, to represent explicitly the durability of housing capital and its impact on housing markets.

Empirical implementation of the notion that the characteristics of durable structures matter is fraught with practical difficulties. In particular, what aspects of housing capital consumers regard as important is imperfectly understood; still, there is reason to believe that structure type, lot size or plot coverage, and structure size are important in housing choices. These dimensions of individual dwelling units are difficult and expensive to alter — lot size may be the most difficult to change, dwelling unit size the easiest, and structure type probably intermediate.

The current version of HUDS represents ten types of structures defined in terms of type of dwelling unit (single-family, small multi-family, large multi-family), size (number of bedrooms), and lot size. Single-family homes may have zero to two, three, or four or more bedrooms. Units in multi-family structures may have zero to one or two or more bedrooms. Large-lot units are assumed to be built at 2.5 units per acre, small-lot units at 8 units per acre, small multi-family structures at 24 units per acre, and large multi-family structures at 32 units per acre. In combination with five neighborhood types, the ten structure types define fifty housing bundles. Each unit is also characterized by a continuous variable representing the quantity of structure services it supplies. HUDS thus achieves a much more detailed representation of housing services than any other analytical simulation model of urban housing markets, but the descriptions are much less detailed than those used in many empirical studies of housing (Kain and Quigley, 1972; Ball, 1973; King and Mieszkowski, 1973; King, 1975; Kain and Quigley, 1975; Dale-Johnson, 1982).

Although many empirical studies of house prices and of demand have documented the importance of neighborhood quality (Kain and Quigley, 1975; King, 1975; Freeman, 1979; Dale-Johnson, 1982), analytical models have generally ignored this dimension of housing, considering only those aspects of housing that are produced by competitive firms. A few analytical models have treated amenities, but these models provide few insights (for example, Polinsky and Shavell, 1978). Virtually everyone would agree that neighborhood quality is important to housing consumers and that real and imagined changes in it have important consequences for urban development; there is no consensus, however, about what neighborhood quality is or how it should be measured. Most housing analysts would include in the list of neighborhood quality indexes such variables as the socioeconomic characteristics of residents, the quality of the housing stock, and the range and quality of local public services, particularly schools. Unfortunately, no conceptual or empirical study convincingly documents the relative importance of these variables or how they influence the behavior of housing consumers. On the basis of our own empirical analyses, HUDS employs an index of average housing quality—that is, the average annual flow of housing services that model dwelling units supply in a particular neighborhood in a given year.

As with the measure of housing services used in most urban models —particularly those derived from Muth's (1969) formulation— model units in HUDS are assumed to supply structure services according to a production function involving both land and nonland factors (Muth, 1969). In contrast to long-run equilibrium models, however, HUDS allows different structure types to supply housing services that are heterogeneous and not directly comparable. Although these differences disappear in long-run equilibrium, we contend that they are important to housing consumers and may have a major impact on housing markets for periods of ten to twenty years or even longer. We do not expect structure services, in contrast to structure type and neighborhood quality, to earn large and persistent quasi-rents.

Workplace as a Determinant of Housing Choice

Like all analytical models of urban economies, HUDS postulates that workplace location plays a major role in the choice of residential location. In contrast to most analytical models, however, which assume that all employment (or all but an inconsequential number of local service jobs) is located in the central area, HUDS identifies twenty specific workplaces throughout the area. Nonetheless, HUDS relies heavily on the same theoretical notions as the analytical models: housing costs tend to decrease with distance from most workplaces, and households trade off the savings against the higher travel costs incurred (Alonso, 1964; Muth, 1969; Solow, 1973; Wheaton, 1977).

Gross prices are used in HUDS to represent these housing cost– travel cost trade-offs and their effect on housing and residential choices. The gross price of a particular housing bundle is the sum of the monthly rent for a particular dwelling, which varies by residence zone, and a particular household's monthly outlays for the journey to work, which depend on residence location, workplace location, and household income. As equation 2.2 reveals, journey-to-work costs include both the out-of-pocket costs of commuting and time costs.

(2.2) $$GP_{khj} = R_{ki} + 0.4W_h M_{ij} + cD_{ij}$$

where GP = Gross price;
R = Monthly rent;
W = Hourly wage of the primary wage earner in cents per minute;
M = Minutes per month required to commute from workplace j to residence zone i by the least cost mode;
D = Highway distance from workplace j to residence zone;
c = Out-of-pocket costs per mile for the lowest cost mode;
k = Bundle type;
h = Household type;
j = Workplace;
i = Residence zone.

Although gross price would ideally include the journey-to-work costs of all employed household members and perhaps the cost of some other predictable types of trips, HUDS calculates only the commuting costs of primary workers. For black households, HUDS also adds a discrimination markup to represent the higher search costs incurred in obtaining housing in all-white neighborhoods far from the ghetto (Courant, 1978).

Gross prices influence choices both of housing bundle and of residential location. In each simulation year, HUDS calculates a minimum gross price for each of the fifty housing bundles and uses these prices in econometrically estimated submarket demand equations. The multinomial logit equations assign each model household participating in the housing market to a particular housing bundle according to its preference (represented by family size, age of head, and race), income, and the relative minimum gross prices of all fifty bundles. Since each of the housing bundles is assumed to be homogeneous with respect to preferences, each household will locate in the residence zone where it can obtain its utility-maximizing housing bundle at the lowest gross price. Spatial competition among model households for units in the various residence zones thus has a central role in HUDS, as it does in most analytical urban economic models.

Housing Capital and the Production of Housing Services

Emphasis on the durability and heterogeneity of housing services and the role of neighborhood quality means that HUDS must also treat housing capital and investment in detail. In contrast to other housing market models, HUDS distinguishes among various kinds of housing capital. In HUDS, as in the real world, consumers do not consider a four-bedroom, single-family unit on a large lot a perfect substitute for an efficiency apartment in a large multi-family structure, even if the quantity of structure services supplied and the market rents of both units are identical. Demand for each of the ten structure types depends on their relative minimum gross prices.

The owner of a dwelling unit can convert it to another structure type at some capital cost. The difficulty and cost of such a conversion depends, of course, on how similar the current and desired structure types are. It is easy, for example, to add a bedroom to a single-family home, but it is both difficult and expensive to convert an efficiency apartment in a twenty-unit building to a four-bedroom, single-family unit. As a result, conversions involving the addition of bedrooms to single-family units are relatively common both in model simulations and in the real world, while conversions of efficiency apartments in large multi-family buildings to four-bedroom, large-lot, single-family homes are exceedingly rare. These distinctions, although they may not be important to the evaluation of all policies, are crucial to many.

The lack of substitution of housing capital in the production of structure services also applies to housing located in neighborhoods of different quality. Many people would consider a four-bedroom, large-lot, single-family home in a high-quality neighborhood quite different from the same structure located in a low-quality neighborhood. These submarkets are not unrelated, however. Again, the demand for a particular structure type in each of the five neighborhood categories depends on the relative minimum gross price of units in each residence zone. Unlike structure type, however, neighborhood quality is not a dimension of housing that individual property owners can change independently. Changes in neighborhood quality depend on the combined locational decisions of hundreds of thousands of households in each metropolitan housing market and on the collective investment and housing production decisions of hundreds of property owners in a particular neighborhood. As in the real world, moreover, the adjustment lags in HUDS are substantial.

Because many kinds of market behavior are due to differences in the durability of housing capital, HUDS incorporates two types of housing capital that depreciate at different rates. As its name suggests, structure capital consists of the more durable components of each dwelling unit —for example, its foundation, load-bearing walls, and other features that are difficult to change. Maintenance capital, in contrast, represents those components of housing capital that must be replaced at frequent intervals, such as appliances, fixtures, and paint.

In HUDS, three construction types represent the effect of structure capital on the production of structure services. Dwellings of the best construction type require 15 percent fewer units of maintenance capital and operating inputs to produce a given quantity of structure services than those of the intermediate construction type, which require 15 percent fewer units than those of the lowest construction type. One additional feature of structure capital in HUDS deserves mention. Even if a property owner pursues a "good-as-new" maintenance policy, such investments can offset only three-fourths of the annual depreciation of structure capital in each dwelling; the amount of structure capital declines steadily until the unit becomes a lower construction type. At that point, the property owner must decide whether to incur the higher annual costs of producing structure services or to make the large capital expenditures necessary to upgrade the unit to its former construction type. Thus, building owners can improve construction type only by undertaking major renovations.

Investments in maintenance and structure capital are subject to other constraints. The amount that a property owner can invest in a particular year depends on the cash flow the building generates and on current and anticipated levels of neighborhood quality. The level of operating inputs can be varied, unlike additions to maintenance and structure capital, within a given year. This year's additions to both maintenance and structure capital, however, affect the level of operating inputs required to produce a given quantity of structure services in subsequent years.

The Role of Expectations and Neighborhood Quality

Neighborhood quality enters directly into the utility function of model households and is included in the definition of housing bundles. Since most households highly value neighborhood quality, its consumption tends to increase with income. The spatial distribution of neighborhood quality therefore will have a major impact on the location decisions of households of different income levels.

Current and anticipated levels of neighborhood quality affect the decisions of property owners to maintain and improve their buildings, the decisions of developers to build new units of various types, and land values. HUDS therefore incorporates an explicit expectations framework that annually projects neighborhood quality for each of approximately two hundred model neighborhoods, as well as rents for some ten thousand actual and hypothetical bundles, for several years into the future. Property owners and developers are assumed to base their projections of future neighborhood quality and of rents on historical trends and on a sense of the long-run supply price of producing both structures and structure services. Using these projections, HUDS then calculates the expected profitability of constructing or converting a structure in a particular residence zone.

In the current version of HUDS, the average quality of units in each residence zone (the average quantity of structure services) is used to represent the externalities that affect investment and production decisions. Our conviction that spatial competition and neighborhood externalities have important, perhaps decisive, effects both on the demand of housing consumers and on the investment and housing production decisions of property owners accounts for the relatively large number of residence zones used in HUDS. A common reaction to HUDS has been that it is too disaggregate and contains too much spatial and other detail. Our concern is the opposite: the model may have too little detail to correctly represent important features of the housing market. We are more convinced than ever that to analyze properly these effects requires the definition of a relatively large number of homogeneous residence areas. Fortunately, there is no practical limit on the amount of spatial detail that can be included in the model. Additional geographic identifiers, representing various levels of geographic aggregation, could be appended to each model dwelling unit. Since HUDS maintains information on between 72,000 and 84,000 individual dwelling units, the behavior of housing suppliers could be made to depend on the characteristics of adjacent units, of other units in the same block, of the micro-neighborhood, and of the political jurisdiction.

The Role of Racial Discrimination

Econometric analyses by Kain and Quigley (1975) and Straszheim (1973, 1975) demonstrate that housing market discrimination restricts the range of housing opportunities available to black families. HUDS, therefore, includes different submarket demand equations for black and white households. In addition, HUDS uses discrimination markups to represent the higher search costs blacks encounter in seeking housing in white neighborhoods. As Courant (1978) has shown, these higher search costs account in part for existing patterns of racial segregation and for the fact that black households tend to pay more than white households for comparable units.

Since discrimination markups enter into the calculation of both gross prices and perceived transportation costs, they affect the bundle choices of black households as well as their residential location decisions. The representation of racial discrimination and segregation in HUDS is relatively crude, but the model appears to account for most of the important ways in which racial discrimination affects blacks and the behavior of urban housing markets. The modeling of racial discrimination and particularly of racial transition, however, would clearly be improved by using smaller, more homogeneous residence zones. Analyses by Schelling (1972) and Vandel and Harrison (1976) suggest the importance of various kinds of dynamics that are not currently well represented in HUDS.

Determination of Bundle Rents and Land Values

The representation of housing as bundles of services greatly complicates the problem of estimating market rents and property values. By assuming that housing services are homogeneous and unidimensional, analytical models of urban housing markets largely avoid these difficulties; they need only obtain a single price schedule which — given sufficient simplifying assumptions, such as that all employment is located in the central business district — yields prices that decline monotonically with distance from the center. More complicated treatments allow for some outlying employment centers and may produce a somewhat more complicated surface (Muth, 1969).

Empirical studies of urban housing markets, in contrast, tend to represent housing as a bundle of attributes and to estimate individual attribute prices (Kain and Quigley, 1975; Schnare and Struyk, 1976; Dale-Johnson, 1982). The treatment of each of the fifty housing bundles as independent but linked housing submarkets reflects the assumption that consumers regard many of these bundles as quite different and that the durability of housing capital and the nonmarket production of neighborhood quality create the necessary conditions for large and persistent quasi-rents. The market clearing sector of HUDS is thus designed with the expectations that both the structure type and neighborhood type (quality) will earn quasi-rents. Equation 2.3 represents the housing bundle price functions used in the current version of the model.

(2.3) $$R_{kqi} = B_k + L_{ki} + r_{qi}$$

where R = Total rent for housing services;
   B = Quasi-rent for structure type and neighborhood;
   L = Location rent;
   r = Rent per unit of structure services;
   k = Housing bundle type;
   q = Actual quantity of structure services supplied by a
      particular dwelling unit;
   i = Residence zone.

The specification of the bundle rent equation has several implications. First, the total rental payment for a particular dwelling unit is the sum of a bundle-specific quasi-rent, a shadow price or location rent that varies by residence zone for each bundle, and a structure services rent that depends on both the quantity of structure services consumed and the residence zone. Second, total bundle rents vary by both bundle type and residence zone. Third, the rent per unit of structure services varies from one residence zone to another and depends on the quantity of structure services supplied; this feature of the model thus permits the price of structure services within a neighborhood to differ from the long-run equilibrium cost of producing structure services.

Estimating bundle rents is a two-step procedure. Exploiting the assumption that the market for housing bundles may be represented as a series of independent but linked housing submarkets, HUDS first uses a linear programming algorithm of the transportation type to simulate spatial competition among those households participating in each of the fifty submarkets. The number of available units of a particular bundle type in each residence zone in a given year was previously determined: it is equal to the sum of existing units vacated during the year by intra-metropolitan movers, out-migrants, and households that cease to exist for a variety of reasons, and of new units of each type produced by new construction, structure transformations, and neighborhood change (neighborhood change has a particularly pronounced effect on the supply of units of each bundle type). The model then assigns model households with particular workplaces to particular residence zones and computes shadow prices for the dwelling units in each neighborhood. Shadow prices, which are the savings in total transport costs that would result from providing another unit of a particular type in a particular zone, indicate how much consumers would be willing to pay to live in this area rather than another. Shadow prices are not considered equilibrium market rents; HUDS uses them only as price signals in an adaptive expectations framework.

To obtain the total rent for a particular type of housing bundle in a particular residence zone, a bundle quasi-rent must be added. In long-run equilibrium the bundle rent is the annual rental payment for the capital required to produce the housing bundle in a specific location; in any given year, however, the quasi-rent may be higher or lower than that amount. The long-run equilibrium cost of producing a particular bundle consists of the construction cost for that structure type plus the value of the land. The current version of HUDS includes a feature that permits construction cost to vary by location, but the simulations described in this book assume that construction cost is constant throughout the metropolitan area. Land values, however, vary from one residence zone to another, depending on both the zones' accessibility to employment and neighborhood quality. Land values for a particular type of housing bundle also include a premium for structure type that represents the effects of zoning and other land use controls.

The quasi-rents associated with neighborhood quality do not have as clear an interpretation in long-run equilibrium. As we have noted, neighborhood quality is a composite good produced by the individual locations of many thousands of households, the investment and housing production decisions of all property owners in a particular neighborhood, and the composition and quality of local public services. Although no theoretical model provides a satisfactory explanation of how these goods are supplied, both casual observation and most systematic empirical studies suggest that quasi-rents for neighborhood quality are quite large (Kain and Quigley, 1975; Grether and Mieszkowski, 1978; Dale-Johnson, 1982).

In the HUDS model, exogenously supplied start-of-decade neighborhood quality markups for each bundle type are increased or decreased at the end of each simulation year according to the extent of marketwide excess supply and demand for the particular bundle type. The magnitude of the excess supply or demand in turn depends on the number of households assigned to a specific housing submarket, on the number and types of units vacated by movers and dissolved households, and on the production of new units by converters and builders. The bundle quasi-rent for a particular bundle in each year, then, is the sum of the previous year's quasi-rent plus an increment or decrement that reflects the extent of the current year's marketwide excess supply or demand for that bundle.

Structure services rents, the third component of total market rents, are computed by multiplying the price per unit of structure services by the quantity supplied by each dwelling unit. The price of structure services varies with the amount supplied, which is determined for each neighborhood by a mini-market clearing algorithm. The price of structure services in each neighborhood depends on the demand for structure services by households assigned to that neighborhood by the submarket linear programming algorithm and on production costs specific to the dwelling unit. In contrast to the situation with quasi-rents for structure type and neighborhood quality, differences in the price of structure services across residence zones are likely to be small and transitory. Since structure capital — and, even more so, maintenance capital — can easily be added to individual dwelling units, any significant quasi-rents and profits from producing larger quantities of structure services should quickly disappear as the owners of other buildings in the neighborhood respond to the higher rents.

HUDS as a Computer Model

As a microanalytic simulation model, HUDS owes a substantial intellectual debt to Guy Orcutt (1957, 1960) and his collaborators (Orcutt et al., 1961, 1976). In the course of a simulation year, HUDS executes a series of seventeen behavioral submodels that represent the activities of 72,000 to 84,000 sample households and 35,000 to 40,000 housing suppliers in Chicago. As figure 2.1 indicates, the seventeen submodels are grouped into three sectors: Demand, Supply, and Market. The Demand Sector of the model represents changes in the level and mix of employment at each of several workplaces; decisions of individual households to move; their choices of housing bundles and residence locations; and their decisions to own or rent housing. The several Supply submodels simulate the production of housing services by individual property owners and owner-occupants; changes in the amounts of maintenance and structure capital embodied in existing structures; alterations in the size and configuration of individual structures through additions or subdivisions; and the construction of new structures on vacant land. The Market Sector assigns households with specific workplace locations to available units in specific residence zones; calculates the market rents for each type of housing bundle in each residence zone; and determines the quantities of structure services consumed by each household and the rents paid for them. In general, housing prices are represented by monthly market rents in the case of rental units and by imputed monthly rents for owner-occupied units.

To facilitate data storage and processing, HUDS employs three distinct zonal systems. The smallest geographic areas in the Chicago simulations are the 198 residence zones, aggregates of census tracts of simi-

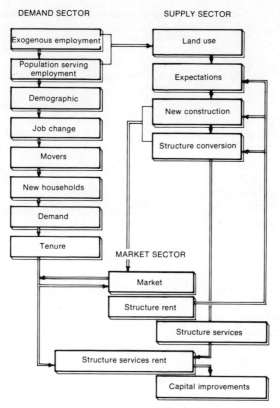

DEMAND SECTOR

SUPPLY SECTOR

Exogenous employment

Population serving employment

Demographic

Job change

Movers

New households

Demand

Tenure

Land use

Expectations

New construction

Structure conversion

MARKET SECTOR

Market

Structure rent

Structure services

Structure services rent

Capital improvements

Figure 2.1. Sequence of major behavior submodels included in the HUDS model

lar neighborhood quality located within each of fifty-eight transit districts. The census tracts constituting each residence zone do not have to be contiguous, but they must be located within the same transit district. Transit districts play an especially important role in the submarket linear programming problems; in combination with the twenty workplace zones (aggregates of the fifty-eight transit districts), they define the transport cost matrix used in calculating gross prices.

Characteristics of households and dwelling units are stored in the Basic List. For the simulations described in later chapters, the Basic List contains between 72,000 and 84,000 occupied dwelling units, with each sample unit representing twenty-five actual ones. As table 2.1 shows, each dwelling unit is classified as one of fifty housing bundle types, defined by ten types of structure and five levels of neighborhood qual-

Table 2.1. Household and dwelling unit information included on the Basic List

Characteristics	Notation	Number of categories
Household		
Income	HY	Continuous, 6
Race of household head	HR	2
Age of household head	HA	Continuous, 3
Family size	HF	Continuous, 4
Tenure	HT	2
Industry of primary worker	HI	11
Occupation of primary worker	HO	3
Labor force status of primary worker	HL	3
Workplace zone	J	20
Years lived at current address	HD	31
Dwelling unit and structure		
Structure type	S	10
Neighborhood quality	N	Continuous, 5
Housing bundle type $(S \times N)$	K	50
Structure services	Q	Continuous, 5
Maintenance capital	MC	Continuous
Structure capital	SC	Continuous
Construction type	CT	3
Structure rent	KR	Continuous
Structure services rent	QR	Continuous, 4
Location rent	LR	Continuous
Residence zone	I	200

ity. Each housing bundle produces a quantity of structure services, represented either as a continuous variable or as one of four levels of structure services. Dwelling units are also described in terms of quantities of maintenance capital and structure capital. The quantity of structure capital embodied in each building in turn defines the construction type.

A simulation year begins as the Exogenous Employment Submodel introduces exogenous changes in the level and composition of export and regional service employment in each of the twenty work zones. The Population Serving Employment Submodel then calculates endogenous changes in population-serving employment by work zone in response to changes in incomes, resident population, and export employment in each residence/workplace zone. The exogenous estimates of export and regional service employment changes are then combined with the endogenous changes in population-serving employment to provide projections of total job growth or decline in each workplace zone by industry. Using a labor force requirements table, estimates for each of eleven industries are then converted to levels of primary employment in three occupational groups.

After obtaining estimates of the number of primary jobs by industry and occupation for each workplace, HUDS completes a number of parallel calculations for each household and dwelling unit on the Basic List at the start of the simulation period. Those submodels that perform operations on sample households belong to the Demand Sector of the model; those that operate on individual dwelling units belong to the Supply Sector. Submodels that match specific households to specific units or determine rents and housing values — for example, the Market, Structure Rent, and Structure Services Rent submodels — function in the Market Sector.

Computer time and the costs of processing the Basic List were major factors in the design of HUDS. In particular, the desirability of processing the Basic List only once during each simulation period strongly influenced the overlay structure of the model and the sequence of operations. The Basic List is maintained in disc storage, and a comprehensive subroutine that integrates the operations of the submodels carries out all list operations simultaneously. The Basic List Subroutine reads a block of records from the disc and performs a number of calculations relating to activities in both the current and previous periods for each record. For example, while the Basic List Subroutine is changing the age of the household head and the household's size and income to begin a new year's simulation, it is also calculating capital investments and the production of structure services that pertain to supply decisions made in the previous period.

The Demand Sector

Basic List operations in the Demand Sector begin with the Demographic Submodel's simulation of the aging of each household head and the changes in household size and income. Changes in the age of household head and family size variables together represent changes in life cycle, which is an important determinant both of moving decisions and of the demand for particular types of housing bundles. Life cycle changes are entirely endogenous and are computed from simple probability matrices that remain constant over the decade. Simulated changes in household income by age of head and race correspond to those actually observed in the Chicago metropolitan area during the decade 1960–

1970. This portion of the Demographic Submodel is one of several components of HUDS that convert exogenous, aggregate projections to changes in individual household or dwelling unit attributes.

The Job Change Submodel, the second of the Demand Sector submodels included in the Basic List Subroutine, simulates the labor market activities of primary workers. Specifically, the submodel determines whether employed primary workers will or will not remain in their current jobs. For those changing work status, it simulates a local job search that produces either a period of unemployment or a new job in a specific industry, occupation, and work zone. In the case of primary workers who are unemployed at the start of the simulation period, the submodel simulates a similar job search that results either in an assignment to a particular industry, occupation, and workplace or in the worker's removal from the labor force.

The Movers Submodel is the third component of the Demand Sector to process the Basic List. Using information provided by the Demographic and Job Change submodels and other household-specific data such as tenure (own/rent) and duration of occupancy, it determines whether a specific household will vacate its unit and seek other housing during the period, either within or outside the metropolitan area. Households identified as intrametropolitan movers are placed on the Demand List in anticipation of their processing by the Demand Submodel; the units vacated by these households are retained on the Basic List and also placed on the Available Units List.

The New Households Submodel, the final Demand Sector submodel included in the Basic List Subroutine, simulates in-migration as well as formation of new households. Age and race of the household head and family size are assigned to these households in such a way that this period's aggregate SMSA population characteristics are consistent with the actual 1960–1970 Chicago distributions for both the baseline and policy simulations. Both in-migrants and new households are placed on the Demand List.

The next two submodels included in the Demand Sector simulate the housing bundle and tenure choices of 12,000 to 18,000 sample households in each period. The Demand Submodel assigns each household on the Demand List to one of the fifty housing bundles, defined by ten structure types and five neighborhood categories. The ten structure types are classified by structure size (single-family units, and large and small multi-family units); by dwelling unit size (number of bedrooms); and by small and large lot sizes, in the case of single-family units. Neighborhood type relates to the average quality of dwellings in each residence zone.

A series of submarket demand equations, econometrically estimated for each of the ninety-six household types defined by life cycle, income, and race of the household head, determine the assignment of specific households to particular housing bundles. The probability that a household type will choose a particular housing bundle depends on the minimum gross price of each of the fifty bundles and its relative share of the available units. The supply of available units consists of those vacated during the period by intrametropolitan movers, out-migrants, and discontinued households, plus units provided by structure conversions and new construction.

After the Demand Submodel has assigned each household on the Demand List to one of the housing bundles, the Tenure Submodel determines whether the household will own or rent its unit. The Tenure Submodel is based on a simple probability matrix that makes the decision to own or rent depend on the household's prior tenure, its current bundle choice, its current income, and the age of its head. After all households are assigned tenure status, the Demand List is again ordered by bundle type, workplace, income category, and race for subsequent use in the Market Submodel. At the same time, the households on the Demand List are summarized in a demand matrix defined in terms of bundle type, workplace, race, and income class.

The Supply Sector

The current version of HUDS has an exact land use accounting system. All developed land is classified according to use: nonresidential or commercial; single-family structures with large or small lots; and large or small multi-family structures. Undeveloped land suitable for development is assigned to the same classifications and is assumed to have appropriate zoning. Land unsuitable for development includes areas with unfavorable topographic features or soil conditions as well as land reserved for parks or other open spaces.

The principal function of the Land Use Submodel is to adjust the supplies of each type of land in each zone to reflect last period's new construction and demolition activities and this period's demand for industrial and commercial land. A series of land absorption coefficients for each industry are used to calculate the land required for employment expansion in each residence zone. The Land Use Submodel in the current version of HUDS is programmed to allocate the necessary land either from the vacant supply or by demolition of the least valuable residential structures. The nonresidential portion of the submodel is not used for the simulations, however, because of a lack of sufficient data.

Decisions to build a new residential structure, to convert an existing building to another structure type, or to undertake major renovations of an existing structure involve major capital outlays that commit the property owner for years and even decades. The Expectations Submodel provides projections of future rents and neighborhood quality that the several Supply Sector submodels use in simulating housing investment decisions. The Expectations Submodel also calculates a series of demand targets for use by the New Construction and Structure Conversion submodels in determining the number of each type of project to initiate. Demand targets for each structure type are based on long-run projections of population, incomes, and rents, modified by current rents and vacancies and recent changes.

The New Construction Submodel determines the profitability of building each type of structure in each residence zone. For the CHIP simulations, the model considers 1,980 distinct construction activities during each period. The most profitable of these potential supply activities are placed on a New Construction List, to be compared with the most profitable structure conversion activities producing the same structure types.

The Structure Conversion Submodel, the first Supply Sector submodel to process the Basic List, is quite similar to the New Construction Submodel. The principal difference is that the Structure Conversion Submodel uses existing structures as inputs, rather than vacant land, to produce new housing units. Structure conversions, which involve changes in the most basic, most durable characteristics of buildings, are the least common type of supply activity. Even so, all rental structures are considered for conversion annually, and owner-occupied structures are reviewed every fourth year.

To determine the profitability of conversions, the submodel calculates the net present value of future rents, minus operating and maintenance costs for the expected life of the structure, and then compares this present value estimate to the sum of the existing structure's current market value and its conversion costs. After processing the Basic List, the submodel places the most profitable potential conversion projects on the Structure Conversion List, which is then merged with the New Construction List; then the composite list is again ordered from the most to the least profitable. The Structure Conversion Submodel selects projects from the composite list on the basis of profitability until the model's demand targets for the current period are satisfied. These structures, however, are not considered available for consumption; the model assumes that completion takes a minimum of two years, with larger and more complex structures requiring more time.

The second Supply Sector submodel to process the Basic List, the Structure Services Submodel, operates after the Market Submodel has assigned particular households from the Demand List to particular dwellings on the Available Units List. It actually performs its calculations at the start of the next period, even though they pertain to the current period. Structure services are produced using varying combinations of operating inputs and maintenance capital; construction type acts as an efficiency parameter, with better construction types requiring fewer units of operating inputs and maintenance capital. The Structure Services Submodel is essentially a production function that determines the least-cost method of producing each quantity of structure services and derives a marginal cost curve for each unit. Since all units of multi-family structures are assumed to have the same quantities of maintenance capital and the same construction type, they all have the same marginal cost curve. The Structure Services Submodel operates annually for all dwelling units in rental buildings, including units occupied by resident landlords of multi-family structures. For owner-occupants of single-family units, the quantities of structure services and capital improvements are determined simultaneously when a new owner moves in and every four years thereafter.

The Capital Improvements Submodel, the final Supply Sector submodel to process the Basic List, calculates the appropriate rates of investment and disinvestment for every existing structure. The model recognizes two kinds of embodied capital: structure capital and maintenance capital. The first of these consists of the most durable elements of the structure and determines structure type and construction type. In new structures, construction type refers to the quality of construction for a dwelling unit of a given size, defined by the number of bedrooms; it includes the quality of interior and exterior finishing, the architectural distinction of the unit, and the unit's spaciousness or average room size. For a given construction type, the quantity of structure capital varies by structure type; that is, large single-family units require more capital than small ones, and low-rise, multi-family units require less than single-family units of the same size.

Structure capital in the simulations is assumed to depreciate at 4.5 percent a year; only two-thirds of this amount can be offset by annual maintenance investments that have first priority on any income from the structure. Consequently, the construction type of existing structures is determined by the original quality of construction, the building's age, and the owner's maintenance policies. Even if the property owner pursues a good-as-new investment policy, obsolescence will eventually reduce the quantity of structure capital in the building so much that the building will be reclassified as a lower construction type. At this point the property owner can upgrade the construction type only by making major renovations, the cost of which is affected by the quantities of structure and maintenance capital embodied in the structure at that time.

Although it does not appear in the submarket demand equations, construction type is important because it strongly influences the quantities of maintenance capital and operating inputs required to produce various quantities of structure services. In deciding whether to upgrade the construction type of an existing building, the Capital Improvements Submodel calculates the savings in annual expenditures for operating inputs and maintenance capital for the current level of structure services and then discounts these savings over ten years. If the discounted savings exceed the capital investment required to upgrade the construction type, the property owner considers making the improvements. The final determination, however, depends on whether current and projected neighborhood quality justify the investment. Calculations relating to the desirability of changes in construction type are made for rental structures every year and for owner-occupied, single-family units every fourth year.

The final investment decisions that the Capital Improvements Submodel simulates are calculations of annual investment or disinvestment in maintenance capital. For rental units, the Capital Improvements Submodel first determines the optimal quantity of maintenance capital for each structure, which depends on the level of structure services currently being produced. If the current stock of maintenance capital is less than the optimal quantity, the Capital Improvements Submodel adds maintenance capital subject to a cash flow constraint, based on the structure's rental income in the previous year, its fixed costs, and its operating outlays. If the structure has more than the optimal quantity of maintenance capital, the Capital Improvements Submodel allows depreciation to occur, up to the maximum of 9 percent a year.

In the case of owner-occupied, single-family units, the Capital Improvements Submodel calculates the structure's optimal capital stock only every four years or when a new household occupies the unit. At that time, the submodel provides the exact quantity of maintenance capital required to reach the optimal level if the structure has less than that amount, or reduces the level of maintenance capital if it has too much.

The Market Sector

Three of the seventeen submodels — the Market, Structure Rent, and
Structure Services Rent submodels — belong to the Market Sector of
the model. All three submodels match households from the Demand
List to vacant units on the Available Units List, or simulate the competition among households for particular housing bundles or for structure
services.

Once the Demand Submodel assigns specific housing bundle types to
specific households, the Market Submodel solves a linear programming
algorithm for each of the fifty housing submarkets. These linear programming problems, which minimize total accessibility costs for each
workplace, simulate the spatial competition among households with
primary workers employed at the twenty workplaces represented in the
model. Accessibility costs consist of transportation outlays plus the discrimination markups incurred by black households and premiums that
reflect accessibility and neighborhood quality. Transportation costs
vary by residence zone, household income, and workplace location;
discrimination markups depend only upon residence zone and, of
course, race.

The linear programming solutions produce estimates of so-called
shadow prices for each residence zone. Shadow prices indicate how
much accessibility costs would be reduced by the addition of one dwelling unit to a particular zone after the households have been reassigned
in a way that once again minimizes aggregate accessibility costs. In the
current version of the model, shadow prices are interpreted as location
rents (the savings afforded by residing in that zone as opposed to the
next best alternative). The Structure Services Rent Submodel estimates
current market rents by adding to this period's location rent an areawide quasi-rent for a particular housing bundle — that is, the weighted
average of the current period's shadow price and the previous period's
location rent. The resulting estimates of market rents by housing bundle and residence zone are used in the next period by the Demand
Submodel to calculate gross prices and by the Expectations Submodel to
project future rental incomes.

The Structure Services Rent Submodel, the final submodel included
in the Market Sector, determines the quantities of structure services
actually supplied during the period and the market rents paid for them.
These quantities are derived from information on the assignment of
specific households to particular dwelling units and from the short-run
marginal cost curves for each dwelling unit. Like the Structure Services

and Capital Improvements submodels, this operation is actually performed as part of the Basic List Subroutine at the start of the next simulation period. And like the Supply submodels that process the Basic List, the Structure Services Rent Submodel performs calculations for owner-occupied, single-family units every fourth year or when a new owner moves into the structure, and annually for all other bundle types.

For all types of units, the quantity and price of structure services are determined by the intersection of the occupant's structure services demand curve and the unit's short-run marginal cost curve, obtained from the Structure Services Rent Submodel. The occupant's demand curve depends on household income, tenure, and last year's rent for structure services for the same type of housing bundle in the same residence zone.

3 Simulated and Actual Housing Market Characteristics

Our analyses of concentrated housing and neighborhood improvement programs require a baseline simulation for a region approximating the Chicago metropolitan area during the decade 1960–1970. Because of time and money constraints, the two metropolitan areas used in previous housing allowance analyses, Pittsburgh and Chicago, were the only feasible candidates for sites. Chicago has a more diverse economic base than Pittsburgh and is more representative of northern and eastern metropolitan areas (Pittsburgh, for example, is one of only two metropolitan areas in the United States that lost population between 1960 and 1970); for these reasons Chicago was chosen. Basing the simulations on a more recent period would have had some advantages, of course, but the availability of sufficient data to develop a good baseline was the decisive consideration.

Chicago in 1960 was the nation's third largest metropolitan area, with a population over 6.2 million. Between 1960 and 1970 the metropolitan area population grew by 12.2 percent and its suburban population by 35.3 percent; the central-city population, however, decreased by more than 5 percent. As in most other northern and eastern cities, rapid increases in the city's black population accompanied central-city decline: constituting 23 percent of Chicago's central-city population in 1960, black households accounted for 33 percent ten years later.

Employment Patterns

Between 1960 and 1970, employment in the metropolitan area expanded by nearly 14 percent. Most of the growth occurred in industries classified as "regional service employment"; this category grew by 26 percent and accounted for 82 percent of the net increase of 342,500 jobs. Regional service employment consists of construction, transportation, utilities, and communications; finance, insurance, and real estate (FIRE); wholesaling; and regional retailing. Of these sectors, wholesaling, regional retailing, and regional government, education, and services grew most rapidly. Employment in regional government, education, and service industries grew by 41 percent and accounted for 45 percent of the region's job growth over the period; wholesaling and regional retailing grew by 38 percent and accounted for 23 percent of the region's job growth. Employment in traditional export industries, primarily manufacturing, declined by 2 percent; in nondurable manufacturing, by 4 percent; and in durable manufacturing, by 0.4 percent. Employment in population-serving industries (local government, primary and secondary education, and local retail) grew by 16 percent, or 78,300 jobs.

These changes in the Chicago metropolitan economy, which reflect changes in the national economy, have important implications for the patterns of urban development. As the previous chapter indicates, the HUDS model places considerable emphasis on the role of workplace in determining both the type of housing particular households will demand and their choice of residential locations. Specifically, the Demand Submodel assumes that a household's choice of housing bundle depends on its preferences and income, as well as on the relative minimum gross prices of the fifty housing bundles represented in the model. (The gross price of each housing bundle is the sum of monthly rent, which varies by both bundle type and location, and the transport costs incurred by the household's primary worker, which depend on workplace location and the value of the worker's travel time.)

Changes in the geographic distribution of jobs have a substantial impact on the housing choices of model households, on the geographic pattern of housing demand, and on the behavior of housing suppliers. Estimates of employment growth and decline in the twenty workplace zones shown in figure 3.1 are thus of considerable importance. The data document a pattern, by now familiar, of employment dispersal marked by extensive central-city decline and vigorous suburban job growth. Employment in zone 7, which includes the central business district, fell by 4 percent, or more than 10,000 jobs, over the decade. Total employment in zones 1 – 11, which make up most of the central city, fell by 5.3 percent. In contrast, suburban zones 12 – 17 all experienced employment growth in excess of 70 percent. Overall employment in these six suburban work zones increased by 81 percent during

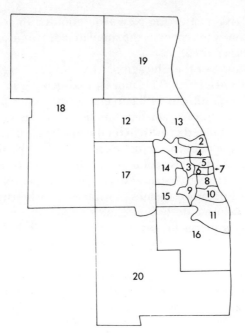

Figure 3.1. Chicago work zones

the decade—403,700 jobs—as contrasted with a combined loss of 92,350 jobs in central-city zones 1–11.

These and other data on the geographic pattern of employment growth and decline are a further reminder of the inadequacy of monocentric models of urban spatial structure. Employment in the central business district accounted for only 10.1 percent of metropolitan area employment in 1960, and by 1970 this figure had fallen to 8.6 percent. Central-city employment, for that matter, accounted for only 69.8 percent of all jobs in 1960 and 58.3 percent in 1970.

Trends in Household Characteristics

Changes in household size and composition have major implications for the region's housing market. The Movers and Demographic submodels are designed to simulate annual changes in individual household characteristics in a manner consistent with parameters estimated from microdata while also conforming as closely as possible to aggregate changes in income, family size, and age distributions for Chicago. Additions to the Basic List by the New Households Submodel provide another opportunity to reconcile the simulated distribution of households with actual experience.

The population of the Chicago SMSA grew by 12.2 percent during the decade 1960–1970. The more rapid growth in the number of households, amounting to 14.9 percent over the same period, reflects a long-term trend toward smaller families that has continued to the present. The simulated growth in total households, moreover, was considerably greater than the actual experience for the decade, totaling 17.1 percent. As the last column in table 3.1 indicates, the largest discrepancies between actual and simulated experience occur in the model's end-of-decade estimates of white elderly households. With the exception of white elderly households with four people, the HUDS model slightly underestimates the growth in elderly households with three or more people. By contrast, HUDS substantially overestimates household growth for the much larger category of white one- and two-person elderly households. As a result, the model's 1970 estimate of white one- and two-person elderly households exceeds the actual number by 42,200, which more than accounts for its 40,175 overestimate of the region's end-of-decade households.

Inspection of table 3.1 also reveals that all six of the one- and two-person household categories increased in number in both the actual and the baseline series; in all, these categories accounted for nearly 80 percent of the growth in households in the baseline simulation. Again, this simulated increase is 20 percent larger than the actual growth of one- and two-person households during the decade. The parameters of the Movers, Demographic, and New Households submodels could have been adjusted—albeit with some difficulty—to achieve more agreement between simulated and actual distributions of the ninety-six household categories used in the model. Because the replication of Chicago's actual 1960–1970 experience was not a primary objective of this study, however, we decided not to expend the time and resources to make these corrections.

The Demographic Submodel also simulates changes in income in such a way that individual model households move through a plausible life-cycle pattern of change, while at the same time achieving a reasonable correspondence to known and exogenously specified changes in the aggregate distribution of real incomes. HUDS obtains annual estimates of household income for each of the 72,000 to 84,000 model households included on the Basic List; six income categories are then used for several kinds of calculations, including the submarket demand equations. The real incomes of Chicago households grew rapidly over

Table 3.1. Actual and simulated number of households by race, age of head, and family size in 1960 and 1970

Household category	1960	1970 Actual	Baseline	B/A (%)
White, <35 years				
1–2 persons	138,900	172,400	172,400	100
3 persons	76,350	93,400	93,400	100
4 persons	82,425	93,300	93,300	100
5+ persons	81,450	85,800	86,650	101
White, 35–64 years				
1–2 persons	360,025	419,800	419,800	100
3 persons	209,575	187,300	188,475	101
4 persons	106,375	182,800	182,800	100
5+ persons	219,475	269,100	269,100	100
White, >65 years				
1–2 persons	203,475	283,700	325,900	115
3 persons	45,150	33,300	32,075	96
4 persons	12,625	10,400	13,675	131
5+ persons	8,600	7,300	6,375	87
Nonwhite, <35 years				
1–2 persons	29,000	33,400	33,400	100
3 persons	14,650	21,800	21,800	100
4 persons	12,125	21,300	21,300	100
5+ persons	26,775	33,100	33,100	100
Nonwhite, 35–64 years				
1–2 persons	58,575	77,000	77,000	100
3 persons	27,275	28,900	29,575	102
4 persons	21,725	26,500	26,500	100
5+ persons	40,400	57,500	57,500	100
Nonwhite, >65 years				
1–2 persons	13,150	31,900	31,900	100
3 persons	3,800	4,000	3,425	85
4 persons	2,775	2,000	1,325	66
5+ persons	2,275	400	400	100

the decade 1960–1970; the number of households with annual incomes between $10,000 and $14,999 increased by 46 percent, and the number with incomes of more than $15,000 grew by 72 percent. The number of households in three of the four remaining categories fell. In the fourth category, households with annual incomes below $3,000, the number of households actually grew by 7 percent. This increase for the lowest income category is undoubtedly related to the rapid growth in the number of small, elderly households.

Comparison of simulated baseline changes in the number of households by the six income categories to the actual Chicago numbers reveals that the baseline overstates the growth in the top income class; the baseline increase is 10 percentage points greater than the actual increase, 82 percent versus 72 percent. Actual and simulated increases are nearly identical for the next-to-highest income category; for the $7,000 – $9,999 category, the simulated increases are substantially less than the actual. Black households experienced a particularly rapid increase in income over the decade, and HUDS exaggerates this trend. Thus the number of black households with annual incomes of more than $15,000 increased by 162 percent, as contrasted with a simulated increase of 192 percent. Similarly, the baseline increase of 151 percent in black households with annual incomes of $10,000 – $14,999 exceeded the actual increase by 10 percentage points. Despite these errors the model's estimates of changes in median household income are fairly accurate. Measured in 1970 dollars, baseline median household income rose by $2,000 during the decade to an estimated level of $10,500, a figure that is only 1 percent higher than the actual end-of-period level.

Fortunately, for the program evaluations that are the core of this book, a precise or even close correspondence between simulated and actual experience is not essential. What is important is whether the model captures the dynamics of housing market behavior. In interpreting the housing stock changes discussed below, however, it is important to recall that differences between actual and simulated experience may reflect errors in the model's representation of housing market behavior, differences in the socioeconomic composition of the modeled and real regions, or data errors or inconsistencies in available descriptions of the Chicago region.

Changes in the Housing Stock

Shown in table 3.2 are annual baseline indexes of the stocks of single-family, small multi-family, and large multi-family units in the model region between 1960 and 1970. Since no reliable annual estimates of the actual stocks exist, no numerical comparisons of simulated and actual stocks are provided. During the second half of the decade, the baseline indicates that additions to the housing stock accelerated, a pattern that is broadly consistent with available data on actual new construction and demolition. The simulated growth in the housing stock overall amounted to 18 percent over the decade, with the most

Table 3.2. Actual and simulated indexes of the number of dwelling units by category, 1960–1970 (1960 = 100)

Year	Single-family	Small multi-family	Large multi-family	Total
1960	100	100	100	100
1961	102	102	100	101
1962	103	106	99	103
1963	104	108	101	104
1964	105	109	104	106
1965	107	111	105	107
1966	108	114	105	109
1967	109	118	107	111
1968	111	119	110	113
1969	113	122	111	115
1970	114	124	113	118
Actual	121	102	129	118

rapid growth occurring in the small multi-family category of dwelling units.

Statistics on the number of dwellings in 1960, as well as the actual and simulated numbers in 1970, are presented in table 3.3. Although these data reveal a close correspondence between total actual and simulated end-of-period housing stocks, some substantial discrepancies occur for individual structure types. The simulated end-of-period number of sin-

Table 3.3. Actual and simulated number of dwelling units by dwelling unit type in 1960 and 1970

Dwelling unit types	1960	1970		
		Actual	Baseline	B/A (%)
Single-family				
0–2 bedrooms	480,075	481,200	506,000	105
3 bedrooms	240,700	297,400	323,775	109
4+ bedrooms	171,750	299,600	187,400	63
Small multi-family				
0–1 bedrooms	242,550	227,100	247,400	109
2+ bedrooms	297,600	324,800	440,925	136
Large multi-family				
0–1 bedrooms	406,800	509,700	441,400	87
2+ bedrooms	102,800	149,100	135,200	91
All structure types	1,942,275	2,288,900	2,282,575	100

gle-family units with four or more bedrooms, for example, is only 63 percent as large as the actual figure. While a more rapid growth in the numbers of units in smaller single-family units partially offsets this underestimate, the total difference between actual and simulated single-family homes of all types amounts to more than 61,000 over the decade. Part of the model's failure to provide enough single-family units is undoubtedly due to the differences in actual and simulated characteristics of the population. It seems likely, however, that the model's submarket demand equations, which rely heavily on parameter estimates obtained for Pittsburgh, may not fully account for some features of the Chicago housing market.

Part of the discrepancy, moreover, may simply be attributable to errors in the actual data. As the figures in table 3.4 reveal, there are substantial inconsistencies in the available estimates of end-of-period characteristics of the region's housing stock. Although estimates of the *total* stock given by the 1970 census's Metropolitan Housing Characteristics (MHC) and the Components of Inventory Change (CIC) are nearly identical, the latter's estimate of the number of single-family units in 1970 is 4 percent larger. Similarly, the CIC estimate of the number of households in structures of five or more units is only 90 percent as large as the comparable census estimate. Since the CIC data are collected by Census Bureau employees while the 1970 census numbers depend on self-enumeration by households, it is likely that the CIC numbers are more reliable. The 1970 census, moreover, was the first to rely on homeowner enumeration; thus the change in data collection procedures between the 1960 and 1970 censuses could easily produce inconsistencies between the 1960 and 1970 estimates.

Table 3.4. Comparison of housing stock estimates, 1970 (in thousands of units)

Structure type	Components of Inventory Change (CIC)	Census Metro Housing Characteristics (MHC)	CIC/MHC (%)
Single-family	1,105	1,063	104
2–4 unit dwelling	576	552	104
5+ unit dwelling	596	659	90
Mobile homes	16	16	100
Total	2,292	2,289	100

The other major discrepancy between actual and baseline estimates of 1970 stocks is in the numbers of small multi-family units with two or more bedrooms. The simulated growth in these units over the decade — 143,325 units — is 36 percent larger than the actual 27,200 new units in Chicago. The previously discussed differences in the socioeconomic compositions of the modeled and real regions undoubtedly contribute more to this discrepancy than to the underestimate of increases in the stock of large single-family units. The underprovision of single-family units, moreover, is probably due in part to the model's overprovision of small multi-family units with two or more bedrooms, since these units are the closest available substitute for single-family homes for many types of households.

Although they are important issues for further research, the differences in actual and simulated changes in the housing stock are not in themselves especially critical to the evaluations presented in later chapters of concentrated housing and neighborhood improvement programs. First of all, the correspondence between simulated and actual housing market behavior is generally quite close, especially if the inherent measurement errors in the actual data are recognized. In addition, some of the discrepancies are attributable to differences in the socioeconomic structures of the real and modeled regions, differences that have little bearing on the analyses because the policies are compared to baseline simulations of the modeled region. If the objective were to evaluate programs that had been or were being considered for implementation in Chicago, the Demographic and New Households submodels could have been calibrated to achieve a closer correspondence between actual and simulated conditions. Since the goal was to determine how a certain class of programs might affect metropolitan housing markets generally, however, we chose to concentrate our resources on more critical conceptual and modeling issues. In this broader agenda, Chicago was simply a convenient source of data for construction of a generic region.

Components of Inventory Change

Changes in the numbers of units by structure type represent the net outcomes of new construction, demolition, and conversion activities. Conversions result in both the loss of units used as inputs and additions to the housing stock. Not surprisingly, actual and simulated estimates of the individual components of inventory change differ more widely than the estimates of aggregate net changes in each category. As the data in table 3.5 indicate, the aggregate simulated level of new construction for

Table 3.5. Comparison of baseline and actual components of inventory change by structure types, 1960–1970

Structure type and activity	Baseline	Actual	B/A (%)
Single-family			
New construction	207,350	261,200	79
Demolition	−46,775	−55,500	84
Net conversion	−35,925	−20,000	180
Total net change	124,650	185,700	67
Small multi-family			
New construction	198,300	32,700	606
Demolition	−61,950	−39,100	158
Net conversion	12,300	18,200	68
Total net change	148,650	11,800	1,260
Large multi-family			
New construction	86,300	187,200	46
Demolition	−81,400	−58,800	138
Net conversion	62,100	20,800	299
Total net change	67,000	149,200	45
All units			
New construction	491,950	481,100	102
Demolition	−190,125	−153,400	124
Net conversion	38,475	19,000	202
Total net change	340,300	346,700	98

the decade 1960–1970 is quite close to the estimated actual level for the Chicago metropolitan area. The simulated number of total demolitions, however, is 24 percent larger than the estimates of actual demolitions, while the simulated net gains from conversions are more than twice as large as the estimates of actual gains. It should be noted, though, that data on aggregate demolitions and conversions for entire metropolitan areas are scarce and notoriously inaccurate; reliable estimates for census tracts or other small areas are almost nonexistent. Given these problems, the overall correspondence between actual and simulated levels is relatively close.

Actual and simulated numbers of individual structure types, however, are much more disparate. For example, the actual increase in the stock of new small multi-family units over the decade in Chicago was only 11,800, compared with a simulated increase of 148,650 units. This error is somewhat offset by a substantial underestimate of the growth in the stock of large multi-family units. The actual growth in the number of these units—which are obviously close substitutes for small multi-family units—amounts to 149,200 units, versus a simulated change of 67,000 units.

Major discrepancies in these estimates are primarily due to the model's failure to replicate Chicago's pattern of new construction by structure type. The simulated number of small multi-family units built in the region during 1960–1970, for example, is 198,300, compared with an actual number of only 32,700. On the other hand, the simulated number of new large multi-family structures—close substitutes for small multi-family units—is only 86,300; the actual number was 187,200. The model's tendency to add too many small multi-family structures and too few large multi-family structures is probably related to construction and land cost differences, to the availability of building sites and the presence of zoning restrictions, to the methods used to determine land values and impute them to particular types of structures, and to the omission of dwelling quality from the definition of housing bundles and the submarket demand equations. The lack of actual data, however, contributes to the problem. Prediction errors of this type could be of considerable importance in forecasting Chi-

Table 3.6. Comparison of baseline and actual components of inventory change by city and suburb, 1960–1970

Activity	Baseline	Actual	B/A (%)
Central city			
New construction			
Private	154,125	104,100	148
Public	23,400	23,400	100
Total	177,525	127,500	139
Demolitions	133,725	112,800	119
Net gain from			
conversions	5,775	1,975	292
Total net change	49,575	16,675	297
Suburb			
New construction			
Private	312,825	351,900	89
Public	1,600	1,600	100
Total	314,425	353,500	89
Demolitions	56,400	40,600	139
Net gain from			
conversions	32,700	17,050	192
Total net change	290,725	329,950	88

cago's actual development, but it is less clear that they have much bearing on the validity of the CHIP evaluations presented in subsequent chapters.

All the data presented thus far refer to the entire Chicago metropolitan area. A primary objective of many housing and urban development policies, however, has been to arrest central-city decline and to retain or attract middle- and high-income households to core areas. The estimates included in table 3.6, differentiating the components of inventory change for the central city from the suburbs, are therefore of some interest. In the simulation, the central city experienced a larger increase in dwelling units (49,575) over the period than actually occurred (16,675). As a result, the simulated increase in suburban dwelling units is only 88 percent as large as the actual increase. Examination of the individual components of change, moreover, indicate that these errors

Table 3.7. Comparison of baseline and actual number of households by ring and sector, 1960–1970

Ring and sector	1960	1970		
		Actual	Baseline	B/A (%)
11	2,275	2,900	1,975	68
12	133,925	129,200	127,325	98
13	107,850	103,600	107,275	104
14	94,500	70,550	86,950	123
15	169,525	163,000	182,975	112
16	162,675	144,525	159,350	110
22	121,525	131,825	122,600	93
23	87,025	96,000	98,625	103
24	250,225	281,025	277,050	98
25	140,300	154,625	163,200	106
26	102,925	115,575	115,350	100
32	142,425	181,725	206,950	114
33	106,150	188,575	146,750	78
34	134,250	194,100	202,850	104
35	78,950	125,375	138,925	111
36	62,425	87,725	74,150	84
Ring 1	670,750	613,775	665,800	108
Ring 2	702,000	779,050	776,825	100
Ring 3	524,200	777,500	769,625	99
Entire region	1,895,950	2,170,325	2,204,100	102

are largely traceable to the fact that the model built 39 percent more new units in the city than were actually completed and only 89 percent as many in the suburbs.

Spatial Distribution of Households

The data in table 3.7 permit a closer examination of how the spatial dimensions of the model region approximate those of the actual Chicago metropolitan area. The areas listed in the table are defined by the system of rings and sectors shown in figure 3.2, where the first digit designates the distance ring and the second designates the sector. With the exception of area 11, which includes the central business district and contains few households, the correspondence between the simulated and actual numbers of households is reasonably close: the 1970 baseline estimates fall within ±5 percent of the actual levels in six of the fifteen areas, nine fall within ±10 percent, and twelve fall within ±15 percent. The simulated number of households residing in ring 1 is 8 percent greater than the actual number, primarily because of the model's ten-

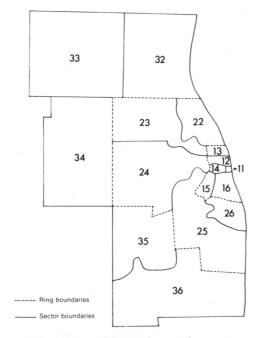

Figure 3.2. Chicago rings and sectors

dency to build too many new units in central locations. Again, it is important to note that the actual numbers are in themselves estimates; given the difficulty of counting inner-city populations, it is unlikely that the true number of Chicago SMSA households is known within 2 percent.

There is widespread agreement that prejudice, housing market discrimination, and racial segregation have major implications that strongly affect how policies operate and how metropolitan areas develop. The ability of the model to represent, at least in general, the character of racial segregation and policy-induced changes in the residential choices of black households is therefore an important issue. The model's estimates of the number of white households by area are more similar to the actual numbers than its estimates of blacks. Comparison of columns 2 and 3 in table 3.8 reveals that the baseline estimates of the

Table 3.8. Comparison of actual and baseline numbers and percentages of black households in 1970 by ring and sector

Ring and sector	Number of black households		Percent black	
	Baseline	Actual	Baseline	Actual
11	0	351	0.0	12.0
12	25,475	8,232	20.0	6.3
13	550	1,583	0.5	1.5
14	62,175	62,022	71.5	87.9
15	37,375	61,246	20.4	37.6
16	117,425	113,113	73.7	78.3
22	4,325	1,538	3.5	1.2
23	4,900	21	4.9	0.2
24	9,275	18,369	3.3	6.5
25	2,175	1,933	1.3	1.2
26	44,200	50,455	38.3	43.6
32	10,425	7,710	5.0	4.2
33	2,175	113	1.5	0.0
34	5,850	2,358	2.9	1.2
35	7,500	10,113	5.3	8.1
36	2,300	5,249	1.8	6.0
Ring 1	243,000	246,547	36.5	40.2
Ring 2	64,875	72,316	8.4	9.3
Ring 3	27,250	25,543	3.5	3.3
All	335,125	344,406	15.2	15.9

number of black households in areas 23 and 33 are many times larger than the actual numbers: 4,900 black households in area 23 versus 21 in reality, 2,175 in area 33 versus 113 in reality. For areas with larger black populations, however, the correspondence is much closer. In 1970, the model estimates that 71.5 percent and 73.7 percent of the households in areas 14 and 16 were black, compared to actual percentages of 87.9 and 78.3. Moreover, the model correctly captures the effects of housing market discrimination, which results in less than 10 percent of the black households residing in the outermost ring.

Simulating Neighborhood Dynamics

An important feature of the HUDS model is its capacity to represent the influence of neighborhood quality on the behavior of housing consumers and suppliers. Since neighborhood quality is one of the dimensions used to define the model's fifty housing bundles, it obviously plays a central role in determining the residence choices of model households. During each simulation year, demanders (that is, households actively participating in the housing market) choose among the model's fifty housing bundles on the basis of their preferences and incomes as well as the relative gross price of each bundle. The submarket demand equations, which are unique to each of the ninety-six types of model households, represent the influence of preferences and incomes on the choice of specific bundles. Neighborhood quality also has a major effect on the behavior of housing suppliers — both builders and the owners of existing structures — since it strongly influences projections of future rents, the characteristics of current and future occupants, and the profitability of new construction or rehabilitation.

For most of the fifty housing bundles, changes in neighborhood quality have a much larger impact on supplies of specific housing types than do new construction activities. An indication of how important the model's endogenous neighborhood change mechanism is in determining each year's supply of particular housing bundles is provided by comparing the estimates in table 3.9 with those in table 3.10. For example, supplies of the ten neighborhood type V bundles increased by 636,300 units over the decade, but new private construction accounted for only 42,825 of those units. Conversions added 20,525 neighborhood type V units, but the combination of new construction and conversion still accounted for only 10 percent of all net additions to the supply of neighborhood type V bundles during the period. Upgrading of lower-quality neighborhoods was the dominant source of new housing in best-quality neighborhoods.

Table 3.9. Simulated change in number of dwelling units by structure type and neighborhood, 1960–1970

Structure type	Neighborhood type					
	I	II	III	IV	V	All
Small-lot single-family						
0–2 bedrooms	75	−6,174	−53,450	−88,200	137,350	−10,400
3 bedrooms	4,650	−1,775	−18,175	−40,175	105,375	49,900
4+ bedrooms	4,950	−3,825	−9,575	−20,900	43,000	13,950
Large-lot single-family						
0–2 bedrooms	150	750	−2,425	−14,375	52,025	36,325
3 bedrooms	925	1,425	175	−8,375	39,025	33,175
4+ bedrooms	400	0	−5,075	−13,600	19,975	1,700
Small multi-family						
0–1 bedrooms	14,475	−41,625	−16,425	11,775	37,125	5,325
2 bedrooms	31,150	−41,625	−13,200	37,575	127,425	143,325
Large multi-family						
0–1 bedrooms	51,800	−60,600	−10,800	2,400	51,800	34,600
2 bedrooms	25,200	−18,400	−1,600	4,000	23,200	32,400
All structure types	135,975	−171,550	−130,550	−129,875	636,300	340,300

The estimates in table 3.10 of new construction activity, however, may be somewhat misleading in that they refer to neighborhood type at the time a particular unit is built. A significant fraction of the new units built in type III and IV neighborhoods after 1960 undoubtedly ended up as type V bundles by the end of the decade. Evidence to support this interpretation is found in the fact that the supplies of type III and IV housing bundles decreased substantially over the decade. While the number of neighborhood type V bundles increased by 636,300 units, type III and IV bundles declined by 129,875 and 130,550 units, respectively.

As the data in table 3.11 reveal, the model's ability to simulate actual patterns of neighborhood change leaves something to be desired. The current version of the model produces substantially more neighborhood improvement than actually occurred in Chicago over the decade 1960–1970. The largest discrepancy by far between the modeled region and the actual metropolitan area of Chicago is the far more rapid simulated growth in type V neighborhoods over the decade. In the baseline, forty-eight type V neighborhoods are added to the seventeen that existed at the start of the decade; the actual increase, however, is

Table 3.10. Simulated additions and losses of dwelling units by neighborhood type, 1960–1970

Activity	Neighborhood type					
	I	II	III	IV	V	All
Private construction	27,200	63,600	167,975	165,350	42,825	466,950
Public construction	21,000	2,000	1,800	0	200	25,000
Conversions (output)	6,150	13,850	16,625	15,125	20,525	72,275
Total additions	54,350	79,450	186,400	180,475	63,350	564,225
Conversions (losses)	5,450	6,925	10,475	4,975	5,975	33,800
Demolitions	69,050	37,625	41,550	31,975	9,225	190,125
Total losses	74,500	44,550	52,025	36,950	15,200	223,925
Total net change	−20,150	34,900	134,375	148,500	48,150	340,300

only slightly more than half that amount. In consequence, the simulated declines in the numbers of type III and IV neighborhoods are both considerably larger than in reality. Somewhat surprisingly, the baseline also overestimates the growth in the worst-quality (type I) neighborhoods. Actual estimates indicate that the number of worst-quality neighborhoods decreased by fourteen, while the simulated number increased by five. This result, which points to deficiencies in the calibra-

Table 3.11. Simulated and actual number of residence zones by neighborhood quality levels, 1960–1970

Neighborhood type	1960	1970			1970 minus 1960	
		Actual	Baseline	B/A (%)	Baseline	Actual
I	40	26	45	173	5	−14
II	42	38	19	50	−23	−4
III	49	47	37	79	−12	−2
IV	50	45	32	71	−18	−5
V	17	42	65	155	48	25
All	198	198	198	100	0	0

tion of the model's Supply Sector, is cause for concern, since the policy analyses focus on the efficacy of certain programs in upgrading low-quality neighborhoods. Nevertheless, evaluation of the policy simulations themselves suggests that the flaw is not a fatal one because those instances where the programs fail to produce significant upgrading are generally explainable in terms of the structure of the model and our understanding of housing market dynamics.

In table 3.12, neighborhoods are cross-classified by the extent of both their simulated and actual changes. The model achieves a match — that is, the same change in neighborhood status as in actuality — for less than half of the neighborhoods, 88 of 198. The major discrepancy between real and simulated changes is that fifty-one neighborhoods that improved in the baseline actually remained at the same quality level during the decade 1960–1970. Moreover, of the sixty-three neighborhoods that actually did improve, the model correctly identifies only thirty-six, or 57 percent; of the twenty-two declining neighborhoods, the model correctly identifies six, or only 27 percent. The errors stem from the model's tendency to understate the number of neighborhoods that changed in quality over the decade. While 113 of the Chicago region's neighborhoods remained the same between 1960 and 1970, only seventy-one neighborhoods remained unchanged in the model. As a result, the model not only overstates both neighborhood improvement and decline in the aggregate but also fails to identify correctly which neighborhoods improved or declined. Part of the explanation is that the model assumes a higher-than-actual growth in household income, and particularly in the number of households with annual incomes of more than $15,000 a year; deficiencies in the calibration of one or more of the Supply submodels, however, are even more likely to be the primary explanation. Once again, although these questions remain a high-priority research objective, we doubt that such errors in model structure or

Table 3.12. Comparison of actual and simulated changes in neighborhood quality, 1960–1970

	Simulated changes			
Actual changes	Improvement	No change	Decline	Total
Improvement	36	19	8	63
No change	51	46	16	113
Decline	10	6	6	22
Total	97	71	30	198

estimation have very serious implications for the results of the policy simulations.

Data on baseline and actual numbers of neighborhood by ring reveal that the largest discrepancy in the numbers of type V neighborhoods occurs in ring 2, where the baseline number of thirty-two is more than twice as large as the actual number. The baseline and actual numbers of type V neighborhoods, in contrast, are identical for ring 1, while the baseline number of type V neighborhoods in ring 3 is six more than the actual number of twenty. The overestimate of worst neighborhoods in the baseline is concentrated in ring 1, where the simulated number of type I neighborhoods in nearly twice the actual number of sixteen. The baseline and actual numbers of worst-quality neighborhoods, however, are identical for ring 3; for ring 2, the baseline number is four more than the actual number.

Baseline and Actual Estimates of Market Rents

HUDS calculates a market rent for each of its 72,000–84,000 model dwelling units in each simulation year by combining an estimated rent for structure services (specific to each model dwelling) and a bundle rent (which varies by bundle type and residence zone). Since each residence zone may have only one neighborhood quality level in a given year, the number of distinct housing bundles is 1,980, that is, 198 residence zones multiplied by ten structure types. Because the Supply Sector requires end-of-planning-period projections of rents for both the current and projected neighborhood quality level, however, the model calculates future market rents for 3,960 housing-bundle/residence-zone/neighborhood-type combinations.

As table 3.13 shows, average market rents (in 1970 dollars) in the model fell by three dollars in the first year and hit a low point in 1964, rising steadily thereafter until they reached their original levels in 1970. Although statistics on real annual rents (market rents for rental units plus imputed rents for owner-occupied units) are not available for Chicago, our estimate in 1970 of $172 a month is some 11 percent higher than the baseline estimate. It should be noted that our estimate of Chicago's average real rents in 1960 is also higher than the comparable baseline estimate. This inconsistency arises from the fact that the baseline 1960 rents were obtained by solving the model for 1960; if we used 1960 actual rents the model's initial rents for model dwelling units would most likely by inconsistent with the other data used by the model.

Examination of table 3.13 also suggests that the pattern of no change in market rents results from a modest decline in average bundle rents in

Table 3.13. Simulated and actual rents, 1960 – 1970 (in 1970 dollars)

Year	Total rent	Bundle rent	Structures services rent
1960	$155	$132	$23
1961	152	129	23
1962	151	128	23
1963	152	128	24
1964	150	127	23
1965	151	127	24
1966	153	128	25
1967	154	129	25
1968	154	129	25
1969	155	130	25
1970	155	129	26
Actual 1970	172	—	—

combination with a significant increase in structure services rents amounting to three dollars a month, or 13 percent of the 1960 levels. Part of the seventeen-dollars-per-month difference between end-of-decade rents in the simulation and in actual experience is due to the fact that the modeled city's start-of-decade rents were two dollars a month less than those of the actual city. In an effort to assess the effect of changes in mix and in the quantities of structure services consumed on market rents, we computed constant quantity indexes, where the bundle rents in each year are weighted by the 1960 shares of each of the fifty housing bundles. These indexes indicate that average real bundle rents declined until about 1965 and then increased steadily, returning to 1960 levels by the end of the decade. Average market rents rose, however, by three dollars as a result of an increase in average consumption of structure services. The remaining difference between actual and simulated rents may be attributed to several factors, the most important being differences in the simulated and actual distributions of dwellings by structure type. Accounting for the differences in average rents is an interesting and useful task, but again the discrepancy is not by itself critical to the policy analyses described in the following chapters.

4 Program Design and Analytics

This book uses the HUDS model to compare the results of three policy scenarios, each a variant of what we have termed concentrated housing improvement programs (CHIPs), in which owners of eligible properties in selected neighborhoods receive an unspecified combination of cash grants and interest subsidies that induce them to upgrade their structures to 90 percent of good-as-new condition. The programs assessed in this book have no exact real-world counterparts but are quite similar in design to a number of actual housing rehabilitation programs such as the federal Section 312 loan program and various locally funded housing improvement programs.

Based on discussions with officials from the U.S. Department of Housing and Urban Development, as well as on an extensive review of the policy evaluation literature, we decided to limit eligibility for CHIP subsidies to owner-occupied, one- to four-family structures located in selected low-income neighborhoods. Although there are numerous examples of programs that provide subsidies for the rehabilitation of large, absentee-owned structures, the vast majority of programs limit eligibility to small, owner-occupied structures.

Current program practices also provided guidance in determining the appropriate scale for the concentrated housing improvement programs and the spatial allocation of funding. Since housing rehabilitation or neighborhood improvement programs have insufficient funds to treat all potentially eligible units or neighborhoods, federal and local policymakers confront difficult decisions about how best to allocate limited program funds among eligible low-income neighborhoods. This targeting issue is usually complicated, moreover, by a desire to achieve two often conflicting objectives — to provide housing assistance

49

to low- and moderate-income individuals, on the one hand, and to encourage neighborhood preservation or revitalization, on the other. Again, federal housing officials were helpful in devising a research strategy that enabled us to explore the effect of different neighborhood targeting practices on program outcomes.

In this chapter we first discuss the design of the concentrated housing improvement programs, explain the criteria used in selecting target zones, and give estimates of participation rates for the CHIP-I scenario, the first of the three programs considered in the analysis. Then a brief explanation is presented of how the provision of CHIP subsidies affects the behavior of households and of housing suppliers.

Program Design

CHIPs provide grants and below-market loans to eligible owner-occupants of one- to four-unit structures in selected target neighborhoods. The subsidies are assumed to induce recipients to make improvements until their properties possess 90 percent as much capital as the average newly built, highest-quality unit of the same structure type. The grants enable eligible owner-occupants to rehabilitate entire buildings — the unit occupied by the owner as well as any rental units. The only other eligibility criterion is that an owner-occupant recipient of a CHIP subsidy have a household income of less than $10,000 a year (in 1970 dollars).

Although experience demonstrates that less than 100 percent of eligible property owners would participate in even such a generous entitlement program, the CHIP simulations assume that all eligible households accept the subsidies. This convention is used because we had no basis for estimating realistic participation rates and, moreover, we were convinced that a more complicated simulation of participation decisions would not improve the analysis. We anticipated that the impacts of CHIP subsidies on nontreated properties in the same or in nontarget neighborhoods would depend primarily on the location and characteristics of target neighborhoods and on the fraction of units receiving subsidies. The exact mechanism used to identify treated units — that is, the specific combination of eligibility and participation rates that leads to a particular profile of program activity — is therefore less important than the share of each neighborhood's units that is subsidized and the location and other characteristics of the target neighborhoods. One advantage of the simulation approach, of course, is that the analysis can be easily repeated using different assumptions about program eligibility and participation, if these judgments prove incorrect.

Selection of Target Neighborhoods

Of the 198 residence zones in the modeled region, 120 are located in the central city; of these central-city zones, only the 65 zones that were of lowest or next-to-lowest quality (neighborhood type I or II) at the start of the simulation period were considered for selection. After calculating eligibility rates for CHIP grants in each of these residence zones, sixteen neighborhoods with less than 5 percent eligibility were eliminated from further consideration. Finally, the panel of fifteen candidate neighborhoods shown in figure 4.1 were selected to provide a range of geographic locations, racial compositions, and shares of eligible units.

As the data in table 4.1 indicate, the racial composition of the fifteen candidate neighborhoods varies from a low of 0.2 percent black (zone 34) to a high of 83.1 percent (zone 86). With the exception of one zone

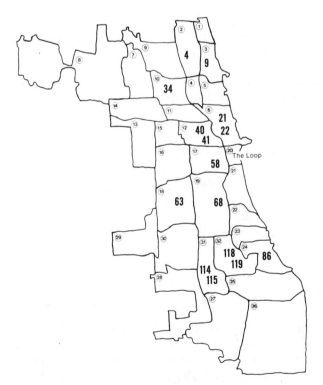

Figure 4.1. Residence zones nominated as target neighborhoods for the simulations (circled numbers indicate transit districts)

Table 4.1. Characteristics of residence zones included in the policy
simulations, 1960

Residence zone	Percent black	Mean income	Percent owner-occupied	Percent eligible
9*	2.2	$8,650	13.5	9.7
4	2.2	8,257	15.3	15.6
34*	0.2	8,618	33.1	40.6
21	2.5	7,535	15.1	22.5
22*	5.0	7,585	15.2	17.2
40	5.8	6,703	17.8	24.0
41*	0.6	7,856	27.3	40.5
58	66.2	5,097	8.7	11.9
68	0.8	7,978	31.8	43.3
63	1.4	8,314	41.2	56.9
118*	64.7	6,990	25.6	33.0
86*	83.1	6,064	10.0	11.6
119	65.6	8,202	30.0	33.0
114	42.5	7,021	22.9	19.8
115	22.6	8,506	41.9	45.2
SMSA	13.3	9,064	60.2	—

*Zones included in the CHIP-I simulation.

located on the western boundary of the ghetto, all the neighborhoods
are either less than 6 percent or more than 40 percent black, reflecting
Chicago's pattern of racial segregation. Mean incomes of the nominated zones vary from $5,097 (zone 58) to $8,650 (zone 9), 56 percent
and 95 percent, respectively, of the regionwide average. It is worth
noting that the requirement that only owner-occupied structures are
eligible for CHIP grants effectively excludes the poorest neighborhoods from being target areas. Of the candidate neighborhoods,
owner-occupancy rates range from 8.7 percent (zone 58) to 41.9 percent (zone 115), while eligibility rates range from 9.7 percent (zone 9) to
56.9 percent (zone 63).

The three policy simulations focus on various subsets of the target
neighborhoods listed in table 4.1. The first concentrated housing improvement program simulation (CHIP-I) includes zones 9, 34, 22, 41,
118, and 86. These six neighborhoods, displayed in figure 4.2, are
paired by location and by high and low levels of eligibility in order to
examine the consequences of different levels of treatment while crudely
standardizing for the effects of geography and racial composition. The

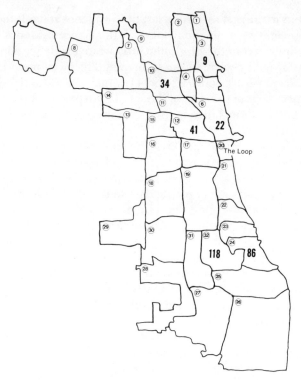

Figure 4.2.   Target neighborhoods in the CHIP-I simulation

first pair of CHIP-I target zones, 9 and 34, are located in the northern part of Chicago. As table 4.1 shows, these neighborhoods have very few black households (0.2 and 2.2 percent, respectively) and relatively high incomes: $8,618 and $8,650, compared to the regionwide average of $9,064. Zones 41 and 22, in contrast, are located in the near north, adjacent to the central business district. These residence zones are also predominantly white but have somewhat lower average incomes than the first pair. The final two neighborhoods, unlike those to the north, have substantial numbers of black households. Zone 118, the high-treatment zone, is 64.7 percent black; zone 86, the low-treatment zone, is 83.1 percent black. These neighborhoods also have by far the lowest incomes of any residence zones included in the four policy simulations: only 77 percent and 67 percent, respectively, of the regionwide average.

The other two CHIP simulations—Concentrated North (CN) and Concentrated South (CS)—provide housing rehabilitation grants to all eligible units in the first seven and last five residence zones listed in table 4.1. The seven target neighborhoods in the Concentrated North scenario are drawn from the predominantly white residence zones to the north of Chicago's central business district. The most integrated areas in the CN scenario are zones 22 and 41, which are 5.0 and 5.8 percent black, respectively, at the start of the simulation period. By contrast, the five neighborhoods included in the Concentrated South simulation are primarily black.

Because of the CHIP eligibility criterion that only owner-occupied, one- to four-family structures qualify, the characteristics of a neighborhood's housing stock are a major factor in determining the program's extent in a particular zone. As the data in table 4.2 indicate, the three target neighborhoods containing a small fraction of one- to four-family structures have low eligibility rates. Other data show that only 11.4 percent of units in the high-treatment zones in the north are of the worst construction type, compared to 39 percent of the units in the high-treatment neighborhood in the south. Similarly, 10.6 and 34.9 percent of the units in these north and south high-treatment neighborhoods belong to the category of structures that provide the least amount of structure services.

The analysis presented in table 4.2 illustrates how housing stock characteristics and household incomes interact to influence the level of treatment in a particular neighborhood. Zones 9 and 34, for example,

Table 4.2. Eligibility for CHIP subsidies by residence zone

Zone location, treatment level, and number	Total units	1 – 4 family dwelling units		Eligible units as percent of all 1 – 4 family owner-occupied units	Eligible units as percent of all dwelling units
		Percent of total	Percent owner-occupied		
North					
High, 34	12,250	67.3	70.6	85.4	40.6
Low, 9	18,500	18.9	65.0	79.1	9.7
Near north					
High, 41	8,700	74.7	60.8	89.2	40.5
Low, 22	6,250	52.0	42.3	78.2	17.2
South					
High, 118	25,550	74.2	53.0	83.8	33.0
Low, 86	34,600	30.6	45.0	84.3	11.6
All target zones	105,850	48.3	55.3	84.3	22.5

have the lowest and highest eligibility rates among the six target neighborhoods included in the simulations. Units in one- to four-family structures account for 67.3 percent of all units in the high-treatment zone, compared with only 18.9 percent in the low-treatment zone. Moreover, 70.6 percent of the one- to four-family units in the high-treatment zone and 65 percent of those in the low-treatment zone are owner-occupied. In the high-treatment north neighborhood, the owner-occupants of 85.4 percent of one- to four-family units pass the income eligibility test; the fraction in the low-treatment north neighborhood is 79.1 percent.

Program Extent

Implementation of the CHIP-I program would result in the renovation of 24,000 dwelling units at an estimated cost of $94 million (1970 dollars). This estimate is based on the data presented in table 4.3, which indicate that program-induced capital improvements would average between $3,289 in zone 34 and $4,255 in zone 118, both high-treatment neighborhoods. These improvements average roughly half of the initial capital value of subsidized dwelling units, excluding land value.

As a percentage of each zone's entire capital stock, the capital improvements induced by CHIP-I range from a low of 5.3 percent in zone 9 to a high of 25.3 percent in zone 41. The estimates in table 4.4 also

Table 4.3. Effects of CHIP-I program on subsidized units (in 1970 dollars)

Zone location, treatment level, and number	Number of subsidized units	Mean initial capital stock	Mean improvement	Mean improvement as percent of capital stock
North				
High, 34	4,975	$8,425	$3,289	39.0
Low, 9	1,800	8,265	3,679	44.5
Near north				
High, 41	3,525	7,679	4,156	54.1
Low, 22	1,075	7,400	4,151	56.1
South				
High, 118	8,425	7,667	4,225	55.5
Low, 86	4,025	7,594	4,023	53.0
All target zones	23,825	7,847	3,951	50.3

Table 4.4. Effects of CHIP-I program on target neighborhoods (in 1970 dollars)

Zone location, treatment level, and number	Value of 1960 capital stock (millions)		Value of total improvement (millions)	Improvement as percent of 1960 capital stock
	All units	Subsidized units		
North				
High, 34	$ 92.9	$ 41.9	$16.4	17.6
Low, 9	124.4	14.9	6.6	5.3
Near north				
High, 41	57.9	27.1	14.7	25.3
Low, 22	40.4	8.0	4.5	11.0
South				
High, 118	167.9	64.6	35.8	21.4
Low, 86	206.6	30.6	16.2	7.8
All target zones	690.1	187.1	94.2	13.7

show that the average value for all six target neighborhoods is 13.7 percent. As a percentage of the aggregate 1960 value of subsidized units, however, CHIP improvements represent between 39 percent (zone 34) and 56.1 percent (zone 22). This range primarily reflects differences in the initial condition of subsidized units: the better-maintained units obviously require less upgrading to meet program standards.

Simple Analytics of the Program

CHIPs cause some housing consumers to choose different structure types and residential locations, induce some housing suppliers to change their housing production and investment decisions, and affect housing prices and trends in neighborhood quality throughout the metropolitan area. In short, such programs set off a complex set of market responses that affect not only the occupants of treated buildings but ultimately the dynamics of neighborhood change and the regionwide housing market. To evaluate the effect of concentrated housing and neighborhood improvement programs on neighborhood dynamics and on urban housing markets more generally, the modeling approach used in this study first determines the impacts on the behavior of the owners and residents of subsidized buildings in target neighborhoods, and then explicitly represents the ways that these first-round effects modify the behavior of the owners and residents of the target neighborhood's unsubsidized buildings. After looking at the target neighborhoods, the model simulates the programs' impact on owners and residents in other neighborhoods and on the pattern of demand, housing prices, construction and renovation, and neighborhood change in other parts of the region.

CHIP grants cause the occupants of rehabilitated units to increase their consumption of structure services by lowering the marginal costs of producing these services and thus their price. Since the HUDS model explicitly represents the way in which property owners combine capital and operating inputs to produce structure services, determining how the CHIP grants and interest subsidies affect investment behavior is fairly straightforward. The average quantity of structure services consumed by the residents of each neighborhood is the index of neighborhood quality, so the provision of CHIP subsidies to a large fraction of units in a particular neighborhood may significantly increase the quality of target zones, thus altering the housing market dynamics in target and nontarget neighborhoods alike.

The sections that follow outline the way in which the HUDS model represents the behavior of individual housing suppliers and demanders as well as linkages between the behavior of individual housing consumers and suppliers and neighborhood and regionwide dynamics. For example, it describes the current model's explicit expectations framework that specifies how the owners of model structures translate past and current market information into forecasts of future neighborhood quality, of rents for specific types of structures, and of the profitability of alternative investments.

The Structure Services Production Function

Structure services are the unobservable flow of services consumed by the residents of sample dwelling units. The CHIP subsidies have no effect on consumption in the year the improvements are made, but in subsequent years the increments to capital they induce lower the annual cost of providing structure services and thereby encourage occupants to demand larger quantities than they would have in the absence of the subsidies. HUDS assumes that housing suppliers produce structure services by combining annual operating inputs with each unit's stock of maintenance and structure capital according to a structure services production function. The effect of structure capital on the annual cost of producing structure services is embodied in the building's construction type. Buildings with more structure capital are better construction types and thus require less maintenance capital and operating inputs to produce a given quantity of structure services.

The current version of the model defines three construction types. The level of structure capital represented by each of these three construction types in turn determines the levels of maintenance capital required to produce a given level of structure services. As equations 4.1–4.4 indicate, each construction type defines a production function in operating inputs and maintenance capital. Since these production functions are of Cobb-Douglas form, they imply constant returns to scale in maintenance capital and operating inputs for each construction type.

(4.1) $\text{SERV}(K) = 1.2 * A * \text{MCAP}^B \text{OPER}^{1-B}$
  for $\text{CT} = 1$, $\text{SCAP}(K) > .8 \ \text{STDDUR}(K)$

(4.2) $\text{SERV}(K) = A * \text{MCAP}^B \text{OPER}^{1-B}$
  for $\text{CT} = 2$, $.5 \ \text{STDDUR}(K) < \text{SCAP}(K) \leq .8 \ \text{STDDUR}(K)$

(4.3) $\text{SERV}(K) = 1/1.2 * A * \text{MCAP}^B \text{OPER}^{1-B}$
  for $\text{CT} = 3$, $\text{MINSCAP}(K) < \text{SCAP}(K) \leq .5 \ \text{STDDUR}(K)$

(4.4) $\text{SERV}(K) = 0$
  for $\text{CT} = 1, 2, 3$, $\text{SCAP}(K) \leq \text{MINSCAP}(K)$

where $\text{SERV}(K)$ = Level of structure services provided by housing bundle K;
   MCAP = Stock of maintenance capital;
   OPER = Operating inputs;
   CT = Construction type;
   $\text{SCAP}(K)$ = Structure capital in housing bundle K;
   $\text{STDDUR}(K)$ = Good-as-new level of structure capital for housing bundle K;
   $\text{MINSCAP}(K)$ = Minimum structure capital required for operation;
   A = Scaling parameter equal to .460;
   B = Parameter equal to the share of rents for structure services which accrue to maintenance capital, set to .667 for the current simulations.

The current version of the model thus assumes that a minimum quantity of structure capital is required to produce structure services and that the quantity of structure services supplied during each period depends on the amount of maintenance and structure capital embodied in the building, the amount of operating inputs used, and the building's construction type. The same production function is used for rental units, for owner-occupied multi-family structures, and for owner-occupied single-family homes; this feature of the model can easily be changed, however, if subsequent research determines that important differences exist among these types of owners.

A structure's construction type depends on the quantity of structure capital it possesses relative to the amount required for a new best-quality unit of the same type. Units of a better construction type — those containing more structure capital — can produce a given level of structure services with less maintenance capital and fewer operating inputs than structures of a worse construction type. Units of construction type 3 (those with the least structure capital), for example, require 44 percent more maintenance capital and operating inputs than units of construction type 1 to produce the same quantity of structure services. Since the CHIP grants in many cases permit an upgrading of eligible units from the worst construction type to the best, they obviously can have a considerable impact on the annual cost of providing structure services.

If the prices of each type of capital and operating inputs are known, unit-specific cost functions may be derived from equations 4.1 – 4.4. Shown in figure 4.3 are intermediate- and short-run structure services cost curves that correspond to the model's three construction types. The curves labeled IRMC(1), IRMC(2), and IRMC(3), the intermediate-run marginal cost curves, are drawn assuming that the quantity of structure capital (construction type) is fixed but that the quantities of both maintenance capital and operating inputs vary; they also assume that the optimal or least-cost combinations of maintenance capital and operating inputs are used. The fact that the three intermediate-run curves have no slope or curvature is due to the assumption of constant returns to scale. In contrast, the upward-sloping short-run marginal cost curves, SRMC(1), SRMC(2), and SRMC(3), assume fixed quantities of structure and maintenance capital; only the quantity of operating inputs is allowed to vary. The shape of these cost curves reflects the fact that when capital stocks are fixed a property owner can produce greater amounts of structure services only by making increasingly large expenditures for operating inputs.

In the long run, property owners can add structure capital and thus change construction type. In addition, structures will eventually deteriorate to lower construction types even if the owners pursue good-as-new maintenance policies. The model assumes that structure capital depreciates by 4.5 percent per year and that owners can offset only two-thirds of this decline through normal maintenance. If the owner of

PROGRAM DESIGN AND ANALYTICS

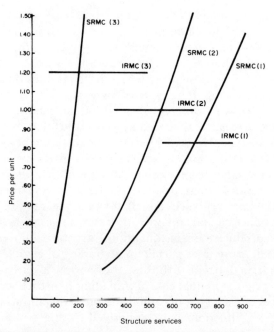

Figure 4.3. Intermediate- and short-run structure services cost curves for a hypothetical dwelling unit

a construction type 2 structure invests in structure capital at the maximum rate, his building will decline to construction type 3 in fifteen years; if he makes no annual additions to structure capital, this process will require only ten years. Property owners who currently provide or expect to provide relatively low levels of structure services will allow their units to depreciate and therefore gradually become a lower construction type.

Since structure capital is so durable, a property owner's decision to upgrade his building depends both on current demand and on expectations about the future demand for structure services. The structure services production function used in HUDS is such that a property owner is rewarded (in terms of saving maintenance capital and operating inputs) for upgrading construction type only if he expects to supply relatively large quantities of structure services for several years. To simplify these calculations, HUDS first determines whether the discounted saving in maintenance capital and operating inputs for providing the quantity of structure services demanded by the current occupant justifies the investment if this quantity were to be demanded indefinitely. The model then considers whether the required outlays to upgrade construction type are prudent given projected changes in neighborhood quality.

The short-run and intermediate-run marginal cost curves incorporate no information about the cost of structure capital or the housing suppliers' optimal construction type. Figure 4.4 depicts the long-run average cost of providing structure services for a specific structure type (a zero- to one-bedroom unit in a small multi-family structure). The shape of the long-run average cost curve depends on the real cost of borrowing or the real interest rate, which is 3 percent in the CHIP simulations. The curve labeled LRAC(1) depicts the average cost of producing structure services using the optimal combination of maintenance capital and operating inputs for a unit of construction type 1; the curves labeled LRAC(2) and LRAC(3) provide this information for buildings of construction types 2 and 3. The envelope of these long-run average cost curves traces out the minimum long-run average cost of producing structure services. Inspection of the cost curves reveals that for less than 500 units construction type 3 is the least-cost method of

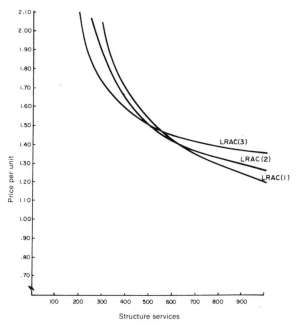

Figure 4.4. Long-run cost curves for a hypothetical dwelling unit of structure type 7

PROGRAM DESIGN AND ANALYTICS

producing structure services, construction type 2 is the least-cost way of producing quantities of 500 to 650 units, and construction type 1 is the least-cost method of producing more than 650 units.

The Demand for Housing Services

The structure services demand functions, illustrated in figure 4.5 for both owner and renter households, are calibrated so that the occupant's demand is decreased by increases in rent per unit of structure services, decreases in household income, or a change in tenure from owner to renter. The functions assume a constant price elasticity of -1.0, implying that increases or decreases in the price of structure services will be exactly offset by proportional and opposite changes in the quantities of structure services consumed. Consequently, a household's expenditures for structure services will remain constant at all rent levels. By assuming that the income elasticity for owners (0.7) is higher than for renters (0.6), the model also captures the fact that owner-occupants are

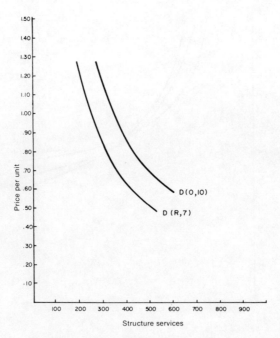

Figure 4.5. Structure services demand curves for two representative households

more willing to pay for structure services and are more likely to spend income on more housing consumption than otherwise comparable renter households.

Direct Effects of CHIP Grants

The model determines the quantity and price of structure services that each structure supplies annually by comparing the unit's supply curve and the structure services demand curve for the current occupant. The supply curve is derived from the marginal cost curve for each dwelling unit, which defines the quantities of structure services a profit-maximizing property owner would supply at each rental level, where rent is defined in terms of the cost per unit of structure services. CHIP grants alter the consumption of structure services by the occupants of rehabilitated units by lowering the marginal cost of producing structure services. Shown in figure 4.6 are the intermediate- and short-run marginal cost curves for a sample unit before and after the subsidy. This example assumes that the same household—a renter with an annual income of $7,000 a year (in 1970 dollars)—occupies the unit in both periods; this household's demand curve is labeled $D(R,7)$. The short- and intermediate-run marginal cost curves before the CHIP subsidies — $SRMC(BC)$ and $IRMC(BC)$ — assume that the unit is of construction type 3, with only 40 percent as much structure capital and 70 percent as much maintenance capital as a new unit. The curves labeled $SRMC(AC)$ and $IRMC(AC)$ depict the same unit's cost curves after CHIP subsidies have upgraded the unit to construction type 1. The intersection of the unit's marginal cost and demand curves determines the quantity of structure services supplied: 208 units before and 348 units after the subsidy.

The effect of the CHIP subsidy on the housing demand of owner-occupants is complicated by the potential wealth effects of the program. Owners of subsidized properties benefit from the improvements both to their own units and to the rental units that they own. Even if the CHIP subsidy is an outright grant, the increase in sale price will not necessarily equal the amount of the grant. In depressed neighborhoods, for example, the additional capital investment may alter little the current or future levels of housing demand and add only marginally to the current value of the property. Alternatively, CHIP may stimulate significant investment by nonsubsidized property owners, an effect that further enhances the value of all properties in target neighborhoods.

The current version of HUDS cannot examine the possible wealth effects of a CHIP subsidy. At present, the model assumes no link between the value of owner-occupied properties, the wealth of owner-oc-

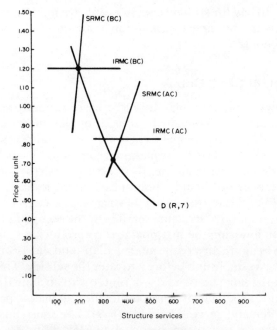

Figure 4.6. Effect of CHIP subsidies on the structure services consumption of a representative renter household

cupants, and the income and housing consumption patterns of owners. In assessing the significance of this omission, it is important to note that most CHIP subsidies do impose restrictions on the owners of subsidized structures; for instance, owners are often required to repay all or some of the subsidy if they sell their property. Moreover, many specific programs impose restrictions on the extent to which property owners can raise the rents following the improvements. These and other restrictions serve to limit the wealth implications of the program for recipients and reduce the significance of the current model's inability to examine the wealth effects of the program.

Effects of CHIP Subsidies on Neighborhood Quality

When the quantity of structure services supplied by individual units is averaged for all dwellings in an area, it becomes the index of neighborhood quality. Thus, in addition to increasing the quantity of structure services that individual households consume, CHIP grants may significantly increase the quality of target neighborhoods. The simulations described in this book employ five neighborhood quality categories defined by the average quantity of services. For the subsidized unit in figure 4.6, for example, the increase in the consumption of structure services from 208 to 348 units in the year following the CHIP-induced rehabilitation implies an improvement in neighborhood quality from level I to IV. Program-induced changes in the quality of target neighborhoods in turn affect the income mix of in-migrants to each neighborhood and the investment decisions of property owners. Each year, HUDS represents the moving decisions of sample households, the dissolution and formation of new households, and migration to and from the metropolitan area. Some 40 percent of the original residents of a typical low-income neighborhood move each year, providing vacancies for approximately the same number of in-migrants. These high rates of mobility permit rapid changes in the composition of target neighborhoods by households of various income levels.

HUDS allows those households actively participating in the housing market in each year (referred to as demanders) to choose from among fifty housing bundles defined by ten structure types and five levels of neighborhood quality. As the distributions in table 4.5 demonstrate, only 7.4 percent of the demanders with annual incomes of $15,000 or more choose the lowest-quality neighborhoods (type I). In contrast, 15.5 percent select middle-quality neighborhoods (type III) and fully 35.9 percent move to neighborhoods of the highest quality (type V). Thus, if CHIP subsidies increase the average quantity of structure services consumed in a particular target zone, they not only improve neighborhood quality but also encourage higher-income households to move into the area.

Table 4.5. Baseline estimate of the percentage of households in each income class who choose each neighborhood type, 1965

Income	Neighborhood type					
	I	II	III	IV	V	All
$0–$2,999	23.8	16.8	10.2	6.6	2.8	13.8
$3,000–$4,999	17.7	16.3	12.7	8.6	4.3	12.9
$5,000–$6,999	16.2	13.8	12.6	9.3	5.0	12.2
$7,000–$9,999	21.2	23.5	25.4	25.8	16.6	22.2
$10,000–$14,999	13.8	20.9	23.5	31.0	35.3	22.9
$15,000+	7.4	9.5	15.5	18.7	35.9	16.0
Total	100.0	100.0	100.0	100.0	100.0	100.0

The Role of Expectations

The attraction of high-income occupants is not sufficient, however, to ensure that the owner of a subsidized building will maintain his building's capital stock at the level induced by the CHIP subsidies, nor does it guarantee that the owners of nearby nonsubsidized properties will rehabilitate their buildings. Decisions to make long-lived capital improvements depend less on current period demand than on expectations about future demand and neighborhood conditions. In the model, each property owner's estimate of future rental income is determined by looking at three pieces of information: projections of future neighborhood quality, estimates of the fraction of property owners who believe that the zone's neighborhood quality will change, and projections of future rents for each housing bundle in each residence zone (see appendix E). To the extent that the CHIP subsidies induce an initial direct increase in the quantity of structure services consumed by the occupants of subsidized buildings and thereby increase neighborhood quality, they affect each of the factors that influence housing suppliers' expectations about future rental income. The extent to which the CHIP subsidies affect the investment behavior of property owners depends on both the relative size of the initial program-induced increase in average neighborhood quality and on a variety of other factors. If only a small share of units in a neighborhood receive subsidies, the program is likely to have only a modest effect on neighborhood quality levels and on expectations.

It seems unlikely that all property owners in a particular neighborhood will have access to the same information about current and past neighborhood conditions, but even if they did, they would probably differ in their interpretation of these data and therefore form different expectations. HUDS thus identifies two types of owner-investors: first, those who assess available data and conclude that the quality of their neighborhood will remain unchanged over the five-year planning period used in the model; second, those who review the evidence and conclude that the neighborhood will improve or deteriorate by one quality level over the next five years. The simulations assume that the proportion of property owners in a particular neighborhood belonging to each investor type is a nonlinear function of the difference between current and predicted levels of neighborhood quality: the more pronounced the projected improvement in neighborhood quality, the larger the fraction of investors who would act on the expectation of that improvement.

After HUDS completes its forecasts of neighborhood quality and assigns an investor type to each sample structure, it projects future rents for each type of housing bundle in each residence zone. Estimates of future rents are based on extrapolations of levels for specific zones and structures in the previous four years. Property owners who expect their neighborhood to remain at the same quality level rely on these simple trend projections of rental income in making investment decisions. Property owners who expect the quality level of their neighborhoods to change, however, use projections of future rents that take into account the anticipated improvement or worsening of neighborhood quality.

Effects of CHIP Subsidies on Investment Behavior

Together, program-induced changes in the capital stocks of eligible buildings, in occupants' incomes, and in expectations about future neighborhood conditions can cause dramatic changes in the investment and production decisions of property owners. While CHIP subsidies will in most cases cause an immediate increase in the quantity of structure services consumed, the extent to which program-induced improvements in neighborhood quality are sustained depends largely on whether the zone attracts higher-income households. Such households demand quantities of structure services that are consistent with the much higher levels of maintenance and structure capital that the subsidies provide. If a building is occupied by higher-income households and if the owner is convinced that future neighborhood quality will improve, he or she is likely to continue to maintain the building at the level afforded by the CHIP subsidy. If the incomes of the occupants do not increase, however, the property owner is likely to allow the building to deteriorate. It should be noted, however, that the original owner-occupants make up a significant fraction of the post-program residents of subsidized units and that significant increases in income among these households are unlikely.

The curves shown in figure 4.7 illustrate the effect of a change in tenant income. In the previous example showing how the CHIP grant would affect structure services, the program-induced reduction in the marginal cost of structure services led to the consumption of 208 more units by the renter household with a $7,000 income. Since the post-CHIP price of $0.72 per unit is below the intermediate-run marginal cost for a unit of construction type 1, the owner of this structure would allow the unit's stock of maintenance capital to decline. As the unit's stock of capital decreases, however, the marginal cost of producing

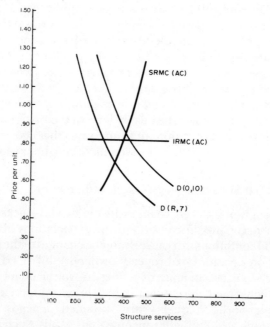

Figure 4.7. Effects of change in household income and tenure on the post-CHIP-subsidy level of structure services

structure services would again rise, leading to further decreases in the production and consumption of structure services.

A change in neighborhood conditions and subsequently in the average income of households living in the zone could, in contrast, induce housing investments beyond the level offered by the CHIP program. As figure 4.7 shows, replacing a renter household whose annual income is $7,000 with an owner-occupant with a $10,000 income would result in the consumption and production of 388 units of structure services at a cost of $0.85 per unit. In this case, the short-run marginal costs exceed the intermediate-run marginal costs, enabling the owner to reduce the cost of producing this level of structure services by increasing the unit's stock of capital beyond CHIP-induced levels. If the building's owner were confident that the demand for structure services would not decline over the period required to amortize his investments, he would add maintenance capital until he achieved the least-cost combination of operating inputs and maintenance capital to produce this level of structure services.

The extent of the investment to be made depends on a relatively complex interaction between current demand and the expectations of property owners about neighborhood improvement or decline. The intersection of the occupant's demand curve and the unit's marginal cost curve determines the quantity of structure services that will be consumed (supplied) by each occupant (housing supplier). In turn, the production function and input prices determine the optimum quantity of maintenance capital necessary for producing this amount of structure services. If the optimum level is more than the amount existing at the start of the period, a property owner must decide whether current and anticipated levels of neighborhood quality justify adding more maintenance capital. Since the simulations assume that property owners are risk-averse, property owners never improve properties in declining low-quality neighborhoods. Indeed, only a fraction of those who expect their neighborhood to improve will increase their structure and maintenance capital investments to the short-run optimal level.

New Construction and Structure Conversion

Program-induced changes in the current and expected quality of target neighborhoods, as well as in the attractiveness of target neighborhoods to high-income households, thus affect investors' decisions to construct new buildings, convert units from one structure type to another, demolish deteriorated units, and maintain existing structures. The levels, composition, and location of new construction activities are based on a profitability calculation that compares construction and land acquisition costs with the present values of projected net rental income. All else being equal, investors are more likely to build new units in higher-quality zones and in zones that they expect will improve in the future. As noted above, no private new construction occurs in middle- and low-quality residence zones that are expected to decline in neighborhood quality.

A decision to convert an existing building to another structure type entails a similar calculation: the capital cost of the newly converted unit is equal to the acquisition cost of the original structure (the present value of the net rental income that is lost as a result of the conversion) plus the capital costs of the conversion itself. If these capital costs are less than the present value of the converted structure's projected net rental income, the conversion is carried out.

CHIP-induced changes in neighborhood quality, in the composition of demand by income class, and in projected rents affect the opportunity costs of building new units and of converting existing units. Assuming that the CHIP subsidies induce higher-income households to move into a target neighborhood, these in-migrants are likely to demand a different mix of structure types than the residents they replace; this change in demand will in turn influence the mix of new construction and structure conversion activities. In areas where households are primarily low income, conversions of single-family houses into small apartment buildings might be profitable. Under the CHIP program, however, decisions to convert small multi-family units back into single-family homes, or to build new structures, are likely to be more appropriate.

Effects on Unsubsidized Units in Target Neighborhoods

The most significant impact of CHIP subsidies may be on the investment and production decisions of ineligible owners in target neighborhoods. If CHIP subsidies succeed in attracting more high-income households to the neighborhood, the owners of nonsubsidized units may revise their expectations about future neighborhood conditions and make more capital improvements than they would otherwise have made.

Although the housing rehabilitation literature emphasizes positive externalities or spillovers, CHIP subsidies may in fact cause the owners of some nonsubsidized buildings to invest less in maintenance and structure capital than they did in the baseline. If the CHIP subsidies do not attract higher-income residents to the target areas, they shift the structure services supply functions but produce no corresponding shifts in demand. Subsidized structures are able to produce structure services more cheaply than nonsubsidized buildings in the same neighborhood and thus capture a larger share of the unchanged number of high-income households. The demand for structure services in nonsubsidized buildings decreases, causing these owners to reduce their investments in maintenance and structure capital.

Impacts on Competing Neighborhoods

To the extent that the CHIP grants produce sustained increases in the average quality of housing units in target neighborhoods, they achieve these gains by drawing higher-income households away from competing neighborhoods. The concentrated housing improvement programs evaluated in this study — and most actual programs — have almost no effect on the aggregate level and distribution of household incomes or on the total number of households living in the metropolitan area; thus any increase in the number of high-income households choosing to live in target neighborhoods is accompanied by a corresponding decline in the number choosing other neighborhoods. Moreover, if CHIP programs displace low- and moderate-income households from target neighborhoods, or, more likely, discourage significant numbers of them from moving to the upgraded residence zones, these low- and middle-income households must necessarily occupy nontarget neighborhoods.

Although this one-for-one substitution of high- for low-income residents appears obvious, it has often been overlooked in the design of concentrated housing and neighborhood improvement programs. About 20 percent of all households move annually. These intrametropolitan movers, as well as a smaller number of new households and in-migrants, compete for units vacated by other intrametropolitan movers, out-migrants, and discontinued households, and for the new units provided by conversion or new construction. A subsidy program that alters the demand for housing in particular neighborhoods affects the entire metropolitan area housing market.

The residents and owners of subsidized buildings who receive important direct benefits of such programs are thus a small subset of those affected. Because they alter regional housing market dynamics, CHIPs — or, for that matter, nearly any government program or policy — will have *some* impact on all participants in the housing market. Households and investors in nontarget neighborhoods, however, may be the most seriously affected because of the program-induced changes in the income distribution of in-migrants to their residence zones. In addition, the programs can also redistribute new construction activities from nontarget to target neighborhoods, rather than significantly increasing their levels.

Even though CHIP subsidies do not significantly change the areawide level or distribution of incomes, they are likely to induce changes in both the net rents and the gross prices of individual housing bundles. These changes might well modify the baseline patterns of new construction, conversions, and demolitions. Because residential capital stocks are so durable, these program-induced changes could last for a decade or longer or even foster permanent changes in the pattern of urban development. The most immediate impact of program-induced shifts in the location of new construction may be to increase regionwide vacancy rates. In response to program-induced shifts in demand, the regional housing market will seek to adjust; eventually, more demolitions or less new construction will occur in nontarget neighborhoods. A major strength of HUDS is its ability to quantify the nature and extent of these substitution effects relative to a baseline. Without careful analysis of such marketwide impacts, any evaluation of concentrated housing and neighborhood improvement programs will necessarily be incomplete.

5 Impacts of Subsidies on Target Neighborhoods

This chapter analyzes the effects of CHIP loans and grants on the residents and housing stocks of six central-city neighborhoods. As the previous chapter indicates, target zones for this scenario, which we call CHIP-I, belong to the lowest or second-lowest neighborhood quality categories and were selected in pairs to reveal the effects of racial composition, location, and the extent of treatment on program outcomes. The analyses that follow emphasize how these factors interact with the CHIP subsidies to produce different responses across neighborhoods.

Effects on Target Neighborhoods

The indexes of annual mean household income for the period 1960–1970, shown in table 5.1, illustrate one of the major impacts of the CHIP subsidies on target neighborhoods. By increasing the quantity of structure services supplied and therefore average neighborhood quality, the subsidies tend to make these neighborhoods more attractive to middle- and high-income households than in the baseline. As the area improves, the better housing and improved neighborhood conditions attract still more higher-income households, thereby steadily increasing the average incomes both of in-migrants and of the neighborhood. Because mobility rates in target neighborhoods are so high, large changes in average income levels and associated improvements in a neighborhood's housing stock can occur without actually forcing lower-income households to move. Indeed, in the baseline simulation, only 16 percent of the 1960 residents of the six target neighborhoods remained in the same zone at the end of the decade, and only 12 percent lived in the same unit. If higher-income persons fill the normal vacan-

Table 5.1. Indexes of mean household income (in 1970 dollars) for target neighborhoods, 1960–1970 ($9,064 = 100)

Year	Zone 34 B	Zone 34 CHIP-I	Zone 9 B	Zone 9 CHIP-I	Zone 41 B	Zone 41 CHIP-I	Zone 22 B	Zone 22 CHIP-I	Zone 118 B	Zone 118 CHIP-I	Zone 86 B	Zone 86 CHIP-I
1960	95	95	95	95	87	87	84	84	77	77	67	67
1961	91	92	100	100	84	84	80	81	82	82	59	59
1962	87	108	99	99	81	109	82	102	82	83	55	57
1963	108	120	94	98	86	126	86	108	81	81	50	22
1964	112	129	92	94	83	139	73	121	89	83	47	48
1965	111	130	89	81	102	135	69	134	88	86	44	48
1966	127	129	83	78	113	139	66	141	91	88	42	47
1967	108	143	80	81	91	139	60	142	88	89	42	45
1968	109	152	70	65	103	142	79	129	94	93	39	44
1969	109	152	68	57	84	152	92	131	98	94	39	45
1970	107	160	68	63	79	163	93	132	99	96	37	42
1970 minus 1960	12	65	-27	-32	-8	76	9	48	22	19	-30	-25
CHIP-I minus B	53		-5		84		39		-3		5	

cies this turnover creates, the policy may significantly raise average neighborhood incomes without displacing any lower-income households.

Some critics of gentrification have used the term "displacement" to refer to losses in the supply of affordable housing available to low-income households. Whether displacement in this sense is a problem depends on whether the higher-income households that the policy attracts to the target neighborhoods vacate comparably located units that become available to the low-income former residents. Since none of the policies considered in this study increase the aggregate number of households seeking units in the metropolitan housing market, the question is whether the policy adversely affects the supply, prices, quality, or accessibility of units available to all low-income consumers. Comparisons of policy and baseline simulations of the kind described in this book provide a basis for such assessments.

Inspection of table 5.1 reveals that subsidy-induced changes in neighborhood incomes vary considerably. The largest income growth relative to the baseline occurred in the near north neighborhood, zone 41, which received subsidies to improve 40.5 percent of its dwelling units. The effects of CHIP subsidies in this neighborhood were sufficient to reverse a modest downward trend in mean income: while average incomes declined by 8 percent between 1960 and 1970 in the baseline, they grew by 76 percent in the policy simulation. The heavily treated north neighborhood, zone 34, which received subsidies to upgrade 40.6 percent of its units, experienced the second largest income growth between 1960 and 1970: 65 percent in the CHIP-I simulation as compared to 12 percent in the baseline.

The data in table 5.1 also indicate that two neighborhoods exhibited a less rapid growth of income in the policy simulation than in the baseline. Between 1960 and 1970, incomes in the high-treatment, predominantly black zone 118 grew by 22 percent in the baseline, but only 19 percent in the CHIP-I scenario. Similarly, the low-treatment, northern zone 9 shows a 32 percent decline in mean income in the policy simulation but only a 27 percent decrease in the baseline. Zone 86, the predominantly black, low-treatment area in the south, exhibits still another pattern: while average household incomes decreased in both simulations, the CHIP subsidies reduced the rate of decline by 5 percentage points. The reasons why average incomes in some target neighborhoods grew less rapidly in the CHIP-I simulations relate to the inability of the subsidies to induce sustained upgrading, and are considered later in this chapter.

Effects on Housing Investment and Production

Data provided in table 5.2 document the effect of CHIP subsidies on the average quantities of structure services supplied in each target neighborhood. These statistics indicate that the CHIP subsidies increase the end-of-decade average quantity of structure services supplied in all but the low-treatment north zone; in addition, the initial level of structure services achieved in the CHIP-I simulations is maintained or increased in four of the six target neighborhoods. The largest 1960–1970 increases in the average quantity of structure services supplied in the CHIP-I simulations occur in zone 41 (35 percent), zone 22 (32 percent), and zone 34 (26 percent); the increase in zone 118, the high-treatment black neighborhood, is only 10 percent. Relative to the baseline, the largest end-of-decade increases are in zone 22 (55 percent), zone 41 (49 percent), and zone 34 (21 percent).

Table 5.2. Mean quantity of structure services supplied per unit by residence zone, 1960–1970

Zone location, treatment level, and number	1960	1962	1964	1966	1968	1970
North						
High, 34						
Base	22.5	22.1	22.5	22.9	23.2	23.5
CHIP-I	22.5	25.3	26.5	27.7	29.0	28.5
Low, 9						
Base	21.6	21.5	20.9	20.1	18.9	17.9
CHIP-I	21.6	22.4	22.1	20.6	19.7	17.1
Near north						
High, 41						
Base	20.5	19.9	19.3	19.7	19.3	18.6
CHIP-I	20.5	23.3	25.2	26.7	27.9	27.7
Low, 22						
Base	19.4	18.9	18.8	17.2	15.8	16.5
CHIP-I	19.4	20.7	22.0	23.8	25.4	25.6
South						
High, 118						
Base	18.6	18.4	17.9	18.3	18.7	19.3
CHIP-I	18.6	21.3	20.7	20.9	21.1	20.4
Low, 86						
Base	17.3	16.3	14.7	13.4	12.5	11.6
CHIP-I	17.3	17.3	15.7	14.5	13.5	12.7

Annual estimates of average net investment or disinvestment in maintenance capital, shown in table 5.3, also illustrate the impact of the CHIP-I subsidies on the behavior of housing suppliers. Each year the Supply Sector of HUDS calculates an optimal capital stock — that is, the amount that represents the least-cost combination of factor inputs for producing the quantities of structure services demanded by the building's current residents. If the building has less than this optimal amount of maintenance capital, property owners attempt to close the gap; as described in chapter 2, they are permitted to increase their maintenance capital up to 25 percent of the difference between current and optimal levels each year, depending on current and expected neighborhood quality. If the building has too much capital, the owners allow it to depreciate.

In four of the six target neighborhoods, the CHIP subsidies induce housing suppliers to increase their average rate of investment in maintenance capital. The exceptions are the low-treatment north and the high-treatment south neighborhoods (zones 9 and 118). In the latter case, maintenance investment averages $2.90 per month per unit over the decade in the baseline, compared with an annual disinvestment of $7.50 per month in the CHIP-I simulation; this disinvestment indicates that the subsidies provide more than the optimal quality of maintenance capital for producing the quantities of structure services that the occupants of zone 118 units demand. The largest increases in average maintenance outlays, in contrast, occur in the two near north zones, where the subsidies convert a decade of steady disinvestment to a healthy rate of new investment in maintenance capital.

The CHIP subsidies affect the end-of-decade numbers of subsidized and unsubsidized units in the target neighborhoods, as well as new construction levels and conversions. As the statistics in table 5.4 reveal, five of the six target neighborhoods contain more dwelling units in the last year of the CHIP-I simulation than in the baseline. The single exception is the low-treatment black neighborhood (zone 86), which has 225 fewer dwelling units in the 1970 policy simulation, or seven-tenths of one percent less than the baseline housing inventory. In the aggregate, there are 4,825 more dwelling units at the end of the CHIP-I simulation than in the baseline.

As expected, the CHIP capital subsidies preserve significant numbers of units that would otherwise be lost. Without the subsidies, only 21,450 of the treated units would remain at the end of the decade; with CHIP, however, an additional 1,325 units are habitable, an increase of 6.2 percent. This stock preservation effect is most pronounced in zones 118 and 86, the two predominantly black South Side neighborhoods. In the

Table 5.3. Dollars of net investment per month in maintenance capital per dwelling unit, 1960–1970

Zone location, treatment level, and number	1960	1962	1964	1966	1968	1970	Average 1960–1970	Net CHIP-I minus B
North								
High, 34								
Base	28.9	−30.0	2.9	31.5	0.6	−0.4	4.7	
CHIP-I	47.1	13.2	23.1	11.2	40.5	39.5	23.0	18.3
Low, 9								
Base	−1.9	−20.1	−21.7	−30.8	−41.6	−25.3	−25.2	
CHIP-I	−4.7	−22.8	−24.4	−40.2	−62.5	−36.2	−27.8	−2.6
Near north								
High, 41								
Base	33.8	−18.9	−29.8	16.8	12.4	−40.3	−11.7	
CHIP-I	40.4	0.6	36.6	32.2	35.4	51.7	26.2	37.9
Low, 22								
Base	11.8	−8.4	−42.8	−46.9	−12.4	32.5	−14.0	
CHIP-I	6.6	22.1	23.7	49.2	19.8	38.1	25.1	39.1
South								
High, 118								
Base	0.4	−13.3	0.6	11.6	12.7	16.2	2.9	
CHIP-I	1.1	−26.0	−17.0	−3.1	9.9	6.9	−7.5	−10.4
Low, 86								
Base	63.4	−44.8	−42.8	−36.8	−26.8	−20.3	−27.2	
CHIP-I	90.7	−52.6	−47.0	−28.1	−20.1	−21.3	−23.9	3.3

Table 5.4. Effects of CHIP-I on the components of inventory change in target neighborhoods, 1960–1970

				Zone			
Unit type	34	9	41	22	118	86	All
Subsidized							
Baseline	4,850	1,700	3,150	975	7,200	3,575	21,450
CHIP-I	4,775	1,550	3,275	1,000	8,175	4,000	22,775
CHIP-I minus B	−75	−150	125	25	975	425	1,325
Unsubsidized							
Baseline	6,225	15,025	4,225	4,550	13,300	26,350	69,675
CHIP-I	6,225	15,000	3,900	4,575	12,975	25,625	68,300
CHIP-I minus B	0	−25	−325	25	−325	−725	−1,375
New construction							
Baseline	1,675	675	600	200	800	0	3,950
CHIP-I	2,100	900	2,625	2,025	1,775	0	9,425
CHIP-I minus B	425	225	2,025	1,825	975	0	5,475
Conversions							
Baseline	0	600	400	175	1,000	400	2,575
CHIP-I	0	625	150	0	725	475	1,975
CHIP-I minus B	0	25	−250	−175	−275	75	−600
Exogenous							
Baseline	0	600	0	0	600	400	1,600
CHIP-I	0	600	0	0	600	400	1,600
CHIP-I minus B	0	0	0	0	0	0	0
Total							
Baseline	12,750	18,600	8,375	5,900	22,900	30,725	99,250
CHIP-I	13,100	18,675	9,950	7,600	24,250	30,500	104,075
CHIP-I minus B	350	75	1,575	1,700	1,350	−225	4,825

baseline, these two neighborhoods lost 10 and 15 percent of their housing stocks to abandonment by 1970; the CHIP subsidies succeeded in preserving 425 units in zone 86 and 975 units in zone 118. In the other target areas, the numbers of treated units remaining in 1970 differed little between the baseline and policy simulations. In zones 41 and 22, the CHIP-I subsidies preserved 125 and 25 of the subsidized units, while in zones 35 and 9 more treated units were lost with the policy than in the baseline.

The data in table 5.4 also demonstrate that the growth in the housing stocks of target neighborhoods is due primarily to new construction, since increased losses of unsubsidized units almost exactly offset the

80

IMPACTS OF SUBSIDIES

numbers of subsidized units that the CHIP subsidies conserve. The neighborhoods experiencing the greatest policy-induced growth in their housing stocks are residence zone 41 (the high-treatment near north neighborhood), which increased its inventory by 18.8 percent, and residence zone 22 (the low-treatment near north neighborhood), which increased its inventory by 28.8 percent. In both instances, new construction accounts for all of the gains.

As table 5.5 indicates, the CHIP-I subsidies trigger a complex series of stock changes in both target and nontarget neighborhoods. Compared to the baseline situation, the CHIP subsidies increase the end-of-decade housing inventories in the target neighborhoods by 4,825 but reduce the housing inventory of the nontarget areas by 1,000 units. In the case of target neighborhoods, the growth is due to a 5,700-unit increase in new construction offset by 350 fewer converted units and 525 more units removed by demolition. CHIP subsidies cause new construction activity to increase in nontarget neighborhoods as well, although these increases amount to less than 2 percent of the total baseline level of new construction in nontarget areas. More significant are the policy-induced changes in demolition activity in nontarget neighborhoods. The CHIP subsidies increase the demolitions in nontarget areas by 8,200, an increase of nearly 5 percent above the total demolitions of 177,625 in the baseline simulations.

Table 5.5 also presents information on CHIP-induced changes in construction type. As noted earlier, the CHIP-I program induces the owners of 23,825 target-area dwelling units to add structure capital and

Table 5.5. Effects of CHIP-I on the components of inventory change, 1960–1970, and on end-of-decade number of units by construction type

| | CHIP-I minus baseline | | |
Change in stock	SMSA	Target neighborhoods	Nontarget neighborhoods
Component of change			
New construction	11,775	5,700	6,075
Net conversions	775	−350	1,125
Demolitions	8,725	525	8,200
End-of-decade units			
Construction type 1	6,950	9,025	−2,075
Construction type 2	8,525	4,750	3,775
Construction type 3	−11,650	−8,950	−2,700
Total units	3,825	4,825	−1,000

upgrade their units to construction type 1. Despite the investment, by the end of the decade CHIP target areas have only 9,025 more units of construction type 1 than were present under baseline conditions. Over the decade, a sizable proportion of CHIP-subsidized structure capital investment depreciated and many subsidized units moved from construction type 1 to construction type 2. Nonetheless, by the end of the decade, target neighborhoods continued to exhibit the effects of the CHIP subsidies by having more units of construction types 1 and 2 and fewer units of construction type 3 than they had under baseline conditions.

The data in table 5.5 suggest that changes in construction type in nontarget neighborhoods are linked to similar changes in target areas. The number of units of construction type 1 in target areas increased by 9,025; in nontarget areas, construction type 1 units declined by 2,075. In addition, with CHIP, the nontarget areas had 2,700 fewer units of construction type 3, but somewhat more of construction type 2. These changes represent a complex process of market adjustment to the introduction of the CHIP subsidies in the six target neighborhoods. It should be noted, however, that the introduction of CHIP subsidies neither changes the number of households nor alters the household income distribution for the metropolitan area as a whole. CHIP does, however, induce many upper-income households to relocate from nontarget to target area neighborhoods. CHIP therefore reduces the demand for higher-quality units in nontarget area neighborhoods and encourages property owners in those neighborhoods to reduce the amount of structure capital in their buildings. As should be expected, this disinvestment process takes time. The movement of properties from construction type 1 to construction type 2 will reduce the number of units of construction type 1 and increase the number of units of construction type 2. Eventually, the number of type 2 units will decline as well, until the housing stock of nontarget neighborhoods has achieved a new distribution of construction types that is consistent with the reduced demand for structure services.

The data presented in tables 5.6 and 5.7 offer some insight into the extent to which CHIP subsidies can induce a permanent shift in the demand for structure services in target neighborhoods. Table 5.6 provides estimates of the 1960 capital stocks of eligible units in both the baseline and the CHIP-I simulation, as well as indexes of the average capital stocks of subsidized units for selected years; table 5.7 then presents comparable estimates for units in each neighborhood in 1960 that did not receive CHIP subsidies.

Examination of baseline trends reveals that the mean capital stocks of

IMPACTS OF SUBSIDIES

Table 5.6. Effects of CHIP-I on capital stock of subsidized units, 1960–1970

Zone location, treatment level, and number	1960 capital stock	Index of capital stock (1960 baseline = 100)					
		1960	1962	1964	1966	1968	1970
North							
High, 34							
Base	$ 8,425	100	97	95	94	93	92
CHIP-I	11,714	139	139	139	138	136	135
Low, 9							
Base	8,265	100	100	101	99	99	95
CHIP-I	11,944	144	140	135	135	140	143
Near north							
High, 41							
Base	7,679	100	99	97	96	94	91
CHIP-I	11,835	154	149	148	147	148	149
Low, 22							
Base	7,679	100	97	97	94	91	89
CHIP-I	11,551	156	156	152	154	157	157
South							
High, 118							
Base	7,666	100	97	95	93	92	92
CHIP-I	11,922	156	155	151	150	150	147
Low, 86							
Base	7,594	100	97	94	91	90	87
CHIP-I	11,617	153	153	152	150	148	148

units eligible for CHIP subsidies decline steadily over the decade in all six target neighborhoods, reaching 87 to 92 percent of their 1960 levels by 1970. The subsidies augment the 1960 capital stocks of eligible units by amounts ranging from 39 percent (zone 34) to 56 percent (zone 118). Although the subsidized units in the CHIP-I simulation also depreciate steadily over the decade, they nonetheless possess substantially more capital in 1970 than in the baseline at either the start or the end of the decade. The experience of zone 34 is typical. CHIP-I increases the average capital stocks of its subsidized units from $8,425 to $11,714, or by 39 percent. Using the average 1960 capital value of eligible units as a base, the average quantity of maintenance and structure capital embodied in the subsidized units of zone 34 declines steadily from 139 in 1960 to 135 in 1970, or by 4 percent. Nevertheless, the capital stocks of these units in 1970 are on average 35 percent greater than the baseline 1960 values and 47 percent greater than the 1970 baseline values.

Table 5.7. Effects of CHIP-I on capital stock of unsubsidized units, 1960–1970

Zone location, treatment level, and number	1960 capital stock	Index of capital stock (1960 baseline = 100)					
		1960	1962	1964	1966	1968	1970
North							
High, 34							
Base	$7,139	100	99	98	97	97	96
CHIP-I	7,139	100	100	101	107	111	116
Low, 9							
Base	6,691	100	99	97	95	92	89
CHIP-I	6,691	100	100	100	100	99	102
Near north							
High, 41							
Base	6,229	100	99	98	95	92	91
CHIP-I	6,229	100	100	103	120	115	116
Low, 22							
Base	6,392	100	98	97	94	90	88
CHIP-I	6,392	100	100	102	105	113	116
South							
High, 118							
Base	6,252	100	98	96	95	94	94
CHIP-I	6,252	100	100	101	101	101	99
Low, 86							
Base	5,932	100	97	94	91	88	85
CHIP-I	5,932	100	100	100	100	100	101

Among unsubsidized units in the six target neighborhoods, those in all but one area (zone 118, the high-treatment south neighborhood) experience less depreciation or more net investment on average in the CHIP-I simulation than in the baseline. The indexes in table 5.7 indicate that the CHIP subsidies actually induce upgrading—that is, positive net investment in unsubsidized units—in three zones: the values for the high-treatment zones in the north and near north both increase from 100 in 1960 to 116 in 1970, while the index for the low-treatment zone in the near north increases from 100 in 1960 to 102 in 1970.

Presented in tables 5.8 and 5.9 are more disaggregate analyses of the changes in capital stocks for two target neighborhoods. The high-treatment near north neighborhood (zone 41) exhibits the greatest income growth relative to the baseline—84 percent—of all target zones, and 1970 neighborhood quality improves from worst in the baseline to best in the CHIP-I simulation. In contrast, 1970 average incomes in zone 86,

IMPACTS OF SUBSIDIES

the low-treatment south neighborhood, grow by only 5 percent in the CHIP-I simulation, an amount that is too small to produce any significant neighborhood improvement.

At the start of the decade, 3,525 — 40 percent — of the dwelling units in zone 41 receive CHIP subsidies. As noted previously, these subsidies reduce the number of eligible units lost over the decade from 325 in the baseline to 250; these gains, however, are more than offset by losses from the unsubsidized portion of the inventory, which increase from 950 in the baseline to 1,275 in the CHIP-I simulation. The combined net loss of subsidized and unsubsidized units induced by the CHIP subsidies over the period amounts to 200 of zone 41's original stock of 7,800 units.

Disaggregation of the capital stocks into maintenance and structure capital reveals some important differences in the response of housing suppliers to the CHIP subsidies. The data in table 5.8 demonstrate that structure capital (long-lasting components of structures) displays the same trends as total capital: the CHIP subsidies increase the stock of structure capital in the average eligible unit from $6,206 in 1960 to $9,723 in 1962, or by 57 percent; by 1970, however, the level of structure capital declines by 10 percent, to $8,736. Relative to the baseline, the decline is much more modest — from an index of 157 in 1962 to only 155 in 1970. Table 5.8 shows that the average quantity of structure capital in zone 86's unsubsidized units in the CHIP-I simula-

Table 5.8. Effects of CHIP-I on the number of units and capital stock in zone 41, 1960–1970

Type of unit	1960 baseline	Index of capital stock (1960 baseline = 100)					
		1960	1962	1964	1966	1968	1970
Number of units							
Subsidized	3,525	100	103	105	109	108	104
Unsubsidized	5,175	100	100	102	98	90	92
Structure capital							
Subsidized	$6,206	159	157	156	154	154	155
Unsubsidized	$4,804	100	100	102	109	113	112
Maintenance capital							
Subsidized	$1,474	115	114	113	117	121	125
Unsubsidized	$1,425	100	100	109	117	125	133
Total capital							
Subsidized	$7,679	154	149	148	147	148	149
Unsubsidized	$6,229	100	100	103	120	115	116

tion increases slightly between 1960 and 1970; relative to the baseline, however, the amount embodied in these units is 12 percent higher in 1970. All of this increased investment in structure capital can be attributed to the indirect effects of the CHIP subsidies.

Since investments in maintenance capital are less durable than investments in structure capital and typically involve smaller outlays, they respond more quickly to changing market conditions. CHIP subsidies thus increase the initial stock of maintenance capital of eligible units by an average of 10 percent; subsequent neighborhood quality improvements and rent and value increases in turn cause the owners of subsidized properties to invest an additional 7 percent in maintenance capital. By the end of the decade, the stock of maintenance capital embodied in units receiving CHIP subsidies is therefore 25 percent higher than in the baseline. The experience of unsubsidized units is even more notable: encouraged by neighborhood improvements, property owners increase the average level of maintenance capital by 13 percent between 1960 and 1970 in the CHIP simulation; end-of-decade levels are 33 percent higher than in the baseline.

Program-induced investments in both subsidized and unsubsidized units in zone 86, presented in table 5.9, are somewhat lower than in zone 41. Like the subsidized units in zone 41, however, structure capital investments in zone 86 in units receiving subsidies decline by 11 percent

Table 5.9. Effects of CHIP-I on the number of units and capital stock in zone 86, 1960–1970

Type of unit	1960 baseline	Index of capital stock (1960 baseline = 100)					
		1960	1962	1964	1966	1968	1970
Number of units							
Subsidized	4,025	100	101	101	103	110	112
Unsubsidized	30,575	100	100	99	99	99	97
Structure capital							
Subsidized	$6,199	160	160	160	159	155	155
Unsubsidized	$4,814	100	100	100	100	100	100
Maintenance capital							
Subsidized	$1,395	118	118	110	105	107	112
Unsubsidized	$1,218	100	100	101	101	104	106
Total capital							
Subsidized	$7,594	153	153	152	150	148	148
Unsubsidized	$5,932	100	100	100	100	100	101

by 1970. Relative to the baseline, moreover, average structure capital decreases from 160 in 1962 to 155 at the decade's end. In contrast to the experience described for zone 41, though, the CHIP subsidies in zone 86 have no impact on the average quantity of structure capital embodied in unsubsidized units in 1970: structure capital depreciates from $4,814 to approximately $4,350 over the decade in both the baseline and policy simulations.

The initial endowment of maintenance capital provided by the CHIP subsidies in zone 86 declines both absolutely and relative to the baseline over the decade. Some evidence of CHIP-induced upgrading is evident, however, in the average quantities of maintenance capital embodied in unsubsidized units. Even though maintenance capital decreased by 28 percent between 1960 and 1970 in the policy simulation, the rate of decline is somewhat lower than the baseline amount of nearly 34 percent.

Impacts on Neighborhood Quality

As the indexes in table 5.10 indicate, the CHIP-I subsidies cause four of the six target neighborhoods — including all three of the high-treatment zones — to improve by at least one quality level over the decade. In the most dramatic case, neighborhood quality in the high-treatment near north residence zone declines from level II in 1960 to level I in 1970 in the baseline; in the CHIP-I simulation, however, zone 41 improves from level II to level V by the end of the decade. The high-treatment north zone also attains the highest neighborhood quality level by the end of the CHIP-I simulation, although it began at level II and reached level III in the baseline. Of the three high-treatment areas, the predominantly black neighborhood (zone 118) exhibits the least improvement: remaining at quality level I throughout the decade in the baseline, the residence zone reaches level II in the second year of the CHIP-I simulation and maintains this level thereafter. Two of the three low-treatment neighborhoods, zones 9 (north) and 86 (south), have identical neighborhood quality levels in every year of the baseline and CHIP-I simulations. The third neighborhood (zone 22) remains at the worst quality level for the entire decade in the baseline, but improves steadily in the CHIP-I simulation to level IV in 1968.

The divergent responses of the six target zones to the CHIP-I subsidies appear to reflect differences in both the levels of subsidies provided and neighborhood location. The two areas achieving the highest neighborhood quality levels in the CHIP simulations, zones 34 and 41, receive subsidies to upgrade more than 40 percent of their 1960 housing

Table 5.10. Effects of CHIP-I on neighborhood quality levels in target neighborhoods, 1960–1970

Year	Zone 34 B	Zone 34 CHIP-I	Zone 9 B	Zone 9 CHIP-I	Zone 41 B	Zone 41 CHIP-I	Zone 22 B	Zone 22 CHIP-I	Zone 118 B	Zone 118 CHIP-I	Zone 86 B	Zone 86 CHIP-I
1960	II	II	II	II	II	II	I	I	I	I	I	I
1961	II	IV	II	II	II	III	I	II	I	II	I	I
1962	II	IV	II	II	I	III	I	II	I	II	I	I
1963	II	IV	II	II	I	III	I	II	I	II	I	I
1964	III	IV	II	II	I	IV	I	II	I	II	I	I
1965	III	IV	II	II	I	IV	I	III	I	II	I	I
1966	III	V	II	II	I	IV	I	III	I	II	I	I
1967	III	V	I	I	II	IV	I	III	I	II	I	I
1968	III	V	I	I	I	V	I	IV	I	II	I	I
1969	III	V	I	I	I	V	I	IV	I	II	I	I
1970	III	V	I	I	I	V	I	IV	I	II	I	I
CHIP-I minus B	2		0		4		3		1		0	

inventories and are both located in the city's high-income north sector. The neighborhoods experiencing the greatest improvement in quality, moreover, are the two near north zones that are highly accessible to the Loop and other centrally located, high-density workplaces. Policy-induced demand among high-income households for units in these residence zones appears to be sufficient to create and maintain these two high-quality neighborhoods.

The significant upgrading of Chicago's two near north neighborhoods was anticipated by the findings of an earlier Neighborhood Improvement Diagnostic (NID) simulation, which indicated that a neighborhood improvement program would encourage development of two high-quality neighborhoods in the same general area of the city (Kain and Apgar, 1980). The decade following the 1960–1970 baseline used for these analyses, moreover, witnessed the emergence of Chicago's New Town and Old Town, as well as the rapid conversion of thousands of North Side apartments to luxury condominiums. The NID and CHIP-I simulations may thus have anticipated the private market renewal that actually occurred. The same locational advantages and other conditions that produced sustained upgrading in these neighborhoods also explain the response of zones 34 and 41 to CHIP subsidies.

In evaluating the effectiveness of neighborhood revitalization programs, an important consideration is whether the upgrading represents a net increase in the aggregate supply of high-quality housing and neighborhoods or whether it occurs at the expense of other residence zones. The statistics presented in table 5.11 on the number of neighborhoods at each quality level in both the policy and baseline simulations bear on this question. The diagonal entries, accounting for 151 of the 198 zones, are neighborhoods that in 1970 were at the same quality

Table 5.11. Number of neighborhoods by end-of-period quality level, baseline and CHIP-I simulations, 1970

Baseline neighborhood quality level	CHIP-I neighborhood quality level					
	I	II	III	IV	V	All
I	35	8	0	1	1	45
II	5	12	2	0	0	19
III	0	7	25	3	2	37
IV	0	2	5	19	6	32
V	0	0	0	5	60	65
All	40	29	32	28	69	198

level in both simulations. Entries below the diagonal are neighborhoods that deteriorated to a lower quality level in the policy simulation than the baseline; entries above the diagonal improved in quality in the policy scenario.

Of the twenty-three neighborhoods that increased in quality one or more levels as a result of the CHIP subsidies, two (zones 22 and 41) improved by three and four quality levels, respectively, while two others (zones 34 and 12) improved by two levels. Only two of the twenty-four zones that deteriorated in quality declined by more than one level. In 1970 both of these neighborhoods were at quality level IV in the baseline; zone 37 had improved from level I since 1960, while zone 42 had improved from level II. In the CHIP-I simulation, however, neighborhood quality in zone 37 increased from I to II but remained at level II for the entire decade — as did zone 42. These results suggest that the program induced some net upgrading (residence zones are of unequal size, however); but there may have been adverse impacts on some areas that did not receive subsidies. Comparing row and column totals in table 5.11 reveals that there are four more highest-quality and five fewer lowest-quality neighborhoods in 1970 in the CHIP-I simulations than in the baseline; in addition, there are four more neighborhoods of quality level IV and ten more residence zones of quality level II.

As indicated in table 5.12, CHIP-I subsidies increase the number of units located in both the best and next-to-best neighborhoods at the end

Table 5.12. Effects of CHIP-I on the number of units in each neighborhood quality level, 1970

Location	Neighborhood quality level					
	I	II	III	IV	V	All
SMSA						
Baseline	540,000	202,900	337,400	335,950	866,325	2,282,575
CHIP-I	520,575	243,500	274,050	348,550	899,725	2,286,400
CHIP-I minus B	−19,425	40,600	−63,350	12,600	33,400	3,825
Target neighborhoods						
Baseline	86,500	0	12,750	0	0	99,250
CHIP-I	49,175	24,250	0	7,600	23,050	104,075
CHIP-I minus B	−37,325	24,250	−12,750	7,600	23,050	4,825
Rest of SMSA						
Baseline	453,500	202,900	324,650	335,950	866,325	2,183,325
CHIP-I	471,400	219,250	274,050	340,950	876,675	2,182,325
CHIP-I minus B	19,900	16,350	−50,600	5,000	10,350	−1,000

of the decade. The table shows that these increases occur in nontarget as well as target neighborhoods. For the entire SMSA, the end-of-decade inventory in the next-to-best neighborhoods is about 2.2 percent higher than baseline levels; in the best neighborhoods it is 2.6 percent higher. The combined gains in these two categories are somewhat less than the declines in level III neighborhoods. The policy also reduces the supply of units in the least desirable neighborhoods by 19,425 units, or 3.6 percent of the baseline end-of-decade levels.

The locations of the twenty-nine central-city residence zones that improve or deteriorate in quality in the CHIP-I simulations are depicted in figure 5.1; the numbers in each district indicate how many quality levels particular neighborhoods changed. It is evident from this map that policy-induced improvements in the two near north target neighborhoods almost certainly have adverse impacts on nearby residence zones. For example, although zone 41 increased in quality by

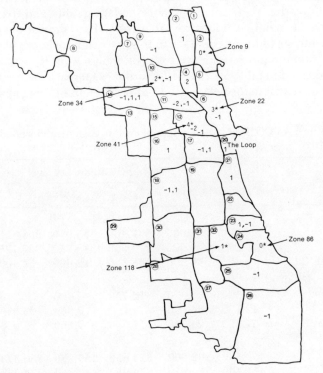

Figure 5.1. Changes in quality levels for neighborhoods in the CHIP-I simulation

four levels in response to CHIP subsidies, two residence zones in the same transit district deteriorated by one and two levels, as did two neighborhoods in the transit district immediately to the north. These declines in the quality of surrounding neighborhoods may also reflect the upgrading that occurred in zones 22 and 34 as well. At the same time, it should be noted that the only nontarget neighborhood to improve by more than one quality level in the CHIP-I simulation is also located in this northern sector.

It is possible that providing subsidies to the six target zones could cause less upgrading in the nearby neighborhoods than would have occurred without the policy. As discussed above, CHIP subsidies produce sustained neighborhood improvements when they succeed in attracting higher-income households to the residence zone; higher-income residents demand more structure services and stimulate housing suppliers to make additional investments in housing capital, which leads to further increases in neighborhood quality and the attraction of still more higher-income residents. The initial increases in neighborhood quality occur because the CHIP-I subsidies reduce the marginal cost and price of structure services, thereby encouraging the residents of subsidized units to consume larger quantities.

Most of the higher-income in-migrants to target neighborhoods in the CHIP-I simulation are attracted from competing zones that are similar in quality and location. When they choose to reside in the target neighborhoods rather than in their baseline residence zones, their absence means a reduction in the number of high-income residents, the quantities of structure services demanded, and the pressures for upgrading in their original neighborhoods. Units formerly occupied by high-income in-migrants to target neighborhoods become available to those "displaced" lower-income residents who lived in the target zones in the baseline. These former residents of target zones also tend to demand units in neighborhoods that are similar in location and quality to those they occupied in the baseline. Although the CHIP-I subsidies may thus produce some net upgrading, their major impact is to attract higher-income households to the improving target neighborhoods while the former low-income residents move to the vacated dwelling units in nontarget neighborhoods.

The preceding description of the movements of high- and low-income households sounds a bit like the children's game of musical chairs. In the real world, however, housing market participants have only one play. Eligible owners of properties in particular neighborhoods either would receive CHIP subsidies or would not. Similarly, higher-income households either would or would not be attracted to the target neighborhoods. The policy simulation described in this chapter suggests that if CHIP subsidies were provided to selected neighborhoods, some, but not all, of these residence zones would experience sustained upgrading. The subsidies would attract more high-income households, induce higher levels of investment among unsubsidized units, and stimulate more new construction of high-quality units than would occur in the absence of subsidies. Most relocations would result from "voluntary mobility." Indeed, in the current version of the model, the only way the program can induce a household to move is by causing the abandonment, demolition, or major rehabilitation (change of structure type) of units available in the baseline. Lower-income households that would have lived in the target zone typically find comparable units in neighborhoods of similar quality and location. Before this issue is discussed further, however, the next chapter compares the results of the CHIP-I scenario with those of the other two simulated concentrated housing improvement programs.

6 Impacts of Spatially Concentrated Policies

Results of the earlier Neighborhood Improvement Diagnostic (NID) simulation suggested that a more spatially concentrated policy might affect nearby residence zones even more severely than the CHIP-I program (Kain and Apgar, 1980). The CHIP-I simulation also indicated that an extensive program of rehabilitation subsidies concentrating on ghetto neighborhoods might have an effect very different from that of a program focusing on predominantly white neighborhoods. To test these possibilities, we simulated two variants of CHIP-I. The first, the Concentrated North (CN) policy, provides loans and grants to eligible owner-occupants in seven predominantly white residence zones located to the north and northwest of the Loop, Chicago's central business district; the second, the Concentrated South (CS) policy, focuses on five predominantly black zones on Chicago's South Side. The target neighborhoods for both programs are shown in figure 6.1.

Although the number of target neighborhoods differs in the two programs, the total populations and numbers of eligible households are approximately the same. Comparing policies that focus separately on black and white neighborhoods provides a better understanding of how discrimination and segregation affect housing market operations, and of the secondary impacts of housing and urban development policies that are oriented toward ghetto neighborhoods. As in the CHIP-I simulation, owner-occupants use the loans and grants to improve their structures to 90 percent of good-as-new condition.

Program Characteristics

As the analysis presented in table 6.1 shows, the eligibility rate of dwelling units in the Concentrated North neighborhoods varies from a high

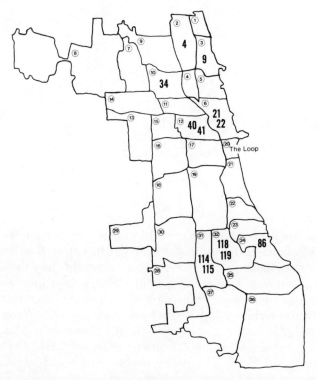

Figure 6.1.   Target neighborhoods in the Concentrated North and Concentrated South policy simulations

of 40.6 percent (zone 34) to a low of 9.7 percent (zone 9); in the Concentrated South simulation, the range is from 45.2 percent (zone 115) to 11.6 percent (zone 86). It should be noted that the target neighborhoods in this and subsequent tables are listed in order by the fraction of units in each zone receiving subsidies — that is, from most heavily to most lightly treated neighborhood.

These data also document the fact that the major difference between the two simulations is that the CS neighborhoods contain much higher proportions of black residents; these zones also tend to have lower mean incomes. While owner-occupancy rates by neighborhood vary considerably, the combined rates of homeownership are 20.4 percent in the CN target neighborhoods and 22.9 percent in the CS zones. Average household incomes in the CN zones are 8.5 percent higher than in the CS zones.

Table 6.1. Characteristics of Concentrated North and Concentrated South residence zones, 1960

Zone	Percent eligible units	Percent black	Percent lowest income category	Mean income	Percent owner-occupied
CN					
34	40.6	0.2	8.6	$8,618	33.1
41	40.5	0.6	14.1	7,856	40.5
40	24.0	5.8	25.9	6,703	17.8
21	22.5	2.5	16.3	7,535	15.1
22	17.2	5.0	22.0	7,585	15.2
4	15.6	2.2	18.6	8,257	15.3
9	9.7	2.3	15.1	8,650	13.5
All	23.5	3.2	18.6	7,698	20.4
CS					
115	45.2	22.6	12.8	8,506	41.9
118	33.0	64.7	21.6	6,990	25.6
119	33.0	65.6	15.7	8,202	30.0
114	19.8	42.6	25.5	7,021	19.8
86	11.6	83.1	28.9	6,064	10.0
All	26.5	64.9	22.0	7,092	22.9

Table 6.2. Effects of Concentrated North and Concentrated South programs on subsidized units (in 1970 dollars)

Zone	Number of subsidized units	Mean initial capital stock	Mean improvement	Mean improvement divided by capital stock
CN				
34	4,975	$8,425	$3,289	39.0
41	3,525	7,679	4,156	54.1
40	7,775	7,313	4,182	57.1
21	2,350	7,649	3,709	45.5
22	1,075	7,400	4,151	56.1
4	1,250	7,910	3,520	40.7
9	1,800	8,265	3,679	44.5
All CN zones	22,750	7,807	3,837	49.2
CS				
115	6,175	8,256	3,759	45.5
118	8,425	7,667	4,255	55.5
119	5,600	7,883	3,904	49.7
114	475	8,189	4,249	51.3
86	4,025	7,594	4,023	53.0
All CS zones	24,700	7,862	4,012	51.0

Shown in table 6.2 are estimates of the number of units receiving subsidies, the average 1960 value of the capital stocks of eligible units in the baseline, the average CHIP-subsidized investment, and the percentage of the capital stocks that these subsidized investments represent. Even though the CN program includes more neighborhoods, the CS program provides subsidies to a larger number of units: 24,700 versus 22,750. The CN simulation, moreover, includes the neighborhood with the lowest average initial capital value for subsidized units (zone 40, $7,313), as well as the neighborhood with the highest (zone 34, $8,425). On average, the structures eligible for CHIP grants and loans in the CN policy contain slightly less capital than those eligible for subsidies in the CS scenario. The average CHIP-subsidized investment provided in the CN policy ($3,837), moreover, is about 5 percent smaller than the average CS subsidized investment. The subsidized investments represent from 39 percent (CN zone 34) to 56.1 percent (CN zone 22) of the initial capital valuation of those units.

Summary statistics included in table 6.3 provide further information

Table 6.3. Effects of Concentrated North and Concentrated South programs on target neighborhoods (in 1970 dollars)

Zone	Value of 1960 capital stock (millions)		Value of total improvement (millions)	Improvement as a percent of 1960 capital stock
	All units	Subsidized units		
CN				
34	$ 92.9	$ 41.9	$16.4	17.6
41	57.9	27.1	14.7	25.4
40	199.5	56.9	32.5	16.2
21	65.1	18.0	8.2	12.6
22	40.4	8.0	4.5	11.0
4	52.3	10.8	4.4	8.4
9	124.4	14.9	6.6	5.3
All CN zones	632.5	177.6	87.3	13.8
CS				
115	106.9	51.0	23.2	21.7
118	167.9	64.6	35.8	21.4
119	125.2	44.1	21.9	17.5
114	16.6	3.9	2.0	12.0
86	206.6	30.6	16.2	7.8
All CS zones	623.2	194.2	99.1	15.9

on the extent of treatment. The CN loans and grants induce investment totaling $87.3 million (in 1970 dollars), while the CS program induces investment of $99.1 million; by comparison, subsidized investment for the CHIP-I policy totaled $94.2. As a percentage of the initial capital stocks of all target neighborhood units, the subsidized investments range from a low of 5.3 percent (CN zone 9) to a high of 25.4 percent (CN zone 41).

Impacts on Household Income

Without long-term subsidies, the attraction of higher-income households to target residence zones is a necessary condition for sustained neighborhood upgrading. The indexes of mean household income in the baseline and in the Concentrated North and Concentrated South policies are thus highly relevant. The first conclusion these data suggest is that the subsidies cause much more income growth in CN than in CS neighborhoods, a result anticipated by the CHIP-I simulation. It is also true, however, that two of the seven CN neighborhoods fared less well under the policy than in the baseline: as table 6.4 indicates, the growth of average incomes in zone 40 between 1960 and 1970 was 11 percentage points less in the CN simulation than in the baseline, and average incomes in zone 9, which over the decade declined by 27 percent in the baseline, declined an additional 5 percentage points with the CN policy. In contrast, all five CS neighborhoods experienced some improvement between 1960 and 1970 relative to the baseline: the smallest improvement, 4 percentage points, was recorded by CS zone 118, while the largest improvement relative to the baseline, 23 percentage points, was recorded by CS zone 115. In the latter case the program reversed a 5 percentage point decline in the baseline, converting it into an 18 percent gain.

Even though two of the CN target neighborhoods had less income growth in the policy than in the baseline, the unweighted average of the 1960–1970 changes in average incomes for the seven CN target neighborhoods is nearly twice as large as for the five CS target neighborhoods, 23.3 percentage points versus 10.4 percent for CS target neighborhoods. The most rapid income growth relative to the baseline in any of the CS target neighborhoods occurs in residence zone 115, which is also the most heavily treated neighborhood: 45 percent of its dwelling units receive subsidies. Three of the seven CN target neighborhoods, however, have income growth rates for the decade that exceed the 23 percent relative income growth in CS zone 115: incomes in zone 34 grew by 52 percent more than in the baseline, in zone 41 by 77 percent

SPATIALLY CONCENTRATED POLICIES

Table 6.4. Indexes of Mean Household Income for Target Neighborhoods in baseline, Concentrated North, and Concentrated South simulatons ($9,064 = 100)

Zone	Simulation	1960	1965	1970	1970 minus 1960	Net
CN						
34*	B	95	111	107	12	52
	CN	95	133	159	64	
41*	B	87	102	79	−8	77
	CN	87	144	156	69	
40	B	74	76	103	29	−11
	CN	74	83	92	18	
21	B	83	88	103	20	8
	CN	83	119	111	28	
22*	B	84	69	93	9	38
	CN	84	105	131	47	
4	B	91	94	92	1	4
	CN	91	78	96	5	
9*	B	95	89	68	−27	−5
	CN	95	76	63	−32	
CS						
115	B	94	87	89	−5	23
	CS	94	114	112	18	
118*	B	77	88	99	22	4
	CS	77	92	103	26	
119	B	90	109	108	18	9
	CS	90	110	117	27	
114	B	77	107	77	0	11
	CS	77	76	88	11	
86*	B	67	44	37	−30	5
	CS	67	49	42	−25	

* Neighborhood appears also in the CHIP-I simulation.

more, and in zone 22 by 38 percent more. With 40.6 and 40.5 percent of their units receiving CHIP subsidies, zones 34 and 41 were almost as heavily treated as the CS zone 115, which received subsidies for 45.2 percent of its units. It should be noted that even though CHIP subsidized only 17.2 percent of its units, average incomes in zone 22 grew by 38 percent.

Comparison of the income changes with figure 6.1 suggests that location is an important factor in determining the extent of program-induced income growth or decline in the target neighborhoods. Of the three Concentrated North zones that experienced the most rapid growth in average incomes, two (zones 22 and 41) are located in transit districts adjacent to the Loop, while the third (zone 34) lies to the northwest of the Loop. The improvement exhibited by these target neighborhoods exceeds that occurring in any of the five Concentrated South areas. Two of the three zones with the lowest rates of income growth in the CN simulation are far from the Loop. Unlike more centrally located target zones, even with CHIP-induced capital improvements these two zones were unable to attract new upper-income residents. Location appears to be a factor in explaining the relative extent of improvement by the five Concentrated South target neighborhoods. CS zones 114, 115, and 119, the three CS neighborhoods exhibiting the most improvement relative to the baseline, are located on or near the periphery of the ghetto. In contrast, CS zones 118 and 86, the two zones experiencing the smallest income growth relative to the baseline, are part of Chicago's large Southside black ghetto. Although these zones are accessible to Chicago's central business district, few upper-income households choose to live in these ghetto neighborhoods.

The rapid upgrading of residence zones 41 and 22 in the CN scenario appears to have occurred partly at the expense of target zones 40 and 21, located in the same transit districts. With a policy-induced income growth of 77 percent relative to the baseline, it is likely that zone 41 attracted high-income households away from nearby zone 40. Despite the fact that 24.0 percent of zone 40 units received subsidies, the neighborhood lost ground relative to the more heavily treated zone 41. CN zone 22, which experienced the third highest income growth rate relative to the baseline, is similarly located in the same transit district as zone 21, where the 28 percent growth in income induced by the Concentrated North policy only slightly exceeds the baseline rate of 20 percent; in effect, competition from nearby target zones appears to have neutralized zone 21's location advantages. It should also be noted that the percentage of zone 21 units receiving subsidies is slightly larger than the percentage in zone 22, even though the latter experienced much more rapid income growth. Moreover, CN zone 34, the only residence zone in its transit district receiving subsidies, experienced the second highest income growth. Despite its distance from Chicago's Loop, the zone benefited from both a high share of subsidized units and the absence of competition from nearby zones.

Four CN and two CS neighborhoods are target zones in the CHIP-I simulations as well. Comparison of the indexes of mean household income in table 6.4 with those for the CHIP-I zones in table 5.1 provides further evidence that target neighborhoods compete with nearby zones for higher-income households. Of the four target neighborhoods that appear in both the CN and CHIP-I simulations, one exhibits the same pattern of relative income growth in both scenarios; two show an income growth 1 percentage point higher in the CHIP-I than in the CN simulation; and one displays a 7 percent greater increase in the CHIP-I than in the CN simulation. These differences would likely be even more pronounced if the CHIP-I scenario provided subsidies to fewer neighborhoods and units in the north and northwest sectors of the city. The number of subsidized units in these areas in the CHIP-I simulation is 50 percent as large as the number in the CN policy. Evidence of geographic competition is less clear for the South Side zones: one of the two common target neighborhoods in the Concentrated South and CHIP-I simulations had an identical time path of net income growth, and the other grew more rapidly in the CS simulation.

Inspection of table 6.4 and figure 6.1 thus suggest that the share of a neighborhood's units receiving subsidies is a major factor in determining whether a given target zone will experience sustained income growth and upgrading. Location—in this instance, accessibility to the Loop and other centrally located, high-density employment centers—and the levels of subsidy provided nearby competing neighborhoods, however, are perhaps even more important considerations.

Impacts on Capital Stock and Maintenance

The initial effect of the CHIP subsidies is to augment the capital stocks of eligible units, thereby reducing the marginal cost and price of structure services and increasing the quantities of services that occupants consume. Policy-induced investments in unsubsidized units lead to further increases in the quantities of structure services supplied and consumed in target neighborhoods, as do increased rates of in-migration of higher-income households. The data in table 6.5 indicate that the consumption of structure services among target neighborhood residents is already greater in the second year of the simulations. Between 1960 and 1962 in the baseline, the average quantity of structure services supplied (consumed) declined in nine of the twelve target neighborhoods; in the policy simulation, however, this quantity was larger in 1962 than in 1960 for all twelve residence zones.

Table 6.5. Mean quantity of structure services per unit in baseline, Concentrated North, and Concentrated South simulations

Zone	Simulation	1960	1962	1964	1966	1968	1970
CN							
34	B	22.5	22.1	22.5	23.9	23.2	23.6
	CN	22.5	25.3	26.5	27.7	28.9	29.1
41	B	20.5	19.9	19.3	19.7	19.3	18.6
	CN	20.5	23.3	25.0	26.7	27.4	27.5
40	B	18.2	17.6	17.1	16.6	17.0	17.6
	CN	18.2	19.8	19.8	19.2	19.1	18.6
21	B	19.5	18.8	17.7	17.6	18.2	18.8
	CN	19.5	20.7	20.9	21.8	22.0	21.7
22	B	19.4	18.9	18.8	17.2	15.8	16.5
	CN	19.4	20.6	21.0	22.1	23.2	24.0
4	B	20.6	19.7	18.9	19.2	19.5	19.1
	CN	20.6	21.1	19.3	18.7	18.7	18.4
9	B	21.6	21.5	20.9	20.1	18.9	17.9
	CN	21.6	22.4	21.9	19.9	18.6	17.4
CS							
115	B	22.0	21.6	21.5	20.9	20.5	20.5
	CS	22.0	25.4	25.8	26.3	26.5	25.1
118	B	18.6	18.4	17.8	18.2	18.7	19.3
	CS	18.6	21.3	21.0	21.5	21.7	21.3
119	B	21.2	21.0	20.9	21.9	22.4	22.4
	CS	21.2	23.7	24.1	24.3	24.4	23.6
114	B	18.9	19.0	19.7	20.7	20.8	20.6
	CS	18.9	21.0	21.3	21.2	21.0	22.1
86	B	17.3	16.3	14.7	13.3	12.5	11.6
	CS	17.3	17.3	15.6	14.6	13.6	12.5

Policy-induced changes in the quantities of structure services supplied exhibit a pattern that is similar, though not identical, to that of average income growth. In the Concentrated North simulation, zone 41 showed both the highest net income increase and the largest percentage growth in the average quantity of structure services consumed. Despite being third in relative income growth, CN zone 22 experienced the second largest increase in structure services consumed relative to the baseline — an increase of 45 percentage points over the decade.

The two CN neighborhoods with the fewest units eligible for CHIP subsidies actually supplied fewer structure services on average at the end of the decade than in the baseline. In contrast, all of the target neighborhoods included in the Concentrated South simulation recorded increases in the average quantities of structure services supplied, ranging from 7 percent (zone 114) to 22 percent (zone 115).

As the 1960–1970 averages in table 6.6 indicate, the CHIP subsidies induce higher private investment in only four of the seven Concen-

Table 6.6. Net monthly investment (in 1970 dollars) in maintenance capital per dwelling unit in baseline, Concentrated North, and Concentrated South simulations

Zone	Simulation	1960	1965	1970	Average 1960–1970
CN					
34	B	28.0	10.7	− .4	4.7
	CN	36.4	28.2	41.4	24.9
41	B	33.8	12.0	−40.3	−11.7
	CN	36.1	31.7	45.8	23.0
40	B	− 5.4	−17.3	29.5	− 4.3
	CN	− 2.4	−11.0	11.4	−12.1
21	B	12.4	− 4.2	11.6	− 1.5
	CN	12.7	30.9	8.3	4.1
22	B	11.8	−42.0	32.5	−14.9
	CN	21.5	12.9	31.0	13.7
4	B	10.1	10.9	− .8	− 8.6
	CN	−15.6	−16.5	−12.9	−18.4
9	B	− 1.9	−23.1	−25.3	−25.2
	CN	− 3.4	−47.3	−29.8	−31.8
CS					
115	B	7.7	−21.0	− 6.3	− 8.4
	CS	11.8	20.0	0.6	4.1
118	B	.4	6.0	16.2	2.9
	CS	6.8	-17.1	12.5	− 2.4
119	B	−16.0	4.8	0.2	3.5
	CS	− 1.6	5.7	5.9	2.5
114	B	23.3	6.0	−46.2	− 1.5
	CS	5.8	−34.6	−20.3	− 9.6
86	B	63.4	−42.8	−20.3	−27.2
	CS	78.0	−41.9	−19.9	−24.9

trated North target neighborhoods and in only one of the five Concentrated South neighborhoods. The exception among the CS residence zones is the most heavily subsidized area, zone 115, where the subsidies turn a disinvestment averaging $8.40 per month per unit into a positive net investment of $4.10 per month per unit. The correlation between the fraction of units receiving subsidies and the propensity for more or less net investment also appears in the CN simulation, albeit less strongly. The two low-treatment neighborhoods, zones 4 and 9, have less capital investment on average in the CN scenario than in the baseline, as did the third most heavily treated area, zone 40. Incomes in zone 40, it may be recalled, grew by only 18 percent in the policy simulation but 29 percent in the baseline.

Impacts on Housing Inventory

As the analysis in chapter 5 demonstrated, the CHIP-I policy led to an increase in housing units in target neighborhoods by inducing new construction activity. In addition, although the CHIP-I program tended to conserve units that would otherwise have been lost during the decade, higher losses among unsubsidized structures almost exactly offset these gains. Although the results of the Concentrated North and Concentrated South scenarios are similar to those obtained in the CHIP-I simulation, important differences emerge. The data in table 6.7 show that the combined increase for all target neighborhoods in the CN simulation amounts to 6,000 units, or some 7 percent of the baseline end-of-period inventory. While all seven CN neighborhoods gained more units than they lost as a result of the policy, this was not true in the CS simulations. Three of the five CS neighborhoods had a net loss in units relative to the baseline, resulting in the net increase of only 900 units, or about 1 percent of the end-of-period baseline inventory.

As in the CHIP-I simulation, new construction accounts for most of the policy-induced growth in the housing inventories of CN target neighborhoods. The statistics in table 6.7 also reveal that the aggregate numbers of both subsidized and unsubsidized units in all CN residence zones remaining in the 1970 policy simulation are higher than in the baseline, although there are fewer units in the two most heavily treated zones. The CN neighborhood with the most new construction activity both in absolute numbers and in percentage terms is residence zone 41, which also experienced the most rapid income growth relative to the baseline: policy-induced new construction in this neighborhood during 1960–1970 amounts to 23 percent of the end-of-period baseline housing stock. The second highest percentage increase in new construction

SPATIALLY CONCENTRATED POLICIES

Table 6.7. Effects of Concentrated North and Concentrated South programs on the components of inventory change, 1960–1970

| | Baseline minus policy | | | | |
| | Remaining initial units | | New | | |
Zone	Subsidized	Unsubsidized	construction	Conversions	Total
CN					
34	−200	−75	425	75	225
41	−50	−375	1,950	−175	1,350
40	650	−150	1,400	−150	1,750
21	0	0	900	−175	725
22	25	−50	1,250	−100	1,125
4	125	150	25	25	325
9	100	550	450	−600	500
All CN zones	650	50	6,400	−1,675	6,000
CS					
115	150	−400	−325	−200	−175
118	1,150	150	1,825	−375	2,750
119	400	−175	−1,550	−150	−1,475
114	25	−500	225	425	175
86	350	−1,300	0	375	−375
All CS zones	2,075	−1,875	175	75	900

occurs in residence zone 22, which had the third highest relative income growth of the CN target neighborhoods. In contrast, residence zone 34—which had the second highest relative income growth and the largest percentage of units eligible for subsidies—had only a 3 percent increase in new construction.

CHIP subsidies have much less of an impact on new construction levels in the Concentrated South target zones. As stated above, the policy-induced net increase in newly constructed units in all five target neighborhoods totals only 175, a number that is less than two-tenths of one percent of the baseline end-of-decade inventory. In contrast to the CN neighborhoods, only two of the five CS target zones experienced more new construction over the decade in the policy than in the baseline simulation.

Neighborhood Change

By 1970 four of the seven Concentrated North target neighborhoods and three of the five Concentrated South zones achieved a higher level of neighborhood quality in the policy simulations than in the baseline. As the data in table 6.8 indicate, the most substantial improvement occurred in zone 41, which deteriorated from quality level II to level I in the baseline but improved to level V in the policy scenario. Residence zones 34 and 22, moreover, increased by two quality levels in the CN simulation, and zone 21 increased by one quality level. Neither of the two target areas with the lowest percentage of units receiving subsidies in the CN simulation improved in neighborhood quality.

Table 6.8. Effects of Concentrated North and Concentrated South programs on neighborhood quality levels of target neighborhoods, 1960–1970

Zone	Simulation	1960	1962	1964	1966	1968	1970
CN							
34	B	2	2	3	3	3	3
	CN	2	4	4	5	5	5
41	B	2	1	1	1	1	1
	CN	2	3	3	4	4	5
40	B	1	1	1	1	1	1
	CN	1	1	1	1	1	1
21	B	1	1	1	1	1	1
	CN	1	2	2	2	2	2
22	B	1	1	1	1	1	1
	CN	1	2	2	2	3	3
4	B	2	1	1	1	1	1
	CN	2	1	1	1	1	1
9	B	2	2	2	2	1	1
	CN	2	2	2	1	1	1
CS							
115	B	2	2	2	2	2	2
	CS	2	4	4	4	4	4
118	B	1	1	1	1	1	1
	CS	1	2	2	2	2	2
119	B	2	2	2	2	2	2
	CS	2	3	3	3	3	3
114	B	1	1	1	2	2	2
	CS	1	2	2	2	2	2
86	B	1	1	1	1	1	1
	CS	1	1	1	1	1	1

SPATIALLY CONCENTRATED POLICIES

In the Concentrated South simulation, the three residence zones with the largest fraction of units receiving subsidies improved in quality relative to the baseline. Residence zone 115, which reached quality level IV by the end of the period, exhibited the largest improvement; the other two zones improved from level I to II and from level II to III. Although the policy also caused zone 114 to improve from level I to II between 1960 and 1962, the residence zone remained at level II until the end of the decade.

Summary statistics on the end-of-decade distribution of neighborhood quality provide comparisons of the CN and CS results with the baseline, with CHIP-I, and with each other. Presented in table 6.9 are the numbers of target zones by end-of-decade quality levels in the baseline and the policy simulations; table 6.10 then gives the end-of-period distribution of all Chicago residence zones by neighborhood quality level. These data offer insights about the direct impacts of CHIP subsidies on target neighborhood quality and about the programs' indirect effects on neighborhoods not eligible for subsidies.

Although the number of target zones is at most seven, both the CS and CHIP-I policies added ten neighborhoods to the second lowest quality level; in both cases, five were upgraded from level I in the baseline and five were initially of better neighborhood quality. As indicated in table 6.9, only one target zone in both the CHIP-I and CS simulations improved from neighborhood quality level I to level II by the end of the decade. In contrast, the Concentrated North program

Table 6.9. Classification of target zones by end-of-period neighborhood quality levels for baseline, CHIP-I, Concentrated North, and Concentrated South simulations

1970 quality level		Number of zones		
B	Policy	CHIP-I	CN	CS
I	I	2	3	1
I	II	1	1	1
I	III	0	1	0
I	IV	1	0	0
I	V	1	1	0
II	II	0	0	1
II	III	0	0	1
II	IV	0	0	1
III	V	1	1	0
All target zones		6	7	5

Table 6.10. End-of-period neighborhood quality levels in baseline, CHIP-I, Concentrated North, and Concentrated South simulations

1970 quality level	Number				Policy minus baseline		
	B	CHIP-I	CN	CS	CHIP-I	CN	CS
I	45	40	46	40	−5	1	−5
II	19	29	21	29	10	2	10
III	37	32	35	29	−5	−2	−8
IV	32	28	26	34	−4	−6	2
V	65	69	70	66	4	5	1
All	198	198	198	198	0	0	0

added only two zones of quality level II, one of which improved from level I as a direct result of the CHIP subsidies, and the other of which was a nontarget neighborhood that deteriorated from a higher quality level. There are also two fewer neighborhoods of level III in the final year of the CN simulation than in the baseline.

The patterns of neighborhood change among high-quality residence zones, in comparison, are much more similar for the CN and CHIP-I simulations. In the CHIP-I simulation, four more highest-quality zones exist in 1970 than in the baseline, and five more in the CN scenario; the CS policy, however, results in only one more highest-quality zone, although two more neighborhoods improve to the next-to-highest quality, level IV. In addition, the CHIP-I simulation includes four fewer zones of next-to-highest quality by 1970; the CN policy includes six fewer. These results suggest that the relatively large number of highest-quality neighborhoods created by the two policies are partially accounted for by less upgrading to level IV; that is, some of the zones that reached level V in the baseline remained at level IV in the policy simulation. The single neighborhood that improved to the highest-quality level in the CS simulation, however, does not seem to have gained at the expense of another zone, since two additional neighborhoods improved to level IV.

Inspection of figure 6.2 suggests that accessibility to Chicago's central area — and, in the case of unsubsidized residence zones, proximity to target neighborhoods — affects the geographic distribution of neighborhood quality changes in the CN simulation. The two target neighborhoods that improve least, zones 4 and 9, are farthest from the Loop; they also, however, possess the smallest fractions of eligible units. The third CN target neighborhood that failed to improve in quality, zone 4,

SPATIALLY CONCENTRATED POLICIES

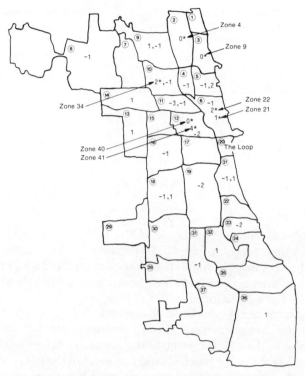

Figure 6.2. Difference in 1970 CN and baseline quality levels for neighbor-hoods changing one or more levels

is located in the same transit district as zone 41, the one that improved the most.

The one neighborhood that deteriorated by three quality levels in the CN simulation is located in transit district 11 and is surrounded by the three districts containing target zones 34, 40, 41, 22, and 21. Of these five neighborhoods, all but residence zone 40 improved by at least one quality level; this same residence zone, moreover, decreased in quality by two levels in the CHIP-I simulation. One of the neighborhoods in transit district 12 (which contains zones 40 and 41) deteriorated by two levels; one located in the same transit district as zone 34 deteriorated by one level; and one in the same transit district as zones 21 and 22 declined by one quality level. Overall, declines in neighborhood quality among unsubsidized zones in the northern and northwestern sectors of the city thus outnumbered gains. It appears, moreover, that providing CHIP subsidies to the northern and northwestern residence zones may

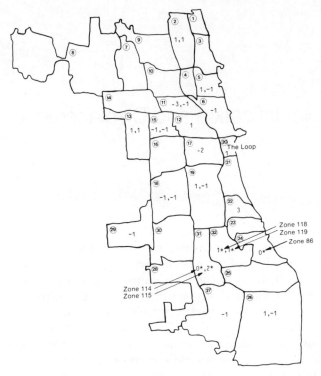

Figure 6.3. Difference in 1970 CS and baseline quality levels for neighborhoods changing one or more levels

have weakened the forces producing neighborhood improvement in
the southern and southwestern sectors. Two unsubsidized neighborhoods south of the Loop declined by two quality levels, and the number
of zones deteriorating by one level exactly offsets the number improving by one level.

A similar pattern appears in the Concentrated South simulation,
where several residence zones to the north and west of the Loop declined in neighborhood quality relative to the baseline. As figure 6.3
illustrates, one zone in transit district 11 deteriorated by three quality
levels and another declined by one level; two zones in district 15 wor-
sened by one level, and neighborhood quality in one district 17 zone
decreased by two levels. Although one or more zones in transit districts
2, 12, and 13 were upgraded by one level, the predominant trend in
neighborhood change was nonetheless downward.

7 Gentrification and Displacement

Since World War II, numerous government programs similar to those described in this book have been intended to halt central-city decline and to attract higher-income residents to inner-city neighborhoods. Government policy and, to an even greater extent, market forces have recently produced some well-publicized instances of neighborhood revitalization, or what is called "gentrification." With these successes occurring in a growing number of cities, however, increasing numbers of tenants'-rights groups and various low-income advocacy groups have begun to complain that gentrification, condominium conversion, and similar activities are causing displacement.

Critics of neighborhood revitalization programs use the term "displacement" in two ways. First, they contend that programs or processes that involve the entry of high-income households into formerly low-income neighborhoods force large numbers of individual residents, particularly renters, from their units. Second, they argue that gentrification, condominium conversion, and similar processes displace low-income households in general from affected neighborhoods by reducing the supply of affordable units.

A major difficulty in assessing the extent and implications of both types of displacement is the lack of systematic analyses of neighborhood change. Specifically, no baseline exists that would permit an evaluation of what would have happened to the residents of upgraded neighborhoods in the absence of the particular policy or market condition that produced the change. The fragmentary data that are available, however, suggest that concerns over the adverse effects of neighborhood upgrading on low-income households are exaggerated. A large fraction of the residents of target neighborhoods are highly mobile renters;

110

indeed, available data indicate that roughly 40 percent of such households are likely to move in any given year. Furthermore, many low-income central-city neighborhoods that are not upgraded experience rapid deterioration, arson, and abandonment, changes that are at least as likely as revitalization to displace households. It can therefore be argued that most people who are "forced" to move by neighborhood upgrading would have relocated shortly in any event; for many of the others, the alternative to displacement through upgrading may be displacement through deterioration. Finally, even casual observation attests to the fact that private market upgrading is quite slow relative to the mobility of central-city residents, particularly renters.

This chapter first presents information on the mobility patterns of residents of the CHIP-I target neighborhoods in the baseline. It then assesses the effect of the housing improvement program on the mobility and housing choices of households that originally resided in the target neighborhoods, and it describes the characteristics of several categories of households that the policy would either encourage to move, or discourage from moving, to the target neighborhoods.

Mobility Patterns of Residents of Target Neighborhoods

In the HUDS model each sample household is assigned a unique sequence number. The numbers allow comparisons between baseline and policy residence locations of each household and between categories of households. Table 7.1 shows the 1960 place of residence of all households residing in the target neighborhoods in 1970, as well as the 1970

Table 7.1 Baseline mobility of households in the CHIP-I target neighborhoods, 1960–1970

	1970 residents of target zones by 1960 residence		1960 residents of target zones by 1970 residence	
Category	Number	Percent	Number	Percent
Continuing households				
Same zone	16,750	17.2	16,750	16.5
Different zone	47,750	48.9	56,550	55.6
Outside SMSA or new household	33,050	33.9	28,475	28.0
All households	97,550	100.0	101,775	100.0

place of residence of households living in the target zone in 1960. Only 16,750 of the 97,550 households residing in the CHIP-I target neighborhoods in 1970 were present ten years earlier; the remaining 80,800 households are thus in-migrants or new households. Since target neighborhoods have low rates of owner-occupancy (from 10 to 33 percent, compared with an SMSA average of 60 percent), turnover is quite high. Moreover, for periods as long as a decade, household formation is an important determinant of total household mobility; decade-long residents therefore account for an average of only 17.2 percent of the 1970 population of all target zones.

The data in the last two columns of table 7.1 present a similar description of the 1970 locations of all households residing in the target zones in 1960. The 16,750 decade-long residents constitute only 16.5 percent of all 1960 residents; fully 28.0 percent of all households residing in the target neighborhoods in 1960 dissolved or moved out of the SMSA during the decade, while another 55.6 percent moved to other zones. These statistics, which again demonstrate the high mobility of target neighborhood households, also suggest that revitalization — whether caused by explicit public policy or by more general market forces — alters neighborhood socioeconomic composition primarily by changing the pool of in-migrants rather than by accelerating the departure of residents.

Relatively few households remain in the target neighborhoods for as long as ten years. In addition to those residents either at the end or at the beginning of the decade, 20,125 households passed through the target areas, arriving after 1960 but leaving before 1970. The HUDS model tracks these transient households by a special flag. As the data in table 7.2 indicate, an estimated 202,700 households lived for one or more years in the approximately 100,000 dwelling units located in the six CHIP-I target zones. Households living in the target neighborhoods for the entire decade thus represent only 8.3 percent of the total number of households ever residing in the six residence zones during the period 1960–1970.

The high turnover rate of target neighborhood residents is a relatively well known but often overlooked consequence of the high mobility rates of renter households. Even without program- or market-induced neighborhood improvement, a large fraction of the households residing in most low-quality neighborhoods would in the course of ten years dissolve, move to other zones, or move out of the SMSA entirely. They would be replaced by newly formed households, households from other residence zones, and in-migrants to the SMSA. To determine the effects of neighborhood upgrading, it is therefore necessary to analyze

Table 7.2 Baseline number and percent distribution of households residing in target neighborhoods for one or more years between 1960 and 1970

Target neighborhood (TN)	Resident in TN in 1960; 1970 residence:		Moved to TN after 1960; 1970 residence:		Households ever living in TN, 1960–1970	Percent resident in TN in 1960; 1970 residence:		Percent moved to TN after 1960; 1970 residence:	
	In TN	Not in TN	In TN	Not in TN		In TN	Not in TN	In TN	Not in TN
34	1,925	9,975	10,400	5,425	27,725	6.9	36.0	37.5	19.6
9	2,350	15,650	15,925	1,650	35,575	6.6	44.0	44.8	4.6
41	1,300	7,025	6,975	3,875	19,175	6.8	36.6	36.4	20.2
22	775	5,250	5,025	750	11,800	6.5	44.5	42.5	6.4
118	4,250	20,250	18,425	6,800	49,725	8.5	40.7	37.0	13.7
86	6,150	26,875	24,050	1,625	58,700	10.5	45.7	41.0	2.8
Total	16,750	85,025	80,800	20,125	202,700	8.3	41.9	40.0	9.9

GENTRIFICATION AND DISPLACEMENT

how the policy would change the mobility patterns and subsequent housing choices of the neighborhood's original residents relative to their baseline behavior. It is also important to distinguish those households that moved into the neighborhood as a result of the policy from those that would otherwise have moved into it. One of the major strengths of the HUDS model is its ability to provide information about these counterfactual scenarios, information that is essential to a complete assessment of concentrated housing improvement programs.

Effects of CHIP-I on the 1960 Residents of Target Neighborhoods

Identifying the households that a policy affects is a difficult task. To begin this process, this section first discusses how CHIP subsidies influence the location decisions of 1960 target zone residents, and then turns to the policy's impact on all baseline residents of target neighborhoods.

Presented in table 7.3 are the numbers of households originally residing in the six target neighborhoods in subsidized and unsubsidized units, classified by their 1970 residence locations in both the baseline and policy simulations. The first two columns identify households by their end-of-period residential locations: still living in the same neighborhood in 1970 (In), in another residence zone in the SMSA (Out), or dissolved and or moved from the SMSA (Left). Interaction of these end-period conditions produces five mobility categories: "Stayers," "Displaced by policy," "Retained by policy," "Voluntary movers," and "Households dissolved/left."

Although a housing or neighborhood improvement policy might also alter the rates at which target neighborhood households leave the SMSA or dissolve, the current version of HUDS does not permit such program-induced mobility. The model assumes that migration to and from the SMSA depends only on household demographic characteristics. The effects of neighborhood improvement policies on patterns of out-migration or household dissolution are probably small, however, especially relative to those already represented in the model.

The CHIP subsidies affected the moving decisions of only a small fraction of the 1960 target neighborhood residents. As the statistics in table 7.3 indicate, under both policy and baseline conditions, only 13.9 percent of all 1960 residents continued to live in the target neighborhoods, 53 percent moved out, and another 28.2 percent of households either dissolved or left the SMSA. The policy thus changed the mobility status of only 4.9 percent of all 1960 residents of the six target neighborhoods, that is, the 2.4 percent who were "retained" and the 2.5 percent who were "displaced."

Table 7.3 Effects of CHIP-I subsidies on the mobility of households residing in all target neighborhoods

Households in target zones in 1960	1970 residence			
	B	CHIP-I	Number	Percent
In treated building				
Stayers	In	In	6,975	30.0
Displaced by policy	In	Out	400	1.7
Retained by policy	Out	In	800	3.4
Voluntary movers	Out	Out	9,250	39.8
Household dissolved/left	Left	Left	5,825	25.1
All	All	All	23,250	100.0
Not in treated building				
Stayers	In	In	7,200	9.2
Displaced by policy	In	Out	2,175	2.8
Retained by policy	Out	In	1,675	2.1
Voluntary movers	Out	Out	44,650	56.9
Household dissolved/left	Left	Left	22,825	29.1
All	All	All	78,525	100.0
All target zone residents				
Stayers	In	In	14,175	13.9
Displaced by policy	In	Out	2,575	2.5
Retained by policy	Out	In	2,475	2.4
Voluntary movers	Out	Out	53,900	53.0
Household dissolved/left	Left	Left	28,650	28.2
All	All	All	101,775	100.0

Two factors explain why the policy has such a small impact on 1960 target neighborhood residents. First, because the target zones are predominantly low-income, renter-occupied neighborhoods, a large fraction of the 1960 residents would have moved under any circumstances. Second, CHIP subsidies have their most pronounced effects on the behavior of the owner-occupants of single-family and small multi-family units that receive subsidies. Since these households tend to have a stronger attachment to their units than renters and are therefore less mobile, a relatively large fraction remain in their units in the baseline. Although only 23 percent of all target zone units received CHIP subsidies, nearly half of the stayers (6,975 out of a total of 14,175 households) in all six neighborhoods lived in subsidized units.

The CHIP subsidies do, however, affect the moving decisions of a much larger fraction of long-term residents. In the baseline simulation,

GENTRIFICATION AND DISPLACEMENT

16,650 households remained in the target neighborhoods for the entire decade; the 2,575 households that the policy displaces are thus 15.4 percent of all long-term residents. This may underestimate displacement, since the model allows displacement to occur only if a structure that houses a long-term resident of one of the target neighborhoods is converted or demolished; it makes no provision for mobility induced by higher rents or other aspects of neighborhood change. But the fraction of long-term residents that the CHIP-I subsidies would displace cannot exceed 16.4 percent (that is, 13.9 percent of all 1960 target neighborhood residents who remain in their original homes plus the 2.5 percent who are displaced). Since 60 percent of the households remaining in their units for the entire decade in the baseline are owner-occupants, the fraction that rent increases or other factors might displace is not likely to be more than 50 percent. Even if the policy displaced 50 percent of the long-term residents, the concentrated housing improvement program would displace no more than 10 percent of the 1960 target zone residents.

Not to minimize the costs that displaced target neighborhood residents may incur, it is important to recognize that neighborhood improvements may also permit some residents who would otherwise have moved to remain in their units. Deterioration of the housing stock in many declining, low-quality neighborhoods leads to the abandonment and demolition of a significant fraction of units, and thus to the displacement of significant numbers of residents. Estimates contained in table 7.3 reveal that the CHIP subsidies allow 2,475 households to remain in the six target neighborhoods, or nearly as many as the program displaces. As might be expected, the fraction of 1960 residents of subsidized buildings that the policy retains in the target zones is somewhat greater than the fraction of residents of untreated buildings. A total of 800 households were able to remain in treated buildings that were actually removed from the housing stock in the baseline. Policy-induced upgrading of untreated buildings in the target neighborhoods also allowed an additional 1,675 start-of-decade residents to remain in the target neighborhoods for the entire ten years.

The preceding estimates of households retained by the CHIP-I subsidies omit families that remain in the target zones because of the indirect effects of neighborhood upgrading. The data in table 7.3 indicate that the number of voluntary movers is nearly four times as large as the number of stayers (53,900 versus 14,175); arguably, some fraction of these movers would have preferred to remain in their 1960 residences in the absence of the deterioration that characterized the target neighborhoods in the baseline. If the fraction of voluntary movers with this predilection is even one-third as large as the fraction induced to move by the policy's indirect effects, the number of 1960 target neighborhood residents that the program retains would exceed the number displaced.

To help clarify the way CHIP subsidies affect the residential choices of target neighborhood households, table 7.4 provides the relative numbers of households in each mobility category for two markedly different neighborhoods. Residence zone 41, the heavily treated near north neighborhood, improved from quality level I in the baseline to level V in the policy simulation; zone 86, the lightly treated south neighborhood, continued to be of the lowest quality throughout both

Table 7.4 Effects of CHIP-I subsidies on the mobility of households residing in target neighborhoods 41 and 86

Households in target zones in 1960	1970 residence		Zone		Percent of category	
	B	CHIP-I	41	86	Zone 41	Zone 86
In treated building						
Stayers	In	In	825	1,425	24.1	36.8
Displaced by policy	In	Out	100	75	2.9	2.0
Retained by policy	Out	In	25	225	0.7	5.8
Voluntary mover	Out	Out	1,650	1,275	48.2	32.9
Dissolved/left	Left	Left	825	875	24.1	22.6
All	All	All	3,425	3,875	100.0	100.0
Not in treated building						
Stayers	In	In	250	3,625	5.1	12.5
Displaced by policy	In	Out	125	1,025	2.6	3.5
Retained by policy	Out	In	25	825	0.5	2.8
Voluntary mover	Out	Out	3,060	15,225	61.2	52.2
Dissolved/left	Left	Left	1,500	8,450	30.6	29.0
All	All	All	4,900	29,150	100.0	100.0
All target zone households						
Stayers	In	In	1,075	5,050	12.9	15.3
Displaced by policy	In	Out	225	1,100	2.7	3.2
Retained by policy	Out	In	50	1,050	0.6	3.2
Voluntary mover	Out	Out	4,650	16,500	35.9	50.0
Dissolved/left	Left	Left	2,325	9,325	27.9	28.2
All	All	All	8,325	33,025	100.0	100.0

the baseline and policy simulations. As might be expected, net displacement (fraction displaced by policy minus fraction retained by policy) is relatively larger for residence zone 41, where few properties were abandoned or demolished in the baseline and where policy-induced upgrading stimulated construction of 2,025 additional units. The CHIP subsidies thus displaced 2.7 percent of zone 41's residents and retained only 0.6 percent. In residence zone 86, in contrast, the policy displaced 3.2 percent of 1960 residents but retained an almost identical number. The retention rate for the 1960 residents of subsidized units (5.8 percent) is more than twice as large as the rate for unsubsidized units. Even so, the number of occupants of unsubsidized buildings that the policy retains is more than three times the number it retains in subsidized buildings.

It may be difficult at first to understand how the CHIP grants could cause significant displacement in residence zone 86 when the policy had so little impact on neighborhood quality. The explanation is that the buildings receiving subsidies come to have a strong competitive advantage in an otherwise declining neighborhood; assuming no change in the level or composition of demand, the subsidized units would attract a disproportionate share of the small number of high-income in-migrants to the zone. In the baseline, however, many high-income in-migrants to the neighborhood live in units that are ineligible for CHIP subsidies. Although the policy may thus decrease the number of households living in units eligible for CHIP subsidies that are forced to move by deterioration and abandonment, it indirectly accelerates the abandonment of units that do not receive subsidies. As a result, the net retention of 1960 residents of subsidized buildings is 150 (225 households retained by the policy minus 75 displaced), while the net displacement from buildings not receiving CHIP subsidies is 200 (1,025 displaced by the policy minus 825 retained).

Like many housing policies, the CHIP-I program is two-edged. To the extent that the subsidies conserve units that would otherwise be lost, they retard displacement; to the extent that they encourage more rapid deterioration of unsubsidized units by drawing away households that would have occupied them, they increase displacement. The relative size of these two effects depends on how attached the occupants are to their neighborhoods or units and on the nature and strength of market forces. Although the simulation results are not precise, they demonstrate that concentrated housing improvement policies have more wide-ranging effects than simply displacing the relatively few long-term residents of target neighborhoods.

Effects of CHIP-I on All Baseline Residents of Target Neighborhoods

Only about half the households residing in the target zones for one or more years over the decade lived there in 1960. As table 7.5 indicates, these "pass-through" households constitute a major category of residents in both the baseline and policy simulations. Since the categories "stayers" and "displaced by policy" consist of baseline residents of target neighborhoods in both 1960 and 1970, they appear twice in table 7.5. To minimize confusion, each of the eleven mobility categories listed in this and subsequent tables has been assigned a unique sequence number.

While the CHIP subsidies have little effect on the moving decisions of 1960 residents, the subsidies have a substantial influence on new households moving into the target neighborhoods. For example, category 6 ("discouraged by policy — existing") consists of 34,400 existing households that moved to the target neighborhoods after 1960 in the baseline, and remained there in 1970. In the CHIP simulation, however, the policy discouraged these households from ever moving into the target neighborhoods. Category 7 ("discouraged by policy — new") includes an additional 30,075 households formed at some time after 1960; like the category 6 households this group actually resided in the target neighborhoods in 1970 but were deterred from moving there in the policy simulation. Finally, the CHIP-I subsidies prevented 7,525 "pass-through" households (those that lived in the six target neighborhoods after 1960 but left before 1970) from moving to the target zones.

As table 7.5 indicates, the number of households that the policy discouraged from moving to a target neighborhood is many times larger than the number displaced. Combining mobility categories 6, 7, and 11, the policy would discourage 82,000 households from moving to the target neighborhoods but force only 2,575 households to move. Critics of neighborhood improvement programs that emphasize displacement effects thus have an exaggerated view of the quantitative importance of these program impacts. The relatively small numbers of affected households suggests the desirability and feasibility of policies that would assist displaced residents — especially long-term residents — rather than halt policy-induced or spontaneous neighborhood upgrading.

The aggregate statistics obscure many important program effects that vary from zone to zone. As discussed above, the CHIP subsidies caused substantial upgrading in residence zone 41, the heavily treated

Table 7.5   Effects of CHIP-I subsidies on households residing in target neighborhoods, 1960 and 1970, by mobility status

Mobility group	Mobility group number	1960 residence	1970 residence B	1970 residence CHIP-I	Number	Percent of all households ever residing in target zones
Households in target zones in 1960						
Stayers	1	In	In	In	14,175	7.0
Displaced by policy	2	In	In	Out	2,575	1.3
Retained by policy	3	In	Out	In	2,475	1.2
Voluntary movers	4	In	Out	Out	53,900	26.6
Dissolved/left	5	In	Left	Left	28,650	14.1
All		In	All	All	101,775	50.2
Households in target zones in 1970						
Stayers	1	In	In	In	14,175	7.0
Displaced by policy	2	In	In	Out	2,575	1.3
Discouraged by policy—existing	6	Out	In	Out	34,400	17.0
Discouraged by policy—new	7	New	In	Out	30,075	14.8
Voluntary in-mover—existing	8	Out	In	In	13,350	6.6
Voluntary in-mover—new	9	New	In	In	2,975	1.5
All		All	In	All	97,550	48.1
Pass-through households of target zones						
Voluntary pass-through[a]	10	Out	Out	Out	2,600	1.3
Pass-through discouraged[b]	11	Out	Out	Out	17,525	8.6
All pass-throughs		Out	Out	Out	20,125	9.9
All households ever residing in target zone in baseline[c]		—	—	—	202,700	100.0

[a] Voluntary pass-through: Household resides in zone for one or more years after 1960 and before 1970 for both baseline and policy simulations.

[b] Pass-through discouraged: Household resides in zone for one or more years after 1960 and before 1970 for baseline, but never a resident of zone in policy simulation.

[c] All households ever residing in target zones in baseline. The sum of all mobility groups identified in this table.

near north neighborhood; in contrast, they had little effect on average incomes or neighborhood quality in zone 86, the heavily treated, predominantly black neighborhood on Chicago's South Side. The income statistics in table 7.6 indicate that households displaced from zone 41 had 1970 incomes about 15 percent higher than the stayers ($11,567 versus $10,051). The opposite is true for zone 86, where the 5,050 households that continued to live in the neighborhood throughout the decade had average 1970 incomes 62 percent higher than the 1,100 households that the policy displaced. In residence zone 86, displacement results primarily from policy-induced abandonment of unsubsidized buildings; since the abandoned buildings tend to be large multifamily structures providing low levels of structure services, the displaced occupants are also among the neighborhood's and region's poorest households.

Existing households that the policy discourages from moving to residence zone 41 — a group consisting of 3,725 highly mobile, primarily

Table 7.6 Characteristics of selected mobility categories for residence zones 41 and 86

Mobility group	Mobility group number	Number of households	Annual income	Percent nonwhite	Percent 65 or older
Zone 41					
Stayers	1	1,075	$10,051	0.0	46.5
Displaced by policy	2	225	11,567	0.0	44.4
Retained by policy	3	50	10,100	0.0	100.0
Discouraged by policy — existing	6	3,725	6,323	0.0	44.3
Discouraged by policy — new	7	2,625	7,763	0.0	0.0
Pass-through discouraged	11	3,050	10,445	0.0	11.0
Zone 86					
Stayers	1	5,050	5,421	89.1	41.6
Displaced by policy	2	1,100	3,341	93.2	54.6
Retained by policy	3	1,050	5,612	95.2	30.9
Discouraged by policy — existing	6	6,825	2,863	78.0	36.6
Discouraged by policy — new	7	4,775	3,428	77.5	0.0
Pass-through discouraged	11	1,475	4,692	95.3	11.1

renter households that moved into the neighborhood after 1960 in the baseline and remained there in 1970—have the lowest average incomes of all household types. This "discouraged by policy—existing" category has the lowest income of all zone 86 households as well. These households have average incomes as low as or lower than those of displaced households, and are much more numerous: 3,725 households versus 225 in zone 41, and 6,825 households versus 1,100 in zone 86. To the extent that low income is a criterion for identifying households with special needs, this group deserves further attention; measures that restrict neighborhood improvement, however, are unlikely to assist these households in any meaningful way.

Further indicators of how the CHIP-I subsidies affect target neighborhood residents are provided in table 7.7 for the same two target neighborhoods in 1970. The 1,075 stayers in zone 41 paid 29 percent more in rent in the policy simulation than in the baseline, reflecting the substantial neighborhood upgrading that occurred as a result of the CHIP subsidies. The households staying in this neighborhood purchased 19 percent more structure services in 1970, lived in units with 39 percent more capital, and benefited from substantially improved neighborhood quality. Since most of these stayers remained in the same dwelling units in both the CHIP and baseline simulations, the policy did not affect the rate of homeownership.

The small number of households displaced by the policy from zone 41 also fared surprisingly well. Relative to the 1970 baseline simulation results, this group paid 17 percent more for their housing but obtained 20 percent more structure services, lived in units with 39 percent more capital stock, and resided in neighborhoods of substantially higher quality than characterized zone 41 in the baseline. In the absence of CHIP-I subsidies, the displaced households would have been living in one of the SMSA's lowest-quality zones in 1970; moving thus meant in most cases an improvement in neighborhood quality.

Households displaced from, or deterred from moving to, zone 86 had a similar experience. Again, these households pay higher rents and receive more housing services, live in buildings with more capital, are more likely to be owners, and are more likely to reside in better neighborhoods than in the baseline. If CHIP-I subsidies had not been introduced, these groups would have lived in very low-quality housing; the policy thus caused many of them to alter their choice of neighborhoods and thereby improve their living conditions. These results again demonstrate that in evaluating the effects of a particular program on selected groups, it is essential to compare what actually occurred with the counterfactual situation of what would have happened in the policy's

Table 7.7 Effects of CHIP-I policy on selected mobility groups in zones 41 and 86, 1970

Mobility group	Mobility group number	Number of households	Mean 1970 CHIP-I as percent of mean 1970 baseline for:				
			Monthly rent	Structure services	Capital stock	Percent owner-occupied	Index of neighborhood quality
Zone 41							
Stayers	1	1,075	129	119	139	100	500
Displaced by policy	2	225	117	120	164	81	377
Retained by policy	3	50	93	79	79	100	100
Discouraged by policy—existing	6	3,725	108	106	114	136	229
Discouraged by policy—new	7	2,625	107	120	124	500	279
Pass-through discouraged	11	3,050	113	110	112	226	300
Zone 86							
Stayers	1	5,050	107	105	114	100	100
Displaced by policy	2	1,100	114	123	132	100	156
Retained by policy	3	1,050	92	90	87	100	55
Discouraged by policy—existing	6	6,825	113	121	133	136	147
Discouraged by policy—new	7	4,775	115	114	119	185	124
Pass-through discouraged	11	1,475	120	138	103	100	160

absence. Although concentrated housing improvement programs may cause some households to change their choice of neighborhoods, "discouraged" households do not necessarily end up in inferior or higher-cost housing, and indeed often improve their living conditions.

Effects of CHIP-I on New Residents of Target Neighborhoods

Because of the high mobility of target zone residents, successful concentrated housing improvement programs may dramatically affect the income mix of a neighborhood but cause little or no displacement. Changes in the income mix of in-migrants can lead to rapid increases in average neighborhood incomes. In the baseline simulation, approximately 100,000 households moved into the six target neighborhoods between 1960 and 1970; in the policy simulation, these in-migrants are replaced by 100,000 different households attracted to the target neighborhood by the improved conditions afforded by the CHIP-I subsidies. The attracted and discouraged groups, although approximately the same size, have quite different average incomes, as shown in table 7.8. Existing households choosing the target zones in the policy simulation have incomes 43 percent higher than those of existing households choosing the neighborhood in the baseline, $9,868 versus $6,907. Similarly, both new households and pass-through households attracted to the target neighborhoods by CHIP-induced upgrading have 31 percent higher incomes than the corresponding groups choosing these neighborhoods in the baseline.

It should be noted that the HUDS model assumes that households consider only neighborhood quality, the supply of available units of each structure type, and the neighborhood's accessibility to the primary worker's job location in choosing a particular residence zone. If households have a special affinity for specific neighborhoods for other reasons, the simulations may thus overstate the amount of turnover. There is no reason to believe, however, that these affinities are so strong or that persons with such preferences are so numerous that the results would differ dramatically.

As table 7.9 indicates, the policy's tendency to raise the average incomes of target neighborhoods by changing the mix of in-migrants is apparent in both the target zones considered. The incomes of both attracted and discouraged households are decidedly lower, however, in residence zone 41. While the CHIP-I subsidies preserve many units and somewhat retard rapid decline occurring in zone 86, the policy fails to induce enough improvement to raise the neighborhood from the lowest

Table 7.8 Effects of CHIP-I on number of households and annual household income in all target zones, by mobility group

Mobility group	Mobility group number	1960 residence	1970 residence		Number of households	Average annual income
			B	CHIP-I		
Groups attracted by policy						
Existing households	12	Out	Out	In	37,975	$ 9,868
New households	13	New	Out	In	30,000	9,978
Pass-through households[a]	14	Out	Out	Out	17,425	10,832
Groups discouraged by policy						
Existing households	6	Out	In	Out	34,400	6,907
New households	7	New	In	Out	30,075	7,622
Pass-through households[b]	11	Out	Out	Out	20,125	9,788

[a] Pass-through households attracted by the policy are those households that never resided in the target neighborhoods during the baseline simulation but in the policy simulation moved into the target neighborhoods after 1960 and left before 1970.
[b] Pass-through households discouraged by the policy are those households that in the baseline simulations moved into the target neighborhood after 1960 but left before 1970, and never resided in the target neighborhoods in the policy simulations.

Table 7.9 Effects of CHIP-I on number of households and annual household income in zones 41 and 86, by mobility group

Mobility group	Mobility group number	Zone 41		Zone 86	
		Number of households	Average annual income	Number of households	Average annual income
Groups attracted by policy					
Existing households	12	4,725	$16,933	6,450	$3,872
New households	13	3,475	17,191	4,775	4,440
Pass-through house- holds	14	3,050	13,536	1,475	5,169
Groups discouraged by policy					
Existing households	6	3,725	6,323	6,825	2,863
New households	7	2,625	7,763	4,775	3,428
Pass-through house- holds	11	3,400	10,445	1,375	4,692

quality level (I). Even so, the subsidies succeed in attracting a somewhat higher income group to the neighborhood.

The change in the income mix of households attracted to residence zone 41 is much more pronounced: the average income of existing households increases more than 2.5 times, from $6,323 to $16,933. A similar differential exists for the new household category, and the pass-through group has average incomes $3,000 higher than those of the deflected group. Residence zone 41 experienced a rapid improvement in quality because of investments in both the treated and untreated housing stock; in effect, the initial subsidies attracted enough higher-income households to induce sustained upgrading.

Since the CHIP-I subsidies cause at least a temporary reduction in the number of lowest-quality zones, they also alter the relative attractiveness of all neighborhoods in the Chicago SMSA. In particular, the policy increases the neighborhood quality level of target zone 118 (located in the transit district adjacent to zone 86) from level I in the baseline to level II in the policy simulation. Both neighborhoods attract largely the same population subgroup—low-income blacks—so the loss of a nearby lowest-quality neighborhood adds to the demand for zone 86, which thus attracts a slightly higher-income, if still absolutely poor, group of in-migrants.

8 Summary of Findings and Directions for New Research

Although the policy simulations described in this book represent particular programs that attempt to induce central-city property owners to upgrade their properties, many of the results are relevant to a larger set of neighborhood and urban development issues. For example, the HUDS model is clearly useful for analyzing mobility and neighborhood change. After briefly reviewing the study's key findings, this chapter will describe the current status and likely future direction of the modeling effort.

Program Effects

Concentrated housing and neighborhood improvement programs have important effects not only on the behavior of both residents and property owners in target neighborhoods but on the entire metropolitan area as well. A major problem in program evaluations is the difficulty of distinguishing policy-induced changes from changes in neighborhood conditions that would have occurred in the program's absence. The most serious deficiency of most evaluations is thus the lack of an adequate baseline; indeed, the major rationale for analytic models and policy simulations may be their capacity to provide such assessments.

This section organizes the summary of results into four categories of program effects: on neighborhood income levels; on the production and investment decisions of property owners in target neighborhoods; on nontarget neighborhoods; and on household mobility.

127

SUMMARY OF FINDINGS

Neighborhood Income Levels

A change in the average income of a target neighborhood is a widely used indicator of the impact of a neighborhood and housing improvement program. In the three CHIP simulations, the policies induce increases in the quantity of structure services supplied by the owners of subsidized units, thereby improving average neighborhood quality in the target zones. These initial improvements in neighborhood quality are sufficient to attract higher-income in-migrants, leading to additional increases in average incomes relative to the baseline.

The simulations also demonstrate, however, that the extent of income growth in target neighborhoods varies substantially with the fraction of units receiving subsidies and with the neighborhood's location and racial composition. In both the CHIP-I and Concentrated North simulations, the same heavily treated, predominantly white near north target neighborhood experienced the greatest income growth relative to the baseline. By subsidizing 40.5 percent of this neighborhood's dwelling units, the CHIP subsidies reversed the marked decline in mean income that actually occurred; the program-induced increases in mean household income, moreover, were sufficient to sustain the improvement in neighborhood quality.

A high fraction of subsidized units is not sufficient, though, to ensure that high-income households will move to a target neighborhood. In the case of the heavily treated, predominantly black neighborhood located on Chicago's South Side, average incomes actually declined slightly relative to the baseline even though nearly one-third of the zone's units were upgraded to 90 percent of good-as-new condition. The simulations also demonstrate that a relatively modest level of treatment may induce substantial income growth in favorably located neighborhoods. In one near north residence zone accessible to Chicago's central business district, introducing the CHIP loans and grants produced only a small initial increase in the level of structure services supplied; the subsequent improvement in neighborhood quality, however, attracted large numbers of high-income white households with primary workers employed in the CBD.

The three policy simulations thus demonstrate the need for careful selection of target neighborhoods in implementing concentrated housing improvement programs. Providing loans and grants to relatively few units in a well-located neighborhood may reinforce or accelerate previously existing market forces favoring revitalization. In contrast, subsidizing a much larger fraction of units in a less well located neighborhood, or in one adversely affected by racial discrimination and segregation, may do little to improve the socioeconomic status of the neighborhood's residents or the quality of its housing stock.

Production and Investment Decisions

To the extent that CHIP subsidies encourage higher-income households to move to target neighborhoods, they induce additional housing investment and the upgrading of both subsidized and unsubsidized buildings. CHIP loans and grants reduce the cost of producing larger quantities of structure services in subsidized units, encouraging occupants to demand more structure services and thereby increasing the average quantity supplied. Upgrading of neighborhood quality in turn attracts more higher-income households to the residence zone, providing the owners of both subsidized and unsubsidized properties with additional incentives to improve their units.

In areas where the CHIP grants induced significant improvements in neighborhood quality, new construction levels also increased substantially. As low-quality residence zones, the target areas experienced little or no new construction activity in the baseline simulations. With the provision of CHIP subsidies, however, one of the near north zones increased its housing inventory by 28 percent and another by nearly 19 percent, primarily as a result of new construction.

Although the concentrated housing improvement program had a less dramatic impact on the predominantly black, South Side target zones, the policy nonetheless had important effects. In the three CHIP simulations, the loans and grants preserved significant numbers of subsidized units that were actually lost to abandonment in the baseline. In the CHIP-I simulation, the program saved nearly one thousand units in the lightly treated South Side target neighborhood, or approximately 12 percent of all subsidized units in the residence zone.

Indirect Effects

Providing capital subsidies to large numbers of property owners in selected residence zones may adversely affect the quality of nearby neighborhoods. In both the CHIP-I and Concentrated North simulations, the subsidies produced impressive increases in the average quantity of structure services supplied and hence in the average quality of the target neighborhoods. Other residence zones in the northern and northwestern sections of the city, however, experienced less improvement or even deterioration relative to the baseline. In effect, the policy redirects high-income demand to target neighborhoods and away from previously attractive zones; instead of the higher-income households that actually moved to these zones in the baseline, the nontarget neighborhoods thus attract the lower-income households that originally resided in the target neighborhoods.

The substitution is not, however, one for one. Although the policy simulations suggest that a program of capital subsidies could, at least in the short run, produce a small overall improvement in neighborhood quality, the subsidies do nothing to change the income distribution of households or to attract higher-income households to the metropolitan area. Over time, a concentrated housing or neighborhood improvement program is only likely to cause a redistribution of households by income and neighborhood quality. Even in the short run, though, the simulations indicate that the advantages of capital subsidies to low-income areas are quickly dissipated.

Gentrification and Displacement

Both spontaneous and policy-induced neighborhood upgrading has evoked concern about adverse effects on low-income residents. The lack of systematic analyses of neighborhood change makes it difficult — indeed, impossible — to assess the extent of displacement that has occurred as a result of neighborhood revitalization: no baseline exists that would permit a meaningful evaluation of what would have happened to the displaced residents of improving neighborhoods in the absence of the particular policy or market condition that produced the change. The ability of the HUDS model to estimate the outcomes of such counterfactual scenarios thus makes it an invaluable tool for evaluating the displacement question.

The results of the CHIP simulations suggest that the extent of program-induced displacement of low-income households is likely to be minimal. The target neighborhoods, like most low-income urban areas, have relatively high shares of rental properties, and as a result mobility rates are also quite high. The process of neighborhood revitalization usually takes a decade or more; for periods of this length, newly formed households or in-migrants to the metropolitan area represent a large fraction of all families participating in the housing market. Indeed, the baseline simulations indicate that decade-long residents account for less than 20 percent of all households living in the CHIP-I target neighborhoods in 1970. Many "displaced" households would thus have moved out of the upgraded neighborhoods even without the program.

This is not to say that CHIP policies cause no displacement. To the extent that significant upgrading occurs, some share of the target zone households that would have remained in the neighborhood for the decade would be induced to leave by the market forces stimulated by the CHIP subsidies. Estimates from the CHIP-I simulation, however, indicate that the policy displaces fewer than 3 percent of the households living in the target zones at the beginning of the period. These displaced households are all long-term residents — that is, those that would have remained for at least a decade — but their numbers are small relative to the total number of 1960 residents who would have moved out of the neighborhood in any case.

Although the costs to long-term displaced residents should not be ignored, neighborhood improvement — whether spontaneous or policy-induced — would nonetheless provide important benefits to many target area residents. Rapid deterioration of the housing stock in many low-quality neighborhoods leads to the abandonment and demolition of significant numbers of units and thus to displacement. By preserving units that would otherwise be removed from the housing stock, the CHIP subsidies may in fact retain as many households as they displace.

Although a program like CHIP-I would have little or no effect on the moving decisions of start-of-decade residents, it would strongly influence the characteristics of in-migrants to target neighborhoods. The policy thus "discourages" many would-be residents and "encourages" other, higher-income households to move to the zones. Of approximately 100,000 households who resided in the target neighborhoods between 1960 and 1970 in the baseline, approximately 75,000 would not have moved into these residence zones if the policy-induced upgrading had occurred. The program would attract almost as many households to those neighborhoods, but the in-migrants would have markedly different demographic characteristics than those of the baseline in-migrants.

The simulations of neighborhood improvement programs provide no evidence that the policies would adversely affect the housing consumption of displaced or discouraged households. Although households remaining in the target zones in both the baseline and policy simulations paid somewhat higher rents, they also lived in rehabilitated units providing significantly more structure services and in better-quality neighborhoods. It is tempting to compare the actual housing consumption of displaced households with the average housing consumption of the residents of target neighborhoods under policy conditions, but such comparisons are misleading: without the policy-induced neighborhood improvement, the target neighborhoods would have been among the worst areas in the city and the displaced residents of these residence zones would have lived in very low-quality housing. Moreover, many of their neighbors would have faced displacement owing to deterioration and abandonment of the housing stock. To the extent that a neighborhood improvement policy does in fact induce displacement, its costs must therefore be measured relative to conditions in the policy's absence.

The Simulation Approach

Despite the extensive theoretical and empirical literature on the dynamics of the housing markets and neighborhoods, there are substantial gaps in our understanding of how individual housing producers and consumers respond to subsidy programs as well as how aggregate behavior produces particular market outcomes. Modeling the adjustment housing consumers must make to changing market conditions is highly complex. Although Americans are highly mobile, for example, many households develop strong attachments to particular types of housing in particular neighborhood settings. As a result, analyses of housing consumption must recognize not only income diversity and other socioeconomic characteristics but also the attachment and inertia that bind many households to particular dwelling units or locations.

Estimating the behavior of housing suppliers is perhaps even more difficult. Housing capital is durable, fixed in location, and difficult to modify. Returns to housing investments thus extend over many years and depend in important ways on both current and future neighborhood quality as well as on general changes in the prices of land, labor, and housing capital, and in the demand for specific types of housing across the entire metropolitan housing market. The spatial distribution of housing of a specific type, vintage, or durability is not only a major factor in current market dynamics but also conditions and constrains future housing market outcomes.

Most recent theoretical and empirical analyses of housing markets agree on the importance of locationally fixed, durable, and heterogeneous housing stock, of diverse household types, and of the attachments of households to specific workplaces and residence zones. As a result most studies of housing market dynamics now attempt to assess the spatial interaction of households, housing demand, housing investment, and employment. What distinguishes the Harvard Urban Development Simulation model from other efforts is its detailed and explicit representation of these spatial interactions as well as of individual consumer behavior.

Technical Issues

The current HUDS model is one of the most complicated applications to date of the simulation technique to social science analysis, and certainly the most technically complex model of urban housing markets that currently exists. For the analyses described in this book, the model annually simulates the behavior of approximately 75,000 model households residing in some 40,000 model structures with one or more dwelling units. Household types are defined in terms of income, race, family size, age of head, employment status, and place of work and residence zone. The housing units they occupy are described in terms of structure type, neighborhood quality, lot size, the quantity of structure services supplied, and the levels of operating inputs and capital stocks used to produce these structure services. The model also identifies twenty separate work zones and 200 residence districts.

Complexity is no virtue per se, of course, but the level of detail achieved in the Harvard model is essential to the evaluation of many issues related to housing market dynamics and neighborhood change. Success in developing the sophisticated software and data processing routines required for a model with the complexity and computational efficiency of the current version of the model is therefore no small achievement.

Empirical Issues

Although the descriptive literature about the historical processes of urban development is growing, our efforts to construct a detailed and accurate record of what occurred in Chicago, Detroit, and Pittsburgh during the period 1960–1970 proved to be surprisingly difficult. Consistent cross-sectional and time series data are limited, and information on basic trends such as the spatial distribution of employment are available for only relatively high levels of aggregation, if at all. Efforts to develop simple cross-classifications of households and housing unit characteristics on neighborhoods or other small areas quickly exhausted 1960 census information. To design, calibrate, and test the HUDS model, we therefore had to construct accurate or at least consistent descriptions of basic development patterns from a limited and frequently contradictory historical data base. Developing a consistent economic history of each of the modeled regions provides valuable insights about urban development processes and the effects (or lack of effects) of government policies; quite apart from its contribution to the formal modeling exercise, such a history proves to be of considerable value.

Efforts to construct the time series data starting in 1960 that were required for the baseline and policy simulations, moreover, increased our awareness of the extent to which most widely held views about urban development are based more on anecdotal evidence or casual observation than on rigorous empirical analysis. Many views are simply incorrect. Fortunately, given our intention to continue this work, the range, extent, and quality of spatially disaggregated data have increased dramatically since the modeling project began in the late 1960s. Better and more extensive data will greatly facilitate our future efforts to simulate housing market behavior for the decade 1970–1980.

Theoretical Issues

Efforts to construct a comprehensive, general equilibrium model of urban housing markets also brought to light serious inadequacies in the theoretical literature. While more limited analyses of household behavior and housing market processes can often avoid certain issues, development of the HUDS model required that we find solutions — often ad hoc — to many largely unexplained theoretical problems. Despite the growing literature on private housing investment behavior, for example, almost no research exists on how property owners form expectations about future housing market conditions. The lack of theoretical work on this subject seriously limits analysis of how neighborhood change affects investment, maintenance, and operating decisions of individual property owners. Similarly, although the literature on household mobility, housing bundle choice, and tenure choice is extensive, there is almost no research on how households simultaneously arrive at a decision to move and choose a housing type, location, and tenure. Moreover, it seems likely that the household's perceptions of current and expected neighborhood quality affect its moving decision and housing choice, but again there has been almost no systematic analysis of these interrelationships.

We do not claim to have solved all or even most of the difficult theoretical problems encountered in designing and calibrating HUDS. Indeed, a major benefit of the modeling exercise has been its tendency to identify important areas for future research. The model itself provides a framework for accumulating and synthesizing theoretical and empirical research about urban housing markets.

Evaluation of Current Baseline Simulations

Although the current baseline simulations do not exactly replicate actual housing market conditions in Chicago, the replication of limited data on market outcomes is a rather weak and potentially misleading test of the model's validity. Data on the Chicago housing market between 1960 and 1970 are surprisingly sparse and disturbingly contradictory. As a result, discrepancies between model-generated results and "actual" market behavior are often due to measurement and reporting errors rather than to flaws in the model. Other discrepancies are traceable to information on actual conditions that the current model does not include because of the high cost of assembling pertinent data or its complete unavailability.

It should be noted that a much closer correspondence between simulated (baseline) and actual data could have been achieved by artfully adjusting the model parameters to fit the available data. Rather than forcing the model to closely track the Chicago experience between 1960 and 1970, however, we chose to base the model on our best judgments and available empirical estimates of how both individuals and markets behave. As our own experience and the rapidly expanding body of theoretical and empirical research on urban housing markets increase, we expect to improve the model's ability to simulate both the general patterns and the important details of metropolitan development without resorting to uninformed, ad hoc adjustments of model parameters.

A Future Research Agenda

The analyses described in this book are the most recent phase of a long-term research program to develop a computer simulation model of urban housing markets with sufficient detail and accuracy to be used as a tool for designing and evaluating a wide variety of programs and policies. Much remains to be done. The simulations of concentrated housing and neighborhood improvement programs clearly provide useful insights about the likely market effects of such policies, and we stand by them; nonetheless, several improvements in model design and calibration are desirable. Although some of these changes will probably lead to different results or interpretations, we doubt very much that even extensive improvements in the model would change the overall character of the findings described here.

Analyses of the several baseline and policy simulations described in this book, as well as those completed for our earlier study of the market effects of housing allowances, have identified numerous model modifications and improvements. Several improvements have already been included in the current version of the model, but time and money constraints have prevented us from investigating and possibly implementing many others. We have gleaned additional ideas for model improvement from the rapidly expanding corpus of high-quality empirical and theoretical research on urban housing markets. When Phase I of the urban simulation modeling project was initiated in the late 1960s, urban economics was in its infancy and the available literature, though of inestimable value in developing the model, was much more limited than the current pertinent literature. Similarly, when the principal decisions about the design and specification of the current version of the model were made a decade or so ago at the start of Phase III, most of the recent high-quality theoretical and empirical research on housing markets had not even been begun. For example, none of the rich and diverse experimental and analytical results from the housing allowance experiment were available, since the current version of the model is itself an EHAP product (see Downs and Bradbury, 1980).

Foremost on our research agenda is to calibrate an improved version of the HUDS model to additional metropolitan areas during the period 1970–1980. Metropolitan housing markets are very different places today than ten years ago: many, if not most, of the factors that determined urban policies during the past decade were barely apparent in 1970. Condominiums, for example, were almost unheard of, and the problems and opportunities associated with conversions were almost completely unanticipated. Similarly, the increase in the Consumer Price Index in 1970 amounted to what we now think of as a modest 6.5 percent, while average effective mortgage rates had grown steadily during the decade to a 1970 high of 8.44 percent (Weicher, 1977). During the 1970s, moreover, changes in household size and composition and in female participation in the labor force — although a continuation of previous trends — began to exert major impacts on metropolitan housing markets (James, 1980; Alonso, 1980). Falling birth rates caused unprecedented numbers of metropolitan areas to lose population in the 1970s; a growing list of central cities also experienced serious losses of both employment and population.

Devising a defensible representation of the dramatic changes that have occurred in the forces affecting metropolitan housing market dynamics will be a challenge to the model's capabilities. The much more extensive data now available, however, should allow improvements in many key parameters. Desirable changes in the model include:

(1) a more detailed and accurate representation of changes in household size and composition;

(2) an improved job search model, and replacement of the Income Dynamics Submodel with an earnings function for each employed household member;

(3) addition of dwelling unit quality to the definition of housing bundles and to the submarket demand equations;
(4) research on the effect of changes in market prices and neighborhood quality on moving decisions;
(5) improvements in the representation of own/rent decisions;
(6) analysis of land value markups for neighborhood and structure types; and
(7) modification of the structure services production function to make structure quality a continuous variable.

Simulating Demographic Change

The current model does only a reasonably good job of replicating actual demographic change in Chicago between 1960 and 1970. As discussed in chapter 3, the discrepancies are only important if the objective is to model a particular real-world region or to replicate the historical experience of an actual market. As we have become more confident about the model's basic structure, however, we have become increasingly convinced that relatively small errors in the simulation of demographic processes may cause rather substantial errors in simulating many aspects of housing market behavior, such as the level and composition of new construction.

Our interest in these questions has been further stimulated by the growing awareness of and interest in the effects of changing population structure on urban development patterns. William Alonso, Franklin James, and others have suggested that recent and probable future changes in the population structure — such as the rapid growth in the number of young households, of two-worker households, of single-person and single-parent households, and of elderly households — have had important impacts on metropolitan development patterns, and that these factors are likely to become more important in the future (see James, 1977; Alonso, 1980; Apgar, 1984). Since the HUDS model is ideal for studying these questions, we hope to carry out a series of simulations to determine how the increase in multiple-worker households, changing patterns of childrearing, and marital stability affect household mobility, housing demand, and ultimately metropolitan development.

Labor Market Behavior and Income Dynamics

The list-processing technique used in the current model maintains information on the characteristics and location of each job and permits us — indeed, forces us — to simulate the job choices of individual sample workers. Since the Job Change Submodel is quite underdeveloped, we plan to review the growing literature on job search behavior and local labor markets and to devise a richer and more empirically sound labor market model (see Moffit, 1977; Nelson, 1977). We also intend to replace the current methods of simulating annual changes in household income with an earnings function that would more closely link income growth to job changes and other labor market activities. Finally, the increasing number of two-worker households in the 1970s suggest that we should reconsider how best to account for the influence of secondary workers on the household's residential location decision.

Improvements in the representation of labor market behavior and income growth would greatly enhance the model's usefulness for urban policy research. For example, the improved model would lend itself to analyses of the effects of spatially targeted job creation programs on specific neighborhoods as well as on urban housing markets generally. The simulations would also provide insights about the likely effects of changing labor force composition on housing demand in particular sections of the metropolitan area.

Modification of the Demand Submodel

In the current version of the model, the Demand Submodel assigns each household on the demand list to one of fifty types of housing bundles, defined by ten categories of structure type and five types of neighborhood. The ten structure types are classified by structure size (single-family units, large and small multiple units), dwelling unit size (number of bedrooms), and small and large lot size in the case of single-family units. Neighborhood type is defined by five quality levels, proxied by the average quantity of structure services consumed (supplied) in each residence zone.

One possible explanation for the problems encountered in simulating the process of neighborhood change is the omission of dwelling unit quality from the definition of housing bundles and thus from the submarket demand equations. In the current version of the model, the quantity of structure services consumed (supplied) is determined by the intersection of the occupant's demand curve and each unit's marginal cost curve, and the price of structure services is set equal to the average price for all dwelling units in a particular residence zone. This approach does not account for persistent differences in the price of structure services among residence zones or allow price differentials to affect the choice of housing types or residential locations. Since the assumptions seem too strong, we plan to investigate the desirability and feasibility of adding dwelling unit quality to the housing bundle definitions and of allowing for variations in the price of structure services among neighborhoods. The price of structure services currently varies by neighborhood, but it is not permitted to affect the demand for housing bundles.

We would also like to reconsider the treatment of lot size. In the current version of the model, single-family units may be built on either large or small lots. Available econometric evidence suggests that lot size has a high-income elasticity of demand; the model's current framework may give too little weight to this dimension of housing bundles. Since dwelling unit quality and lot size are, of course, highly correlated with neighborhood quality, it may ultimately be impossible to distinguish these effects adequately. Nonetheless, we feel a careful reexamination of the model's representation of lot size and its role in the demand for housing bundles could lead to important improvements in model design and estimation.

Household Moving Behavior

One of the major issues addressed by the policy simulations is the extent to which neighborhood revitalization causes displacement of low-income households. Neighborhoods of the type usually selected as targets for community development efforts often contain a large share of rental housing stock. Empirical estimates based on census statistics demonstrate that relatively few units are occupied by the same household for a period as long as a decade. Simulated rates of mobility are quite close to actual rates. As a result, concentrated housing improvement programs like CHIP-I will have only a limited tendency to displace target area households because most of these households are highly mobile. At the same time, there is a real possibility that the model understates the affinity households develop for particular neighborhoods. If so, the policy simulations may underestimate the extent to which neighborhood revitalization causes households to move out of a particular neighborhood. Because displacement is a highly sensitive concern in designing neighborhood improvement policies, we place a high priority on reviewing this aspect of the model.

A better representation of household mobility might also improve our ability to explain changing patterns of housing demand. The decision to move and the choice of a new housing bundle may be simultaneous. Moving decisions in the current version of the model depend solely on current levels or changes in such variables as prior tenure, family size, and income; they involve no explicit comparisons of the utility and price of a household's current unit with those of alternative units. While we do not expect to estimate joint move/bundle choice functions, we may introduce a more explicit utility-maximizing framework to account for this simultaneity.

Modification of the Tenure Choice Submodel

The Tenure Choice Submodel is a simple probability matrix in which the decision to own or rent depends on a household's prior tenure, current bundle choice, current income, and the age of its head. We plan to consider several possible changes in representing the own/rent decision, including how unexpected appreciation, mortgage rates, and changes in income tax schedules affect the probability of homeownership. Since condominium conversion is often associated with neighborhood revitalization, we also plan to improve the representation of the supply and demand for condominiums.

Determination of Neighborhood Quality, Land Values, and Market Rents

Analysis of the baseline simulations suggests that many aspects of land value determination and market rents need reconsideration, especially the representation of neighborhood quality and lot size effects. There is only limited knowledge about how changes in the relative accessibility of particular neighborhoods, for instance, affect land values, and our understanding of how these changes in turn affect the pattern of new construction is not much better. Given sufficient data, research funding, and time, we would review these critical aspects of model design and attempt to develop better empirical estimates of their effects. Even if empirical evidence is unavailable, we would like to design and execute a series of diagnostic simulations to test the effects of alternative specifications of the determinants of neighborhood change.

Modifications in the Structure Service Production Function

It is likely that the methods used to decompose rents and housing services in the HUDS model assign too large a share of both quantities to structures and neighborhoods and too little to structure services. Since an imputation error of this kind could account for at least some of the model's difficulties in simulating changes in neighborhood quality, we plan to carefully examine this issue. The estimates used in the current model were obtained using hedonic techniques from rather poor data. The larger number of high-quality samples of housing data, and particularly the availability of parcel files in a growing number of cities, should enable us to make some significant improvements in this area.

In the current version of the model, structure capital appears in the structure services production function as a step function; the index of structure capital — that is, construction type — affects the quantities of maintenance capital and operating inputs that must be used to produce a given level of structure services. The best construction type can produce the same level of structure services as the intermediate one with operating and maintenance inputs that are 15 percent lower; the worst construction type requires 15 percent more of each type of input than the intermediate one. The use of only three construction types appears to be the source of some difficulty in the simulations and we no longer see any reason for not including structure capital as a continuous variable. When we chose this specification, available data did not seem to justify the use of more categories. Data remain a problem, but we now believe the structure services production function should be modified and reestimated so that structure capital is represented as a continuous variable. Such a function would be easier to use, would eliminate potentially troublesome discontinuities, and places no more weight than the current approach on the limited available data.

History of the Modeling Project and Comparison with Other Models

The intellectual origins of the HUDS model are traceable to the early 1960s, when several researchers were attempting to develop better methods to forecast land uses in conjunction with the urban transportation studies then being carried out in a number of U.S. metropolitan areas. These large-scale comprehensive transportation studies, typically costing several millions of dollars, collected unprecedented quantities of data on both household behavior and land uses (Chicago Area Transportation Study, 1960). Home interview surveys of 30,000 to 50,000 households in individual SMSAs were common. It was inevitable that the availability of large study budgets, the need to process huge quantities of data, and the desire to obtain better projections of urban development patterns would create an interest in using an emerging computer technology.

As part of the RAND Study of Urban Transportation, John F. Kain and John R. Meyer (1961) set out a prospectus and a conceptual outline of a computer simulation model to study land use – transportation interrelationships. At about the same time, building on the work of John Herbert and Benjamin Stevens (1960) on the use of linear programming to represent residential location choices, Britton Harris (Harris, 1962a, 1962b, 1966) and others involved with the Penn-Jersey transportation study proposed developing a computer simulation model for projecting future land use, and Ira S. Lowry began work on a model to simulate the spatial distribution of employment and population in the Pittsburgh metropolitan area. In comparison to the Kain-Meyer and Penn-Jersey proposals, the model framework suggested by Lowry was exceedingly modest, consisting of little more than a journey-to-work function for projecting residential distributions and a journey-to-shop function for projecting the location of population-serving employment. In spite of, or perhaps because of, its simplicity, the Lowry model (1964) has had great influence, serving as the core of a score of operational land use forecasting models (Goldner, 1968, 1971; Batty, 1970; Putman, 1980).

These and other early attempts (Hill, 1965; Lowry, 1967; Brown et al., 1972; Hill, Brand, and Hansen, 1975) to use systematic methods of quantitative analysis and computer simulation techniques to forecast land use patterns faced immense intellectual and operational difficulties. Data, and particularly historical data, on urban development patterns were sketchy, and the body of relevant and systematic empirical research was exceedingly limited. Moreover, there existed little experience that was directly relevant to building large-scale computer simulation models; and the computers available at the time had limited capabilities. The decision in most cases to carry out the research in conjunction with operational transportation studies only exacerbated an already difficult task (Batty, 1979). Lowry's (1964) work was an important exception. Lowry proposed his model while employed by a research study, the Pittsburgh Metropolitan Area Study, and only completed the model's programming and several illustrative simulations with unrestricted research funds after joining the RAND Corporation.

Considering the formidable obstacles to success, the achievements of the developers of the early computer simulation models were substantial. Nonetheless, their sponsors were often disappointed with the resulting models and had little confidence in the forecasts they produced; the response of these sponsors and many others was to blame the method rather than its imperfect execution. The widespread disappointment with these early efforts to build urban simulation models is documented in a number of publications, of which a paper by Lee (1973) and a book by Brewer (1973) are perhaps the best known. Although the critics of early simulation modeling efforts acknowledged the need for better methods of projecting urban development patterns, their critiques created a widespread, though unsubstantiated, impression that cheaper and superior techniques existed. This view was reinforced by a widespread tendency to vastly overstate the costs of computer modeling by attributing the entire cost of comprehensive transportation studies to the land use modeling efforts. The critics of computer modeling efforts generally overlooked the fact any other forecasting methods would have required similar data and as a result would have cost as much or more. As Batty (1979) points out, moreover, the resources devoted to land use modeling were never more than a tiny fraction of the total transportation study budgets.

Although the HUDS model owes important intellectual debts to the efforts to develop land use forecasting models for use in urban transportation studies, its purpose and design are more similar to the computer simulation models developed for the San Francisco and Pittsburgh Community Renewal Programming (CRP) studies (Crecine, 1964; Steger, 1965; Little, 1966). The San Francisco and Pittsburgh CRP studies had as their objective the design and evaluation of large-scale urban development projects, including an assessment of the impacts of these projects on urban development patterns, on central city tax bases, and on the welfare of central-city residents. While there was great enthusiasm and support for the San Francisco and Pittsburgh computer modeling projects at their inception, the CRP model builders also promised too much too soon and their achievements, though considerable, fell far short of the expectations they had created. Criticism of the projects was intense (Lee, 1973; Brewer, 1973). Again the critics failed to compare the successes and failures of these analyses to other studies of the same kind. There is no evidence that analysts working in other cities on CRP studies performed any better, that they encountered any fewer problems, that their sponsors were any happier with the results, or that their policy recommendations and projections were any more accurate.

HUDS and Other Third-Generation Models

HUDS might be thought of as a third-generation computer simulation model. As such, it is most similar in conception and purpose to the model that Frank de Leeuw and Raymond Struyk (1975) developed at the Urban Institute and that their colleagues subsequently elaborated and applied to a number of policy issues (Marshall, 1976; Vanski, 1976; Struyk, Marshall, and Ozanne, 1978). Both the Urban Institute model and HUDS (as well as HUDS's precursor, the NBER Urban Simulation Model) were intended for use in simulating the impacts of various government policies on urban housing markets. Both, moreover, received a substantial portion of their funding from the Experimental Housing Allowance Program (EHAP) sponsored by the U.S. Department of Housing and Urban Development to assess the market effects of full-scale housing allowance programs. Since then the Urban Institute model has been used to evaluate the market impacts and benefits and costs of construction programs, various tax policies, and several other housing and urban development programs.

Although the HUDS and Urban Institute models are both economic models and simulate housing market behavior, there are some major differences between the two. For example, the Urban Institute model simulates only decade-long changes; HUDS obtains annual solutions and therefore may be used to study within-decade changes in house prices and other short-run phenomena. Furthermore, HUDS explicitly treats urban housing markets as a disequilibrium process: annual model solutions are viewed as exchange equilibria rather than the traditional long-run equilibria of comparative statics. The solutions of the Urban Institute model, on the other hand, appear to be much closer in spirit to the long-run equilibria assumed in most analytical models (de Leeuw and Struyk, 1975); indeed, the Urban Institute model bears more than a little resemblance to a number of earlier analytical models and particularly to Richard Muth's (1969). The Urban Institute model departs from these analytical models principally in the methods it employs to obtain market clearing solutions, in explicitly enumerating start-of-decade housing stock characteristics, and in providing a more detailed representation of household characteristics.

The most striking difference between HUDS and the Urban Institute model, however, is the level of detail in each. The Urban Institute model uses between twenty-five and forty-five model households and dwelling units to represent the population and housing stock of the Chicago metropolitan area during the decade 1960–1970; HUDS uses samples of between 72,000 and 84,000 households and dwelling units. Similarly, HUDS employs just under two hundred residence zones or neighborhoods to represent the Chicago metropolitan area; the Urban Institute model divides the SMSA into six zones. HUDS identifies twenty workplace locations; the Urban Institute model uses instead an exogenously specified average journey-to-work travel time for the residents of each zone. Differences in the level of detail reflect some disagreement about what factors are important or necessary for an accurate representation of the behavior of consumers and suppliers in urban housing markets and the consequences of public policies. To evaluate the different modeling strategies, it is therefore useful to describe HUDS's structure and some of the principal theoretical assumptions imbedded in its design, and compare them with those employed in the Urban Institute model and existing analytical models of urban spatial structure.

Like structure services in HUDS, housing services in the Urban Institute model are produced by combining capital and operating inputs. Because the Urban Institute model obtains only end-of-decade equilibrium solutions, however, the distinction between capital and operating inputs is much less important than in HUDS. In addition, the capital stocks in the Urban Institute model are homogeneous except for their location in one of the six model neighborhoods. Model households and housing suppliers in the Urban Institute model thus perceive no differences between a five-bedroom, single-family unit on a large lot and an efficiency apartment in a high-rise building, as long as the units have the same quantity of homogeneous housing capital.

Accessibility to employment has a less central role in the Urban Institute model than in HUDS. The Urban Institute model's zonal accessibility variable, an exogenously determined average journey-to-work travel time for each residence zone, is included in the utility functions of model households and affects the assignment of sample households to particular model dwellings, albeit in a limited way (de Leeuw and Struyk, 1975). Since the job locations of model households are never identified in the Urban Institute model, however, it is not clear just how accessibility to work influences housing choices.

In HUDS the amount that a property owner can invest in a particular year depends on the cash flow the building generates and on current and anticipated levels of neighborhood quality. To our knowledge, this feature of HUDS has no counterpart in any existing analytical or simulation model of urban housing markets. In the Urban Institute model, for example, a housing investor's decision to add capital to a unit depends solely on current period profitability, with no explicit consideration of the future. Of course, the longer periods and the higher level of aggregation in the Urban Institute model make such considerations less critical than in HUDS.

HUDS and the Community Analysis Model (CAM)

At first glance, the Community Analysis Model (CAM) developed by Dave Birch and others (Birch et al., 1974, 1977a) appears to be very similar to HUDS in both purpose and structure. Indeed, in describing the relationship of CAM to historical antecedents Birch and his co-authors state:

> Structurally, it most closely resembles the NBER model; many of its submodels contain the same labels and perform the same functions . . . Both treat explicitly a stream of events that begins with movers leaving units, continues through a system of vacancy accounting, a set of demand preferences for available units, a supply response (ours is lagged) both for the existing stock (filtering) and for new construction, and includes a market clearing algorithm . . .

At a more general level, both modeling groups reject the simplicity of Alonso's and Muth's static cross-sections and their feature-less-plain cities with all employment located at the center. Moreover, we both reject the concept of long-term equilibrium as an achievable state . . .

The mechanics by which both models clear the housing market are quite different, but it is not a fundamental conceptual difference. In fact, we suspect with a significant amount of work, we could employ the NBER strategy, and vice versa. We feel that ours is more realistic and, at present, it is considerably less expensive to operate (1977a, pp. 7–8).

It should be noted first of all that the NBER model referred to is the Detroit Prototype, which is very different from the model used for the simulations described in this book. Nonetheless, CAM more closely resembles HUDS than the Urban Institute model does in terms of the extent of spatial detail it employs and in terms of its emphasis on household and housing supplier behavior and patterns of metropolitan growth and development. Furthermore, CAM obtains estimates of prices for six types of housing defined by rent level and tenure, of new construction, and of demolitions, and it models maintenance outlays, deterioration of stock, and the abandonment of existing units.

In spite of these similarities, CAM and HUDS differ fundamentally in conception, design, and purpose. The conceptual differences are especially great in the demand and market clearing sectors. CAM is not a market model in the same sense as HUDS and the Urban Institute models. In modeling residential location and housing choices, CAM's authors assume that "people first choose a neighborhood and then a unit." To predict the neighborhood choices of moving households each year, CAM calculates probabilistic choice equations for twenty-seven types of households defined in terms of race, ethnicity, income, and family size. CAM then uses six variables to obtain initial or provisional estimates of the probabilities (frequencies) that each of its household types will choose a particular neighborhood. Equations calibrated to these variables, apparently on the basis of actual 1960–1970 choices of each area's households, are then used to calculate a desired 1970 demand by each household type for each neighborhood each year. Similarly, provisional estimates of the demand for each of the six unit types for each of the twenty-seven types of households are obtained from existing occupancy patterns, with adjustments made for renters' tendency to shift to owned units and for all movers to move up in price at each move (Birch et al., 1977a). CAM's demand model thus tends to assign each household category to the neighborhood and unit types they previously occupied, based on the ethnic and racial composition of demander households and on the social class of candidate neighborhoods. CAM's demand equations, however, contain neither gross nor net housing prices.

HUDS, in contrast, uses econometrically estimated submarket demand equations to predict the housing choices of ninety-six types of households on the basis of preferences and incomes and the relative gross prices of the fifty housing types. Given their choice of a particular housing bundle, specific model households are assigned to particular residence zones using a procedure that simulates spatial competition among households for locations that minimize transportation costs to work. For black households, discrimination markups are used to represent the higher search costs they would encounter in searching for housing in predominantly white neighborhoods and areas distant from the ghetto. Although accessibility to employment opportunities in general (the number of jobs within thirty-five minutes of the residence zone) apparently influences the desired demand for specific neighborhoods in CAM, only in HUDS does the specific workplace location of each household's primary worker has an impact on the household's housing and residential choices.

Since neither net nor gross prices have any effect on the neighborhood or housing type choices of model households, the phrase "clearing the market" in CAM obviously has a very different meaning than it does in HUDS and the Urban Institute model. In CAM clearing, "the market" merely refers to an algorithm that is used to reconcile first-round, provisional estimates of desired demand with independently determined supplies of available units by neighborhood, using a standardization technique attributed to Frederick Mosteller (Birch et al., 1977a). This algorithm obtains the market clearing solution that equates supply and demand while modifying desired demands by the least amount possible. Even after the independent projections of supply and demand by residence zone and unit type have been reconciled, differences remain in vacancy rates from one neighborhood to another and from one unit type to another; these differences are interpreted as measures of excess demand and supply and are used to adjust rents and housing values in each neighborhood. Unlike the adjustments that HUDS makes in the bundle quasi-rents, the resulting price changes in CAMS have no effect on demand. Mills (1978) provides a useful discussion of these issues in a critical evaluation of CAM prepared for the U.S. Department of Housing and Urban Development. This discussion also presents limited comparisons of CAM to the Urban Institute and NBER models; the version of the NBER model featured in Mills's discussion, however, is once again the Detroit Prototype.

HUDS and the Detroit Prototype

As table A.1 shows, major changes have occurred in the emphasis and orientation of the NBER-HUDS modeling effort over its two-decade lifetime. The modeling effort has, of course, been influenced by many factors, particularly funding, which in turn has reflected the major policy concerns at any given point in time. For example, the U.S. Department of Housing and Urban Development's initial grant to the NBER was for the development of a computer model to analyze the relationship between land use and transportation. At the time the Urban Mass Transit Administration (UMTA) was still part of HUD. This phase of research ended with the publication of *The Detroit Prototype of the NBER Urban Simulation Model*, a description of the theoretical and empirical foundations of the modeling effort (Ingram, Kain, and Ginn, 1972). HUD then funded further model development oriented toward analyzing housing abandonment, but in 1973 asked the NBER to change the project's focus to the market effects of housing allowances. The most recent HUD-funded analyses are concerned with the consequences of concentrated housing and neighborhood improvement policies.

The current version of the model retains many of the basic theoretical notions characterizing the Detroit Prototype—for example, emphasis on the importance of specific workplace location and of durable housing stocks, and on the disequilibrium nature of urban development—but it also incorporates many improvements. Indeed, these improvements and elaborations are so extensive that the current model is best thought of as completely new, despite its clear parentage. One purpose of this appendix is to document the changes that have been made in the design, empirical estimation, and programming of the model over the past fifteen years, and in paticular to clarify the relationship between HUDS and the better-known Detroit Prototype.

Phase I: Development of the Detroit Prototype

The emphasis of Phase I on land use – transportation interrelationships reflected the concerns of the Urban Mass Transit Administration (then located in HUD) as well as of Kain and Meyer's earlier research and continuing interest in urban transportation. As the NBER Urban Stud-

Table A.1. Chronology of Model Development

Date	Activity
1963	Publication of "A First Approximation for a RAND Model to Study Urban Transportation."
Phase I	
1967	NBER establishes Urban Simulation Modeling Project.
1968	HUD-UMTA awards grant to develop computer simulation model for studying land use–transportation interrelationships.
1968–71	Development of Detroit Prototype and calibration to Pittsburgh and Detroit.
1972	Publication of *The Detroit Prototype of the NBER Urban Simulation Model.*
Phase II	
1972	HUD awards contract to study housing abandonment.
1972–73	Modification of Detroit Prototype for abandonment study, implementation of list storage and processing, and reestimation of submarket demand equations.
1973	Completion of HUD report describing improvements in model design and improvements.
Phase III	
1973	Redirection of model development and research toward evaluation of the market impacts of a full-scale housing allowance program.
1974	Interim report sent to HUD describing housing allowance demand simulations (HADS).
1975–76	. Complete redesign of model, calibration to Pittsburgh and Chicago, and completion of baseline and policy simulations for Pittsburgh and Chicago for 1960–1970.
1976	Publication of three-volume report, *Simulation of the Market Effects of Housing Allowances.*
Phase IV	
1977	Modeling project moves to Harvard University.
1978	HUD awards contract to evaluate the impacts of spatially concentrated housing and neighborhood improvement programs.
1980	Completion of diagnostic simulations to improve model calibration.
1981	Submission of report, "The Market Effects of Concentrated Housing and Neighborhood Improvement Programs."

ies group began to consider the problem of modeling the processes of urban development, however, the project began to focus less on land use – transportation interrelationships and more on housing market behavior, and particularly on explaining changes in the characteristics of the existing housing stock. This important shift in emphasis reflected our growing belief that previous land use models had given too much attention to development at the urban periphery and too little to the processes by which the characteristics and use of the existing housing stock in built-up areas are modified (Kain and Meyer, 1968; Brown et al., 1972).

The research program leading to the current version of HUDS had to deal with four kinds of constraints: an inadequate theoretical understanding of the structure and behavior of urban housing markets and of the processes of urban development; the unavailability of empirical estimates of critical model parameters; limited computer capabilities; and too little experience and understanding of how to translate theoretical notions about housing market behavior into workable, computationally efficient computer programs. The modeling effort has therefore been an iterative process; progress in one area has permitted improvements in each of the other three. Although we had to solve most of these modeling problems ourselves, we nonetheless benefited from numerous complementary advances in each of the four areas by other researchers. During the project's lifetime the capacities, speed, and cost of computers has steadily improved; the amount and quality of both theoretical and empirical research in urban economics have increased enormously; and through our own growing experience as well as that of other modelers we have been able to exploit advances in computer capabilities.

The first operational version of the NBER Urban Simulation Model, the Detroit Prototype, was crudely calibrated to Detroit data, and a small number of test runs were completed. The test runs proved that a computer simulation model with the spatial detail and complexity we felt were necessary for evaluating many housing and urban development policies was computationally feasible. Our concept of computational feasibility also embodied a budget constraint. Specifically, we felt that if the model was to be useful for policy analysis, the computational cost per decade-long simulation and per simulation year had to be "modest." We chose a cost of $250 for a ten-year simulation (in 1972 dollars) as an appropriate target in developing the model.

Calibration of the Detroit Prototype to the Detroit metropolitan housing market was problematic, however, because of severe data deficiencies. The model's emphasis on workplace location in determining housing choice meant that estimation of the critical submarket demand equations was not possible without information on both the specific workplace locations and the housing choices of a large sample of households. Fortunately, we obtained a large, high-quality sample of Pittsburgh households, collected as part of the Pittsburgh Area Transportation Study. Using these data, J. Royce Ginn and Gregory K. Ingram made minor changes in model structure, achieved a much improved calibration, and completed a small number of test simulations for Pittsburgh (Ingram, 1971).

Phase II: Abandonment Research

The second phase in the development of the NBER urban simulation model was funded by a grant from HUD to study housing abandonment, a nationwide phenomenon that was of growing concern to local, state, and federal policy makers. Signed in 1972, the contract called for further improvement of the model and for the completion of several simulations. The first series of simulations were meant to assess the hypothesis that abandonment was no more than an efficient market response to post–World War II job suburbanization, rising incomes, and declining commuting costs, which altered the relative attractiveness of various kinds of housing. A second series of simulations were to investigate the possible role of market imperfections, externalities, and interneighborhood variations in the cost of producing housing services. Some analysts, for example, claimed that abandonment was traceable to the high costs of producing housing services in declining neighborhoods and that these high costs were due to the high incidence of vandalism and crime, the overassessment of property taxes, and the high cost or unavailability of financing and insurance in declining neighborhoods. In the absence of little direct evidence, we proposed to do sensitivity analyses involving several simulations that assumed a range of values for neighborhood variations in housing input and production costs. After evaluating these competing hypotheses about the market and nonmarket causes of housing abandonment, we were to investigate the efficacy of several policies intended to improve the living conditions of low-income households, encourage use of the existing housing stock, and discourage abandonment of structurally sound units. The abandonment simulations, however, were never completed. Before the necessary model improvements were made, HUD asked us to redirect our modeling efforts toward an evaluation of housing allowances. We agreed, and in spring 1974 HUD specified a new program of model development and several new simulation exercises.

In the eighteen-month period covered by the abandonment contract, however, a number of important improvements and modifications were made in the urban simulation model (Kain, 1974). Among the most important advances were improvements in data processing and storage techniques that were permitted by a dramatic increase in the size, speed, and reliability of direct-access storage devices. When we began work on the Detroit Prototype, available disc storage was limited to the IBM 2344 or its equivalent. By the time Phase II of the research began, most large computer centers had acquired the capability to mount the IBM 3330 disc, a unit four times as large and twice as fast as its predecessor. Despite these advances, with the Detroit Prototype version of the model, data storage requirements and computational costs continued to be real constraints in representing the characteristics of households, property owners, and dwelling units. As table A.2 shows, the Detroit Prototype simulated the behavior of seventy-two types of households defined by the income and size of the household and the age and education of the household head. Sample workers competed for jobs defined by nine industry groups in one of nineteen work zones; sample households selected one of 1,350 types of housing units from among twenty-seven housing bundle types in fifty residence zones. What may at first appear to be rather modest model dimensions thus produce 16,621,200 unique combinations of work zones, industries, residence zones, household types, and housing bundles.

Since it would be impossible to store even a fraction of the full matrix, the Detroit Prototype used a series of marginal matrixes to summarize the information needed by the model. For example, the model maintained a matrix consisting of the types of housing bundles consumed by workers employed at each workplace, but not the specific residence zone location of these bundles. Similarly, summary matrixes for each workplace included information on the characteristics of the residents, but not on the number of each housing bundle type in each residence zone. Some arrays were maintained in permanent storage; others were created, used in the year's simulation, and then aggregated or discarded. In addition, many of the summary matrixes were reduced in size by omitting empty columns and rows. These procedures added to the complexity of the Detroit Prototype programs and frustrated efforts to expand or add new variables to the model.

The most compelling reason for abandoning the summary matrix method, however, was concern about the accuracy of the procedures used to expand and collapse the marginal arrays. Serious cumulative errors arose in earlier versions of the model, particularly in matching moving households to available vacant units. Identifying movers and

Table A.2. Household and dwelling unit information included on the Basic List

Characteristics	Detroit Prototype	Current model
Household		
Income	4	Continuous or 6
Race of household head	1	2
Age of household head	3	Continuous and 3
Family size	3	Continuous and 4
Tenure	NI[a]	2
Industry of primary worker	9	11
Occupation of primary worker	NI	3
Labor force status of primary worker	1	3
Workplace zone	19	20
Education	2	NI
Years lived at current address	NI	31
Dwelling unit and structure		
Structure type	9	10
Nieghborhood quality	NI	Continuous and 5
Housing bundle type	27	50
Residence zone	50	200
Structure services[b]	3	Continuous or 4
Maintenance capital	NI	Continuous
Structure capital	NI	Continuous
Construction type	NI	3
Structure rent	Continuous	Continuous
Structure services rent	NI	Continuous and 4
Location rent	Continuous	Continuous
Residence zone	50	200
Market rent	Continuous	Continuous

a. NI = Not included.

b. In the current model, the concept of structure services replaces the Detroit Prototype use of housing quality categories.

available vacant units required information on household characteristics and workplace locations kept in one array, and information on dwelling unit choices by workplace, work-trip patterns, and dwelling unit locations kept in three other arrays. When a particular household moved, the characteristics of the unit it vacated could only be approximated; over time these approximations tended to produce cumulative errors.

Experience with the Detroit Prototype convinced us that more housing bundle types and a larger number of more homogeneous zones had to be included if the model was to be useful for many types of policy analysis — specifically, for simulating the impact of housing allowances. In addition, we concluded that meaningful analyses would require at minimum the inclusion of race, tenure, and employment status in the description of model households. Of course, increases in the model's dimensions would only increase the frequency and severity of the cumulative errors that plagued the summary matrix method.

The availability of larger and faster disc storage devices enabled us to replace the summary matrix data storage and processing approach used in the Detroit Prototype with what we refer to as "list processing." The list technique involves storing information about individual households and dwelling units as a list rather than attempting to summarize these data in matrixes. We were by no means the first to use this approach; Guy Orcutt and his associates (Orcutt et al., 1961), for example, had used list storage techniques in their pioneering studies of microanalytic simulation models. The list storage approach enabled us to expand substantially the model's representation of household and housing unit characteristics (see table A.2).

HUDS explicitly quantifies neighborhood quality and assigns one of five quality levels to each of its two hundred neighborhoods. The Detroit Prototype did not represent neighborhood quality as a separate housing attribute; rather, both neighborhood quality and dwelling unit quality were included in a single index of dwelling unit quality that was assigned one of three values. Dwelling units of each structure type were classified into three quality groups: sound, in need of repair, or dilapidated. The Detroit Prototype's concept of dwelling unit quality is quite similar to the current model's quantity of structure services, which measures both the quantity of structure services provided by the individual dwelling unit and the household's consumption of these services.

The most important benefit of list storage is that it permits a much more direct mapping of theory to the behavioral relations included in the model. The Detroit Prototype's counterpart of HUDS's elaborate microanalytic representation of the structure services supply and investment decisions of individual property owners is represented by a simple filtering function. The Detroit Prototype used this filtering function to adjust the quality level of model dwelling units in each year depending on a calculation of the profitability of supplying housing of greater or lesser quality.

HUDS's elaborate representation of expectations and the procedures it uses to project future rental income are also completely absent from the Detroit Prototype, which uses current-period prices in determining both consumption and investment decisions. (Current prices are a weighted average of the shadow prices obtained from the solution of linear programming algorithms for each of the fifty housing submarkets in each simulation year.) As appendix G indicates, we also made several changes in the algorithms used in calculating each period's prices, including the addition of premiums to reflect the extent to which black households face price and other forms of discrimination in the market.

The Job Change Submodel used in the current version of the model is also entirely new. Part of the information that was lost in the summary matrix method of data storage and processing used by the Detroit Prototype was the specific job location of primary workers. Although specific workplace location was used in determining the bundle choices of each household in the market, this information was not kept. With the adoption of the list processing method of data storage and processing, however, this information could be retained for each sample household. Thus, during each period the current version of the model simulates the labor market activities of each primary worker, his or her decision to change jobs or remain at the same job, and, if the worker changed jobs, his or her choice of a new job defined in terms of workplace location, industry, and occupation. A job change in turn influences the household's decision to move or remain in its current unit.

The Job Change, Demand, Market, and Supply submodels underwent the most extensive modifications, but substantial changes were made in most of the other submodels as well. For example, the Movers Submodel was significantly improved, a change motivated by the current model's much richer representation of labor market behavior and the addition of tenure (own/rent), race, and duration of occupancy to the variables maintained by the model. Similarly, the treatment of income change was improved, although we have yet to link the labor market and income changes more closely by including an earnings function in the model.

During Phase II of the modeling project, William C. Apgar, Jr., and John M. Quigley worked out a solution to the difficult problem of estimating the gross price parameters for the model's crucial submarket demand equations. Their adaptation of Daniel McFadden's multinomial logit technique to the econometric estimation of housing demand represented a major breakthrough in the development of an operational computer simulation model of urban housing markets (McFadden, 1968; Charles River Associates, 1972). Although we still have some reservations about the quality of the estimates used in the current version of the model, they clearly represent an enormous improvement over those we had been able to obtain using other methods (Ingram, Kain, and Ginn, 1972; Kain et al., 1974).

Phase III: Analysis of the Market Effects of Housing Allowances

The first year of the abandonment study thus entailed major changes in both the conceptual and programming structure of the Urban Simulation Model and produced solutions to several critical estimation problems (Kain et al., 1974). Before the abandonment research could be completed, however, HUD asked NBER to redirect the modeling effort toward an analysis of the market impacts of housing allowances. HUD was concerned primarily with short-term market effects, and in particular with the nature and extent of rent inflation that might result from implementing a large-scale housing allowance program. This shift in focus again required major changes in model structure and design, especially in the Supply and Market sectors.

Amended in spring 1974, the revised contract specified two goals that were largely complementary in the long run but somewhat competitive in the short run: to refine the model for the purpose of analyzing housing allowances and housing abandonment; and to provide HUD with interim analyses of the probable market impacts of housing allowances for a fall 1974 internal evaluation of proposed programs. It was agreed that development efforts should receive priority in the hope that a suitable model could be completed for the internal evaluation. When it became clear that the full model would not be available in time, however, development began on the Housing Allowance Demand Simulator (HADS) to provide HUD with an interim assessment of the probable effects of a full-scale housing allowance.

HADS combined the Demand Sector of the NBER Urban Simulation Model with a much simpler market clearing algorithm that alternately assumed that supply was perfectly elastic or perfectly inelastic. Unlike previous analyses that treated housing as a homogeneous good and considered only the aggregate effects of housing allowances on expenditures and prices, the HADS simulations traced out how the policy would affect the demand for individual housing bundle types. Simulations using HADS indicated that an effectively earmarked program would produce a significant change in the demand for and supplies of certain types of housing units (Kain, 1974; Kain and Apgar, 1976). Policymakers were concerned that allowances would induce price and rent increases, but the HADS analyses suggested that a greater problem might be that they would induce large declines in the demand for some less desirable housing types, thus inducing widespread abandonment.

After completing the HADS simulations, the modeling project focused once again on completing the full model and carrying out baseline and housing allowance policy simulations for Pittsburgh and Chicago. The version of the model used for these housing allowance simulations is quite similar to HUDS. Findings of the housing allowance research were presented in a three-volume report and in several papers (Ingram, Leonard, and Schafer, 1976; Kain, Apgar, and Ginn, 1977; Kain and Apgar, 1977).

One of the most striking of the findings obtained from the NBER housing allowance simulations was a decline in average rents relative to the baseline experience. Along with the NBER simulations' somewhat surprising result that a full-scale housing allowance could cause average rents to fall, they also determined that the particular allowance program evaluated using the simulations could cause 20 percent of Pittsburgh's dwelling units to experience rent increases of more than 10 percent and another 22 percent to experience rent decreases of the same magnitude. Comparable statistics from the Chicago policy simulations are 19 and 24 percent respectively.

The widely held expectation that a full-scale housing allowance would cause average rents to increase illustrates the tendency to rely on models with homogeneous housing in thinking about the probable effects of policies. If housing services were in fact homogeneous, a housing allowance would simply shift the demand curve for these homogeneous services, causing an unambiguous increase in the price of housing services. The size of this increase would be uncertain, depending on the period examined and the responsiveness of housing supply to changes in demand, but its direction would be certain. When the heterogeneity of the housing stock is recognized, however, as in the NBER and HUDS models, the effect of a housing allowance on average prices becomes less obvious. A housing allowance would not affect the demand for all types of units uniformly. In both the HADS and full-model simulations, provision of an effectively earmarked housing allowance increased the demand for housing of moderate quality in good neighborhoods and decreased the demand for the lowest-quality housing in the least desirable neighborhoods. Although on average rents fell, they increased in those submarkets where the allowance led to an increase in demand and decreased in those submarkets where the allowance led to a decrease in demand. These increases and decreases produced a small net average decline in rents.

There has been considerable confusion about how the results of the Housing Allowance Program supply experiment should be interpreted and particularly about the relationship of its findings to the housing allowance simulation results obtained from the Urban Institute and NBER models (Barnett, 1979; Kain, 1980). The supply experiment was conducted in two midwestern metropolitan areas — Green Bay, Wisconsin, and South Bend, Indiana — because of a widespread concern that a full-scale housing allowance would produce either small or no increases in the consumption of housing services by recipients because the hope of increased expenditures by recipients would be disappointed by increased rents. Worse yet was the possibility that a full-scale allowance program would cause large increases in the prices of units occupied by nonrecipients as well as huge windfall profits for the owners of rental property.

The best-known finding of the supply experiment is that the full-scale housing allowance program tested in Green Bay and South Bend caused no increase in rents beyond background inflation. Barnett (1979) argues that this result was completely unexpected; he points to the widespread expectation that such an allowance would cause sharp increases in rents and housing prices and in particular cites the increases in rents obtained from the Urban Institute and NBER housing allowance simulations. The supply experiment finding of no price increase, he concludes, demonstrates the inadequacy of these models.

Barnett's interpretation of the Urban Institute and NBER model results is deficient in two major respects. First, his discussion of the NBER simulation results confuses the HADS simulations with those obtained using the full model. Second, he provides a seriously incomplete explanation for the difference in supply experiment and simulation findings about the probable market impact of a full-scale housing allowance program. In particular, he never mentions that the housing allowance program tested in Green Bay and South Bend differ in important respects from the programs evaluated using the Urban Institute and NBER models. Both the Urban Institute and NBER simulations tested versions of housing allowance programs that produced substantial increases in housing expenditures by recipient households; in contrast, the program tested in the supply experiment had almost no effect on recipients' housing expenditures.

The Urban Institute and NBER housing allowance simulations both employed variants of minimum quantity or rent earmarking and assumed that an effectively earmarked housing allowance would produce a substantial increase in housing expenditures by recipients. The allowance programs tested in both the Urban Institute and NBER simulations, which produced the significant price effects cited by Barnett, moreover, induced substantial increases in housing expenditures. In contrast, the housing allowance program tested in Green Bay and South Bend had little effect on prices and supplier behavior because it had almost no impact on demand. Supply experiment analyses make it clear that the minimum quality standards employed by the supply experiment were typically not binding on recipients and that as a result the program tested had virtually no effect on demand. The supply experiment's "no earmarking, no price effect" result, incidentally, was anticipated by HADS simulations of several unearmarked housing allowance programs (Apgar and Kain, 1974). Few would have predicted substantial rent and house price increases if they had been told in advance that the program in question would not increase housing expenditures.

In fairness to the designers of the supply experiment it should be acknowledged that the effects of the housing standards used in the supply experiment on housing expenditures are far more obvious today than they were before the experiment began. This fact, however, should not be allowed to obscure the fact that the housing allowance program tested in Green Bay and South Bend produced almost no increase in the housing expenditures by recipient households. Furthermore, other program variants tested in the demand portion of the experiment produced larger increases in expenditures, although none produced increases as large as were obtained in the Urban Institute and NBER housing allowance simulations. The Brookings volume edited by Downs and Bradbury (1980) provides a compact discussion and critical assessment of demand experiment findings; the chapter by Kain (1980) considers the effects of housing standards on housing expenditures by recipients in both the supply and demand experiments.

The NBER Pittsburgh and Chicago simulations identified a wide variety of indirect effects of an earmarked housing allowance program that could easily prove more important than the more commonly recognized impacts on housing prices and rents. Changes in neighborhood quality are probably the most significant, though least understood, of these indirect effects. As the analyses presented in this book demonstrate, neighborhood quality strongly affects the demand for housing and the investment behavior of both owner-occupants and suppliers. Simulated improvement and deterioration of neighborhoods caused larger annual changes in the supply of particular housing bundles, and therefore in rents, than new construction and renovation activities.

The housing allowance simulations also suggest that an effectively earmarked program would have a different impact on the residence location choices of black and white households. The allowances would increase the supply of units in high-quality zones and decrease the supply in low-quality zones, blacks and whites would not share equally, however, in the resulting housing stock improvements. The analysis thus concludes that a housing allowance program would not by itself substantially reduce racial discrimination or significantly change the geographic distribution of black households.

Phase IV: Evaluation of Concentrated Housing and Neighborhood Improvement Programs

The fourth, and current, phase of the modeling project began in November 1978 when HUD awarded Kain and Apgar a contract to investigate the issues in this book. Phase IV also included the analysis of two diagnostic simulations, one assuming that household incomes grew 20 percent faster between 1960 and 1970 than in the baseline, the other assuming a substantial exogenous increase in the perceived quality of seven central-city neighborhoods. This income growth simulation was carried out primarily to test and improve the model; the second scenario, referred to as the Neighborhood Improvement Diagnostic (NID) simulation, was used in designing the policy scenarios presented in this book.

Although the model used for the CHIP simulations is quite similar to the one used to analyze housing allowances, both the lessons learned from evaluating previous simulations and the specific requirements of housing rehabilitation led to a number of model modifications and improvements. The principal changes in model design and programming completed in Phase IV include:

1. *An increase in the number of variables on the Basic List and a decrease in the processing cost of list-handling operations.* The central data storage system, the Basic List, consists of a random sample of 72,000 to 84,000 housing units and their occupants. Each period, the model reads the Basic List and uses the information to simulate the supply and demand behavior of households and property owners. Two of the added variables are used for household and dwelling unit sequence numbers, another for a public housing variable, and one for a variable indicating the length of residence in the unit. Two of the five remaining spaces in the CHIP simulations are used to record the quantity of structure services supplied by each dwelling unit and the unit cost of producing these structure services; the other three are used for variables that facilitate subsequent analyses of the effects of housing rehabilitation subsidies: identification of treated buildings (those receiving subsidies), of all

households that ever lived in a treated building, and of the building's residence zone.

2. *Redefinition of the model's residence zones to achieve compatibility with the zonal system used in the spatially disaggregate 1970 Public Use Sample Files and the 1975 and 1979 Annual Housing Survey for the Chicago SMSA.* This modification greatly enriches the model's data base and permits additional tests of its reliability. Indeed, several of the model improvements described below result from our ability to use these spatially disaggregate samples.

3. *Development of annual estimates of subsidized new construction by zone and structure type.* As part of the Phase IV research, we collected information on the number of newly constructed public housing and subsidized dwelling units by residence zone in each year. In the current simulations, these subsidized units are supplied as exogenous inputs.

4. *Addition of household and dwelling unit sequence numbers to the Basic List.* Earlier efforts to analyze the market effects of housing allowances and of housing rehabilitation programs were frustrated by our inability to track individual households and to compare their behavior under baseline and policy conditions. We were therefore unable to answer a number of important questions relating to the impacts of these policies, such as whether the former residents of target neighborhoods paid more or less rent at their new locations and whether they lived in better or worse housing.

5. *Addition of the capability to change perceived neighborhood quality exogenously.* This new feature, added for the Neighborhood Improvement Diagnostic simulation, provides the model with greater flexibility in representing the impacts of a variety of programs.

6. *Modification of the model to allow owner-occupancy of multi-family units.* Recent increases in condominium conversions have focused attention on the ownership of multi-family structures. Experience gained in Phase IV of the modeling effort suggests that it would be even more desirable in future versions of the model to make individual dwelling units rather than structures the sampling unit represented on the Basic List. Among other advantages, this change in model structure would enable us to increase the spatial disaggregation of the model.

7. *Addition of a duration-of-occupancy variable.* Analyses of household moving behavior in particular neighborhoods clearly indicated that the model underestimated the number of households remaining in the same unit for the entire decade. The model now maintains a variable that indicates the number of years the household has lived in the unit. Duration of residency is used as a variable in determining the probability that a household will move during the period.

8. *Development of a technique for freezing the random draws used in the simulations.* Because earlier versions of the model used different sequences of random numbers in the baseline and policy simulations, the behavior of individual households could differ in ways unrelated to the program impacts being studied. As long as no effort was made to analyze the impacts of programs on individual participants, these small random disturbances were unimportant; when we added household and dwelling unit sequence numbers to the Basic List, however, the problem became more apparent.

9. *Changes in the model's input-output routines to permit writing of the Basic List in any year.* In earlier versions of the model the entire list of approximately 80,000 households and dwelling units was written out in only the first and last years, thus limiting the ability to study various market dynamics as they applied to particular categories of households or units. For the simulations described in this report, a copy of the Basic List was written out every other simulation year.

10. *Addition of an output file to retain the characteristics of households and dwelling units that "disappear."* Efforts to track individual households and dwelling units highlighted the failure of earlier versions of the model to retain information on households that disappear because of death, dissolution, or out-migration, and on dwelling units that are demolished or used as inputs in producing other structure types. A full analysis of program-induced changes should account for these categories both in the baseline and policy simulations. The new output file, which we term the "graveyard," facilitates these analyses.

11. *Addition of the capability of providing spatially targeted capital subsidies to specific sample dwelling units.* This subroutine determines the eligibility of each unit, calculates the amount of capital required to bring the structure to 90 percent of good-as-new condition, and augments the unit's stock of structure and maintenance capital by this amount.

12. *Development of a price index.* The findings of our housing allowance simulations were somewhat ambiguous because simulated rents for location, structure type, neighborhood, and the quantity of structure services supplied were not completely standardized. In Phase III, we added information to the Basic List and developed programs to construct price indexes at virtually any level of aggregation.

13. *Changes in the calculation of profitability of new construction activities.* This change in model structure largely corrects a tendency in earlier baseline and policy simulations to build unrealistically large numbers of new units in low-quality neighborhoods.

Employment Location and Land Use Accounting

This appendix describes how the current version of the HUDS model deals with three important tasks: determination of the level and location of jobs by industry within the region; calculation of primary jobs by occupational class; and land use accounting.

The model maintains information on eleven industry groups, corresponding closely to the one-digit Standard Industrial Classification System. For the CHIP simulations, these eleven industries are assigned to one of three industry groups: export employment; regional service employment; or population-serving employment. Both the aggregate level and location of export jobs are exogenous to the model; in 1960, the initial year of our baseline simulations, export employment accounted for 940,250 jobs, or 37 percent of total employment in the Chicago SMSA. In contrast, the level and location of population-serving employment, which accounted for approximately 20 percent of jobs, are determined endogenously by the Population Serving Employment Submodel. Regional service employment, which in 1960 accounted for 43 percent of total employment, consists of enterprises that serve the resident population and other industries in the region, and tends to concentrate in the CBD, in other major commercial centers, in large regional shopping centers, and near airports. Both the location and aggregate number of regional service jobs are determined exogenously.

The explicit representation of both workplaces and residences in HUDS makes it possible to trace in some detail the impact of changes in the level, composition, and location of employment on the demand for specific types of housing.

The Exogenous Employment Submodel

The Exogenous Employment Submodel is simply the entry point for exogenous projections of changes in export and regional service employment by workplace zone. In the Chicago simulations the metropolitan area is divided into twenty discrete work zones, which range from rather compact and dense zones, corresponding to a rather generous definition of Chicago's central business district, to large, low-density zones located at the periphery of the region.

Data to make even a crude representation of historical trends in the level of export and regional service employment by workplace zone are almost nonexistent. Our estimates of total employment by industry and workplace location for the period 1960–1970 rely heavily on data collected by the Chicago Area Transportation Study. The 1960 and 1970 census data provide very little spatial detail, but they do include more specific information on the occupational and industrial composition of the labor force. These two sources were combined to make an estimate of the spatial distribution of the Chicago work force by industry, type, and location in 1960 and 1970. Although no annual data exist on employment by work zone for the eleven industries used in the model, information collected by the Chicago Area Transportation Study and other agencies provides estimates of employment changes over the decade by detailed location. These data were combined with annual industry employment control totals to estimate annual changes in employment by work zone and industry for the decade 1960–1970.

Although the employment data used for the Chicago baseline simulations are uncomfortably primitive, they are the best available and probably capture the gross trends in employment by work zone and industry. The exogenous specification of employment changes precludes consideration of the impact of changes in land prices and other endogenous variables on employment and employment location, but it provides a flexible structure for considering the impact of changes in the spatial distribution of employment on housing markets. In addition, the model could also be used for parametric analyses of the effects of changes in the spatial distribution of employment on urban housing markets.

The Population Serving Employment Submodel

The location and level of population-serving employment are endogenous in the current version of the HUDS model, unlike the Detroit Prototype. As the name implies, population-serving employment consists of those jobs that provide services to community residents. In contrast to export and regional service industries, population-serving employment tends to be uniformly distributed throughout the metropolitan area. The primary activity of the Population-Serving Employment Submodel is to simulate changes in the level of these jobs by work zone.

The CHIP simulations consider two categories of local employment: local government, education, and services; and local retail. We assume that annual changes in employment levels for the former category depend on changes in the spatial distribution of households, income, and employment, and that changes in local retailing depend only on changes in the spatial distribution of households and income. Thus, the Population Serving Employment Submodel calculates the number of population-serving jobs for each zone in each year using equations B.1 and B.2.

(B.1) $\text{ELR}(J) = a * \text{HOU}(J) + b * \text{INC}(J)$

(B.2) $\text{ELS}(J) = c * \text{HOU}(J) + d * \text{INC}(J) + e * \text{EXBASE}(J)$

where $\text{ELR}(J)$ = Local retail employment in work zone J;
          $\text{ELS}(J)$ = Local government, education, and services employment in work zone J;
          $\text{HOU}(J)$ = Total households living in residence zones located within work zone J;
          $\text{INC}(J)$ = Total income of households living in residence zones located within work zone J;
          $\text{EXBASE}(J)$ = Total export and regional service employment in work zone J;
          a, b, c, d, e = Scaling parameters.

Summation of equations B.1 and B.2 over work zones gives total population-serving employment as a function of total household income, the total number of households, and the number of workers in export and regional service employment. Since the total number of households in the metropolitan area and household income are exogenously specified for each simulation period, care must be exercised to insure that areawide estimates of population-serving employment are consistent with the exogenous projections of export employment, regional service employment, and households.

Even though the Population Serving Employment Submodel is relatively simple in design, it does permit the evaluation of complex relationships between employment and residence locations. For example, if incomes grow more rapidly in one part of the metropolitan area than in another, these changes will produce secondary increases in employment and changes in the demand for housing in adjacent areas.

Occupation

In addition to the eleven industry groups discussed above, the current version of the model classifies sample workers into three major occupational categories: white collar, blue collar, and service. Unpublished econometric research by J. Royce Ginn and Charles Revier indicates that rates of job change and moving behavior differ by occupation, and these distinctions must therefore be incorporated into the Job Change Submodel.

Unfortunately, available sources do not provide estimates of either the 1960 level or the changes over the decade in employment by industry and occupation in each work zone. For the Chicago simulations we assumed that the occupational composition of each of the eleven industries in each zone is equal to the SMSA distribution in 1960 and did not change over the decade. These estimates are used in the Exogenous Employment Submodel and the Population Serving Employment Submodel to convert job change estimates classified by industry and work zone into job change estimates classified by industry, occupation, and work zone.

Primary Employment by Zone

The assumption that the primary wage earner's workplace location influences both the type and location of housing consumed by urban households is central to the design of the HUDS model. The model considers the workplace location of only primary workers for two reasons. First, although it would be possible to include the journey-to-work costs of secondary workers in the calculation of gross prices and thus allow their travel to affect the housing choices of model households, the calculations required would be prohibitively expensive. Second, econometric work assessing the workplace location effects of secondary workers on housing choices is presently inadequate to justify their consideration in the analysis.

Since the current version of the model keeps track of the detailed location of only primary workers and since the employment submodels provide estimates of total employment by industry and workplace, it is necessary to convert total employment into estimates of primary employment by zone. The required estimates are obtained from equation B.3, which is simply a labor force requirements table.

(B.3) $\text{PWORK}(HI,HO,J) = \text{PROBHEAD}(HI,HO) * \text{WORK}(HI,HO,J)$

where $\text{PWORK}(HI,HO,J) =$ Number of primary workers by industry, occupation, and work zone;
$\text{PROBHEAD}(HI,HO) =$ Probability that a job is filled by a head of household;
$\text{WORK}(HI,HO,J) =$ Count of total jobs by industry, occupation, and work zone.

As is evident from equation B.3, the labor force requirements tables used for the simulations presented in this report assume that the proportion of primary workers in each industry is the same for all workplaces. Of course, since the eleven industries are not uniformly distributed across work zones, the ratio of total primary workers to total employment does vary by zone. The ratio will be highest in zones dominated by manufacturing activity, and lowest in suburban zones with relatively high proportions of population-serving employment.

Land Use Submodel

The Land Use Submodel maintains an enumeration of available vacant land by residence zone. At the beginning of each period, the supply of available vacant land is adjusted to reflect changes during the previous period in land used for employment, housing, or other exogenously specified activities such as public parks or public transportation.

Although the Exogenous Employment and Population Serving Employment submodels can produce estimates of employment change by industry, occupation, and work zone, translation of these estimates into land use changes requires a series of land absorption factors. Unfortunately, we were unable to obtain reasonable estimates of the relationship between job expansion or contraction and land use change for the aggregate industry categories used in the current model. To calibrate such relationships requires an estimate of the extent to which new jobs lead to new plant or office space development (extra jobs are sometimes accommodated within existing facilities). Equally difficult questions are posed for zones with declining employment: although it seems likely that small declines in employment do not increase the space available for residential use, major declines may encourage selective demolition or conversion of commercial and industrial buildings to residential use. Rather than deal with these complex issues at this time, we did not engage the mechanism that accounts for industrial land use changes for the CHIP simulations. Changes in employment thus do not affect the amount of vacant land available for residential development in the model. This omission is not very serious, since the land devoted to industrial or commercial activities is a small percentage of total land in most metropolitan areas, and since land use patterns change only slowly over time.

The land use accounting problem is much easier for residential land. Each type of housing bundle used in the Chicago simulations requires a particular quantity of residential land. Single-family homes are assumed to occupy either one-fourth or three-eighths of an acre; small multi-family structures with an average of three units occupy one-eighth of an acre; and large multi-family structures containing eight units occupy one-fourth of an acre. The Land Use Submodel uses these areas to calculate the effects of demolitions, conversions, or new construction activities on the supply of available vacant land in each residence zone. These available supplies of vacant land in turn affect the level of new construction, which we discuss in more detail in appendix F.

Demographic Change, Job Change, and Moving Behavior

This appendix describes the logic, calibration, and operation of four major components of the HUDS model: the Demographic, Job Change, Movers, and New Households submodels. Each of these submodels makes important changes in the characteristics of households included on the Basic List, the central data base of the model, which is composed of a household and dwelling unit sample arranged by structure type and residence zone. For the baseline and CHIP simulations reported in this book, each sample household represents twenty-five actual Chicago households, thereby producing a list with as many as 84,000 individual records. Programming and computational efficiency are obviously major considerations in a model designed to simulate the behavior of such a large number of households and nearly as many property owners.

Having noted the programming difficulties, we should mention that the current version of the model has a relatively flexible structure and is quite easily modified to incorporate new model features. For example, the Basic List used in the housing allowance simulations contained only twenty-two items, while the Basic List for the CHIP simulations includes thirty-one variables. Two of the added variables were used for household and dwelling unit sequence numbers, another for a public housing variable, and one for a variable indicating the length of residence (or duration of tenure) in the unit. In the current simulations the five remaining spaces maintain the quantity of structure services supplied by each dwelling unit and the unit cost of producing these structure services, as well as three variables to trace the effects of housing rehabilitation subsidies: one that identifies treated buildings (those receiving capital subsidies), another that identifies all households that ever lived in a treated building, and the third giving the building's residence zone.

Because of the experience gained since the allowance simulations were completed, this increase in the number of variables included in the Basic List was achieved with a simultaneous reduction in the processing cost of list-handling operations.

Despite these programming advances, processing the list is one of the major contributors to the cost of model operations. Thus, to avoid the heavy cost of processing the Basic List more than once in a simulation period, these four submodels—the Demographic, Job Change, Movers, and New Households—as well as the Structure Services, Structure Conversion, and Capital Improvements submodels, are combined into a single comprehensive Basic List Subroutine.

All seven operations represented by these submodels are performed for each sample household and dwelling unit one at a time. During the processing of the Basic List Subroutine, three additional lists are created: the Structure Conversion Submodel places structures being considered for conversion on a Structure Conversions List, and the Movers Submodel selects moving households and places them on a Demand List and simultaneously places the corresponding vacant units on an Available Units List. The occupied units in these structures are also included on the Available Units List to maintain the order of sample dwelling units by structure and permit more efficient processing.

After the Demographic, Job Change, Movers, Structure Services, Structure Conversion, and Capital Improvements submodels have performed their calculations for each sample household and dwelling unit and the New Households Submodel has added households to the Basic List to satisfy exogenous population forecasts, the Demand Submodel simulates the selection of specific housing bundles by all movers, new households, and in-migrants on the Demand List.

With the exception of the Movers Submodel, none of the submodels described in this appendix were included in the Detroit Prototype, although many of their functions were performed in less explicit ways by other submodels in that version of the model. The development of these new submodels was required by our use of the list technique. The old summary matrix method aggregated the job locations of primary workers; in contrast, the list technique identifies the specific type and location of these jobs, enabling, if not forcing, us to simulate the job choices of individual workers and thereby begin to model urban labor markets. While the Job Change Submodel is still quite primitive, it has allowed us to make modest progress in understanding potentially important interrelationships between housing and labor markets.

Accurate modeling of demographic and employment changes is crucial to the understanding of housing market dynamics. Changes in household characteristics, such as increases in family size and composition and changes in jobs, can influence the demand for different dwelling unit characteristics. The Movers Submodel combines the demographic and job changes of individual households previously determined by the Demographic and Job Change submodels, with other household characteristics, such as tenure, determining whether a specific household will vacate its present unit and enter the housing market this year.

The Basic List Subroutine simulates changes in the size and composition of existing households, out-migration, in-migration, and the addition of new households, along with changes in the workplace location of primary wage earners. It should be emphasized, however, that the principal task of the submodels included in the Basic List Subroutine is to identify moving households; the other activities, though important, remain less central and their calibration more primitive. The other aspects of behavior simulated by the Basic List Subroutine are included less out of a conviction that we can adequately model them endogenously than out of the need to modify individual household records in response to exogenous aggregate projections of population, household income, and similar variables.

The Demographic Submodel

The Demographic Submodel, summarized in equation C.1, simulates two kinds of demographic processes: changes in family size, including those caused by death of the household head for one- and two-person households, and changes in household income.

(C.1) $\quad$ NHOU(H,I,J) = FAMSIZ(HA,HF) * AGE(HA)
$$* \text{ INCOME}(HA,HY,HR) * \text{HOU}(H,I,J)$$

where $\quad$ NHOU(H,I,J) = Characteristics of each household by household type H, residence zone I, and workplace zone J, after operation of the Demographic Submodel;

HOU(H,I,J) = Characteristics of each sample household at the beginning of the simulation period;

FAMSIZ(HA,HF) = Function that simulates changes in family size for each household on the basis of family size HF and age of the household head HA, at the start of the simulation period;

$\text{AGE}(HA)$ = Function that simulates changes in the age (HA) of each household head;

$\text{INCOME}(HA,HY,HR)$ = Function that simulates changes in household income. Changes depend on household income at the start of the period (HY) and on the age (HA) and race (HR) of the household head.

As equation C.1 indicates, the simulation of changes in household size and income are based on two probability functions. Changes in family size for the Chicago simulations, including the elimination of particular households, are represented by a simple family size change probability matrix, $\text{FAMSIZ}(HA,HF)$, which determines changes in family size as a function of household size and the age of the household head at the beginning of the period.

The probabilities used in the Chicago simulations are calculated from a ten-year retrospective random sample of households in the San Francisco–Oakland SMSA, adjusted to various control totals that reflect differences between the behavior of those households and that of Chicago households. The resulting estimates represent the combined effects of factors such as birth and death of family members, or divorces and separations, on family size and composition. The probabilities used for young, one- or two-person families in the Chicago simulations require that 87.5 percent of households in this life-cycle category will remain in that same family size category next year; 10.5 percent will become three-person and 1.7 percent four-person families. The rates for middle-aged, five-person families indicate that 6.9 percent of these households will decrease in size through loss of one or more household members during the year.

The estimates of family size change are used stochastically in the model. That is, the Demographic Submodel draws a random number for each household and compares this number to a cumulative probability function created from the simple probabilities depicted in equation C.1 to determine what change in size, if any, the household will experience.

Aging of the household head, simulated by the function $\text{AGE}(HA)$, is straightforward: for annual simulations the age of the household head included in each household record is incremented by one each year; for simulations of less than a year, ages are increased probabilistically. Thus, if the simulation period is six months, one-half of the household heads will be aged one year during each period. Although the Chicago simulations are calibrated for one year of real time, the model's programming is flexible enough to permit simulations with any periodicity.

The final task of the Demographic Submodel is to simulate changes in family income for each sample household. Using the income change probability matrix INCOME(*HY,HA,HR*) in equation C.1, the Demographic Submodel determines changes in income level as a function of the household's previous income, and the race and age of the household head. Although we lack data on the dynamics of individual income changes required to represent these changes in detail, the income change probabilities used for the Chicago simulations have been calibrated to move each household through a reasonable age profile of earnings in consonance with the aggregate changes in income distributions observed in the Chicago metropolitan area. Again, our objective is to simulate individual household changes in a manner consistent with known exogenous control totals for each region during the decade 1960–1970, or exogenous regionwide projections if the model is used to evaluate policies pertaining to some future period.

The Job Change Submodel

Before the processing of the Basic List begins, the estimated total changes in primary employment by industry, occupation, and work zone obtained from the Exogenous Employment and Population Serving Employment submodels are converted by the Job Change Submodel into estimated occupation- and industry-specific job change probabilities for each work zone. The Job Change Submodel uses these job change probabilities to make a stochastic determination of whether a particular primary worker will change jobs. The outcome of the job search process may be a change in the status of the primary worker to unemployed, complete removal from the labor force, or a new job. For those workers who do find a new job, the submodel determines the industry, occupation, and work zone.

To convert the estimates of aggregate and zone-specific employment by occupation and industry to changes in the jobs held by specific workers, the Job Change Submodel computes a job change probability for each household from data on primary job reductions by industry, occupation, and work zone and total primary employment in the same categories at the start of the period. The appropriate job change probabilities are thus formed by equation C.2.

$$(\text{C.2}) \qquad \text{PROBDEL}(J,EI,EO,ER) = \frac{\text{JDEL}(J,EI,EO)}{\text{PRIMWKR}(J,EI,EO,ER)}$$

where   PROBDEL(J,EI,EO,ER) = Number of job deletions by work zone J, industry EI, occupation EO, and race ER;

            JDEL(J,EI,EO) = Number of job deletions by work zone, occupation, and industry;

      PRIMWRK(J,EI,EO,ER) = Number of primary workers in work zone J by industry, occupation, and race.

We assume that when there is an absolute decline in the number of jobs in a particular work zone, industry, and occupation, at least an equal number of primary workers with these employment characteristics must lose their current jobs. When the job separation rates have been determined on the aggregate level, they are applied to each sample household in the same manner as the demographic change probabilities.

Of course, there are many more determinants of job change than absolute employment decline; an average of three of every hundred workers quit or lose their jobs within a given year. The Job Change Submodel simulates these voluntary and involuntary job changes with a series of occupation-specific job separation rates. Exogenous additions and normal turnover determine the total number of available jobs for primary workers seeking employment during the year, while exogenous deletions of jobs and probabilistic job turnover rates determine which primary workers will engage in job search.

The job turnover rates used for the Chicago simulations are based on an unpublished study of occupational mobility by J. Royce Ginn and Charles Revier using the Parnes panel analysis. They established that turnover rates vary systematically by occupation, industry, and race in the manner summarized in table C.1. To incorporate race into the job change probabilities for each workplace, we derived the job turnover function defined by equation C.3 on the assumption that an absolute decline in employment in a specific occupation, industry, and work zone produces job losses for blacks and whites proportional to their share of jobs in each category.

Table C.1. Rate (in percent) of job turnover by industry, occupation, and race of primary worker

Industry	White workers			Nonwhite workers		
	White collar	Blue collar	Unskilled	White collar	Blue collar	Unskilled
Basic industries						
Agriculture	8.6	24.2	11.6	21.3	25.0	13.0
Mining	4.0	17.6	11.6	11.0	4.0	13.0
Construction	17.7	32.7	38.3	11.0	34.6	8.9
Manufacturing	7.0	11.3	2.6	4.3	9.4	12.3
Primary metals	4.0	7.4	11.6	11.0	8.1	13.0
Transportation, utilities, and communication	6.7	7.6	14.8	15.9	9.4	3.8
Wholesale and regional retail	18.5	12.2	20.7	15.7	18.8	19.0
Finance, insurance, and real estate	10.8	22.1	11.6	7.6	30.6	14.8
Regional government, education, and services	12.7	13.7	13.9	9.7	18.5	15.0
Local industries						
Local government, education, and services	4.4	7.2	5.0	3.5	3.2	8.9
Local retail	12.7	13.7	13.9	9.7	18.5	15.0

178

APPENDIX C

(C.3)   JOBTURN(J,EI,EO,ER) = PRIMWRK(J,EI,EO,ER)
                                    * JOBSEP(EI,EO,ER)

where   JOBTURN(J,EI,EO,ER) = Job turnover rate by work zone
                                J, industry EI, occupation EO,
                                and race ER;
        PRIMWRK(J,EI,EO,ER) = Count of primary jobs by work
                                zone, industry, occupation, and
                                race;
        JOBSEP(EI,EO,ER) = Rate of job turnover by
                             industry, occupation, and race.

The probability of job change for each type of primary worker,
PRJOBC(J,EI,EO,ER), is simply the sum of job deletions and job turnover
divided by the original number of workers in each category, as shown by
equation C.4. (The subscripts HI, HO, and HR are used to refer to the
characteristics of households, while the subscripts EI, EO, and ER refer
to the characteristics of jobs.)

(C.4)   PRJOBC(J,HI,HO,HR) =
$$\frac{\text{JOBDEL}(J,EI,EO,ER) + \text{JOBTURN}(J,EI,EO,ER)}{\text{PRIMWRK}(J,EI,EO,ER)}$$

where   PRJOBC(J,HI,HO,HR) = Probability of job change for a
                               primary worker employed in
                               work zone J, of race HR,
                               industry HI, and occupation HO.

Finally, as equation C.5 indicates, the number of job openings is the
sum of exogenous job creations and normal turnover.

(C.5)   JOBOPEN(J,EI,EO) = −JDEL(J,ET,EO) + JNEW(J,EI,EO)
$$+ \sum_{ER} \text{JOBTURN}(J,ET,EO,ER)$$

where   JOBOPEN(J,EI,EO) = Total number of job openings
                             in work zone J, industry EI,
                             and occupation class EO;
        JDEL(J,ET,EO) = Total number of exogenously
                          specified job deletions in work
                          zone J, industry EI, and
                          occupation EO;
        JNEW(J,EI,EO) = Total number of exogenously
                          specified job additions in work
                          zone J, industry EI, and
                          occupation EO;

JOBTURN(J,ET,EO,ER) = Jobs available as a result of normal turnover in work zone J, industry EI, occupation EO, and race ER.

Conceptually, the Job Change Submodel may be thought of as representing a local job search by each primary worker seeking employment during the period. The search algorithm first attempts to assign a particular job seeker to an available job in the same industry, occupation, and work zone as the one he or she just left; this effort produces a match for most job seekers. When employment of a particular type is declining in a particular work zone, however, there may be too few jobs to provide all primary workers with jobs in their same industry, occupation, and work zone. In these cases, the Job Change Submodel first attempts to assign the worker to an available job at a new work zone but within his or her original industry and occupation. In attempting to make these worker/job matches, the job assignment algorithm tries to match the individual to a job in the worker's residence zone. If this fails, an effort is made to match the worker to a job in the central business district, and then to jobs in other work zones.

If the search over all twenty Chicago work zones fails to produce a match within the worker's previous occupation and industry, the Job Change Submodel searches for a job match in other industries, beginning with the industry with the largest percentage of available jobs. If the submodel still fails to achieve a match, the worker is classified as unemployed, and the Job Change Submodel again attempts to locate a job for him in the next period. If the job assignment algorithm fails in the second period as well, the worker is classified as being out of the labor force. Household heads out of the labor force are considered unemployable and are not returned to the labor market.

Little weight should be given to the geographic pattern of job search produced by the Job Choice Submodel. Even so, the required changes in the geographic distribution of employment and the number and characteristics of primary workers are accomplished in a manner consistent with projected changes in employment and with our qualitative understanding of job search processes. It should be noted, however, that because job openings are not identified by race, we have a limited ability to simulate changes in the geographic distribution of black employment. Previous studies have shown that the location of black employment is also influenced by the constraints blacks experience in choosing residence location (Kain, 1968; Mooney, 1969; Kain, 1975). We hope to deal more explicitly with these relationships in future versions of the model.

It should be evident from the preceding discussion that the Job Change Submodel simulates only the most basic dimensions of labor market activity. It does, however, incorporate those aspects of the labor market which most directly influence housing market dynamics through the effects of employment mobility on household moving decisions. Studies of intrametropolitan household location and moving behavior indicate that an important link exists between employment location and job change, and between the residential location and moving decisions of urban households (Brown, 1975; Weinberg, 1977). The Job Change Submodel used in the Chicago simulations is a first attempt to model these relationships.

The Movers Submodel

The Movers Submodel selects those households from the Basic List that will vacate their current dwelling units and participate in the housing market during the year. The units they vacate are retained on the Basic List and are repeated on a separate Available Units List. Moving house-

Table C.2. Probability of intrametropolitan move by age of head, tenure, family size change, and job change

	Job change			
	No job change	New job	Becomes unemployed	Retires
Owner, age < 35				
Increase size	12.5	16.3	15.6	22.9
Same size	4.4	5.5	4.9	12.2
Decrease size	5.6	6.8	6.2	13.5
Owner, age > 35				
Increase size	5.5	7.0	6.4	13.6
Same size	4.4	5.5	4.9	12.2
Decrease size	6.4	4.3	3.6	10.9
Renter, age < 35				
Increase size	36.5	41.9	43.6	81.0
Same size	27.3	31.0	37.8	70.2
Decrease size	40.7	46.3	48.0	85.5
Renter, age > 35				
Increase size	29.9	25.9	27.6	65.0
Same size	22.3	31.0	32.8	70.2
Decrease size	30.1	55.3	57.0	94.5

holds are, in turn, placed on a separate Demand List, where, along with new households and in-migrants, they will be processed by the Demand Submodel.

The Movers Submodel selects four variables in predicting moving behavior: the age of the household head, prior tenure, change in employment, and change in family size. The actual movers' probability functions used in the current version of the model are defined in equation C.6 and exhibited in table C.2.

(C.6) $\text{MOVE}(H,I,J) = \text{PROBMOV}(HT,HA,CHF,JOBC) * \text{HOU}(H,I,J)$
$* \text{DURTEN}(IYTEN)$

where

$\text{MOVE}(H,I,J) =$ A move/no-move decision for each household;

$\text{PROBMOV}(HT,HA,CHF,JOBC) =$ Matrix of probability that a household will move;

$\text{HOU}(H,I,J) =$ Households by household type, residence zone, and workplace;

$\text{DURTEN}(IYTEN) =$ A matrix of the probability that a household will move as a function of the duration of tenure or the number of years the household has lived in the unit;

$HT =$ Tenure class (own or rent);

$HA =$ Age of head of household;

$CHF =$ Change in family size (no change, increase, or decrease);

$JOBC =$ Job change (change in employment status and location).

In contrast, moving decisions in the Detroit Prototype depend on family size, income, education, and age of head, adjusted to reflect aggregate changes in employment by work zone.

The basic moving rates used in the current version of the model combine information from two sources: the 1970 Census data on the relationships among income, tenure, and moving behavior of Chicago households; and data from a special retrospective ten-year history of job and residence choice conducted by the San Francisco Bay Area Transportation Study. The retrospective survey provides estimates of the conditional probability of a move for households of various sizes whose primary workers do or do not change jobs, for each income level and tenure class. Since data relating employment location, job change status, and moving behavior were not available, the San Francisco estimates were combined with Chicago data to form composite moving rate estimates. The alternative would have required us to use a less complete matrix of moving probabilities based solely on Chicago data. The procedure used to combine the Chicago and San Francisco data involved the use of iterative scaling to estimate the joint distribution that satisfied the known distribution of Chicago moving households by income and prior tenure, and incorporated the conditional probabilities of moves involving family size change and job change. A discussion of the use of iterative scaling in housing market analysis is presented in Apgar (1981).

Despite our careful efforts to calibrate the moving rates from available data, analysis of simulation results suggested the need for further refinement. In particular, although each year the model-designated pattern of household movers corresponded quite closely to the pattern observed in the Chicago SMSA, the cumulative moving patterns were in error. That is, analysis of earlier baseline simulations suggested that the model underestimated the number of households remaining in the same unit for the entire decade. To correct for this failure, the model now maintains a variable that indicates the number of years the household has lived in the unit. Duration of residency, then, is used as a variable in determining the probability that a household will move during the period.

New Households Submodel

The New Households Submodel simulates the in-migration of households to the region and adds new households to the model to satisfy exogenous projections of population characteristics for the metropolitan area. To the extent possible, the income, age of household head, race, and family size assigned to these new households and in-migrants by the New Households Submodel conform to exogenous projections of these characteristics for the aggregate distribution of Chicago households. The submodel operates after all households on the Basic List at the start of the period have been processed so that aggregate changes in the characteristics of Chicago households can be represented by the socioeconomic characteristics assigned to new households.

As each in-migrant or new household is added to the model, the Job Change Submodel assigns their primary worker to a work zone, occupation, and industry, starting with the work zone with the largest number of available jobs. If a job match is not immediately found, the Job Choice Submodel searches in the work zone having the next largest number of job openings and so on until the primary worker is matched to an occupation, industry, and work zone. The household is then placed on the Demand List, where, along with intrametropolitan movers, it will be assigned a housing bundle type and residence zone by the Demand and Market submodels.

APPENDIX D

The Demand and Tenure Choice Submodels

The heart of the Demand Submodel is a series of econometrically estimated submarket demand equations that predict the choice of individual sample households among fifty housing bundles defined by ten
structure types and five levels of neighborhood quality. The submarket
demand equations used in the current version of the HUDS model are
estimated by multinomial logit. The method and its theoretical justifi-
cation were adapted by William C. Apgar, Jr., and John M. Quigley
from research by Daniel McFadden (Charles River Associates, 1972) on
urban travel demand. Quigley (1976) subsequently applied the technique to an analysis of the demand for housing by Pittsburgh rental
households, and Apgar (Apgar and Kain, 1974) used it to estimate
submarket demand equations for renters and owner-occupants in the
Chicago and Pittsburgh housing markets.

The theoretical model underlying the use of multinomial logit estimates assumes that each household can rank each housing bundle in
relation to all other bundles, where X_i is a vector containing a description of each bundle attribute. For simplicity, it is assumed that the
ranking, or utility, function for any particular socioeconomic group S
can be expressed as a function of a vector of housing attributes X and a
stochastic term E, as depicted in equation D.1.

(D.1) $$U(X_i) = V(X_i) + E$$

The probability that a particular household of socioeconomic class S
will choose bundle i over any other bundle depends on the probability
that the utility ranking of bundle i exceeds that of each other bundle k. If
H_i denotes the probability of choosing bundle i and there are K bundles,
then:

(D.2) $H_i = \text{Prob}(U(X_i) > U(X_k))$ for $i \neq k$, $k = 1$, to K

By substitution we obtain:

(D.3) $H_i = \text{Prob}((V(X_i) + E_i) > (V(X_k + E_k)))$ for $i \neq k$, $k = 1$, to K

Equation D.3 states that the probability of choosing a particular bundle X_i depends on the attributes of all possible bundles and on a vector of stochastic terms. In this formulation the gross price of a bundle is treated as one of its attributes. If the vector of stochastic terms is jointly distributed with a known cumulative distribution, it is possible to derive an explicit formula for H_i (Apgar and Kain, 1974).

In summary, if the ranking function $V(X_i)$ is assumed to be a linear function of the vector of attributes X_i and a vector of coefficients B, and if the vector of stochastic terms is independently distributed with the reciprocal exponential distribution, then the probability of choosing any particular bundle is:

(D.4) $H_i = e^{X_i B} / \Sigma e^{X_k B}$

The relative probabilities of choosing two bundles H_k and H_i are given by equations D.5 and D.6.

(D.5) $H_k / H_i = e^{X_k B} / e^{X_i B}$

or, in log form:

(D.6) $\log (H_k / H_i) = B(X_k - X_i)$

The left-hand side of equation D.6 gives the log of the probability of choosing H_k and H_i, while the right-hand side is a vector of coefficients times a vector of differences between the attributes of the two bundles. Thus, equation D.6 indicates that the log of the probability of choosing bundle k over bundle i is a linear function of the differences in the attributes of the two bundles. This implies that the relative choice between two bundles is independent of the characteristics of other bundles, even though the probablity of choosing any one bundle depends on the attributes of all bundles. Although this independence assumption is often pointed to as a limitation of the logit framework, it causes no difficulty in our analysis. All dwelling units belonging to the same housing bundle type are assumed to be identical in every respect, and we assume that each household can rank all bundle types according to their preferences. The ranking of a particular bundle type is determined by a series of pairwise comparisons and therefore does not depend on the characteristics of other bundle types.

The multinomial logit demand equations which serve as the core of the Demand Submodel are computed separately for each of the ninety-six discrete household categories defined by six income categories, eight life-cycle categories, and two races. In addition to these socioeconomic determinants of housing demand, the multinomial logit equation, which takes the form depicted in equation D.7, recognizes the influence of workplace and labor force status on gross prices.

$$(D.7) \qquad \text{DEMAND}(K,HY,HL,HR,J) = \frac{e^{X(K,HY,HL,HR,J)}}{\sum_{KK} e^{X(KK,HY,HL,HR,J)}}$$

where $X(K,HY,HL,HR,J) = A(HY,HL,HR,K)$
$+ \text{BETA}(HY,HR,HL)$
$* \text{MINGP}(K,J,HY,HR)$
$+ S(HY,HR,HL)$
$* \log(\text{STOCK}(K));$

$\text{DEMAND}(K,HY,HL,HR,J) =$ Probability that a particular household defined by income HY, race HR, life cycle HL, and workplace J, would choose bundle type K;

$A(HL,HR,HY,K) =$ Matrix scaling factors;

$S(HY,HL,HR) =$ Matrix of coefficients measuring the impact of available stock on the probability of demand;

$\text{BETA}(HY,HL,HR) =$ Matrix of price coefficients;

$\text{STOCK}(K) =$ The available vacant units of bundle type K;

$\text{MINGP}(J,K,HY,HR) =$ Matrix of gross prices.

The Demand Submodel solves equation D.7 for each sample household included on the Demand List, which consists of all intrametropolitan movers, selected this period by the Movers Submodel, and new households and in-migrants, provided by the New Households Submodel. The formidable expression shown by equation D.7 simply states that the probability of a particular household choosing a particular type of housing bundle K depends on the difference between the gross price of that bundle and each of the forty-nine other housing bundles; the number of available vacant dwelling units of type K relative to the number of vacant units of each other bundle type; and on the income, life cycle, and race of the household. The household characteristics included in the Demand Submodel—that is, household income, life cycle, and race — are represented by different parameter values, the BETA and A in the equation.

The submarket demand equations used for the CHIP simulations are calibrated so that the BETA(HY,HL,HR) parameters in equation D.7 are based on estimates obtained for a sample of Pittsburgh households; the Chicago equations used for the simulations described in this book employ Pittsburgh parameters for the same income, life cycle, and racial group. The remaining parameters of equation D.7, $X(HL,HR,HY,K)$ and $S(HY,HL,HR)$, are estimated from Chicago data and correspond to parameters that correctly predict end-of-decade proportions that correspond to actual proportions for each household category.

The submarket demand equations were estimated in two stages. First, Pittsburgh data on household characteristics, bundle characteristics, gross prices, and actual bundle choices were used to estimate full multinomial logit demand equations for each of the ninety-six household categories. The more limited Chicago data were then used to estimate the remaining parameters of equation D.7 on the assumption that the gross price parameters for Pittsburgh were applicable to Chicago households of the same type. Multinomial logit bundle demand equations obtained for a sample of San Francisco households provide some support for the portability of these estimates. In the future, it would be valuable to estimate full submarket demand equations for a number of cities, including Chicago, to test whether the gross price parameters are true structural estimates that depend only on household characteristics and do not vary across metropolitan areas.

Because of the complexity of solving equation D.7, the Demand Submodel precalculates the probabilities of choosing each of fifty types of housing bundles for the 2,208 household categories defined by income, life cycle, race, labor force status, and work zone. Each household appearing on the Demand List during each simulation period is assigned to a household category and matched to one of the fifty housing bundle types by comparing a random number drawn for it with a cumulative density function. To suggest the magnitude of the Demand Submodel calculations, it may be pointed out that the Demand List processed in the CHIP simulations contains between 5,000 and 18,000 households per year.

Econometric Analysis of Housing Demand

The structure of the Demand Submodel included in the current version of the HUDS model permits a highly detailed specification of the effect of housing prices on demand. It should be recalled that the gross prices used in the submarket demand equations incorporate the effects of both the market rent and the travel costs a household incurs by selecting each alternative housing bundle in each residence location. Inclusion of the travel costs associated with each possible residence allows us to analyze how the choice among housing bundles is affected by variations in transport cost to specific workplace locations, effects that cannot be considered in most conventional analyses of housing demand.

In addition, the particular functional form of the multinomial logit model used for the submarket demand equations allows the effects of gross price on housing demand to vary by type of household. This feature of the model is accomplished by estimating separate demand equations for each of the ninety-six types of households included in the Demand Submodel. As the statistics presented in table D.1 illustrate, the effect of gross prices on bundle choice varies substantially across socioeconomic groups, and depends in complex ways on the race, life cycle, and income class of the household head. For example, the gross price coefficients in table D.1 tend to decrease in absolute value as household income increases, suggesting that lower-income families, who must devote a larger share of their income to housing, may be more sensitive to differences in gross prices than otherwise similar but higher-income households. There is also a slight tendency for the gross price response to be absolutely smaller for white families.

Differences in household responsiveness to gross price variations are even more clearly demonstrated by estimates of the own gross price elasticity of demand for particular housing bundles. The own gross price elasticity of demand is calculated using equation D.8.

$$(D.8) \qquad N_{KK} = GP_k B_k (1 - H_k)$$

> where GP_k = Gross price of the bundle;
> B_k = Gross price coefficient;
> H_k = Probability of choosing bundle k.

From equation D.8 it is evident that a 1 percent change in the price of the bundle will result in $GP_k B_k (1 - H_k)$ percent change in the probability of choosing bundle k. Thus, the gross price elasticity of demand for a particular bundle depends on both the gross price of the bundle and the probability of choosing the bundle type.

Since the gross price elasticity of demand for particular housing bundles depends on the gross price and the probablity of choosing the bundle, equation D.8 must be evaluated at a particular point to obtain a set of representative price elasticities. Shown in table D.2 are illustrative estimates of the gross price elasticities of demand for a zero- to one-bed-

Table D.1. Gross price coefficients by income class, life cycle, and race

Race and life cycle	Annual income					
	$0–2,999	$3,000–4,999	$5,000–6,999	$7,000–9,999	$10,000–14,999	$15,000+
White, age < 35						
1–2 persons	−.012	−.011	−.011	−.010	−.006	−.005
3+ persons	−.012	−.011	−.011	−.010	−.006	−.005
White, age 35–64						
1–2 persons	−.009	−.008	−.011	−.008	−.007	−.005
3 persons	−.011	−.010	−.006	−.009	−.008	−.007
4 persons	−.013	−.011	−.008	−.010	−.012	−.006
5+ persons	−.014	−.010	−.013	−.009	−.008	−.007
White, age 65+						
1–2 persons	−.012	−.010	−.009	−.013	−.012	−.004
3+ persons	−.012	−.010	−.009	−.013	−.012	−.004
Nonwhite, age < 35						
1–2 persons	−.012	−.011	−.011	−.010	−.006	−.005
3+ persons	−.012	−.011	−.011	−.010	−.006	−.006
Nonwhite, age 35–64						
1–2 persons	−.013	−.009	−.008	−.010	−.010	−.007
3 persons	−.016	−.012	−.010	−.013	−.008	−.005
4 persons	−.018	−.014	−.017	−.012	−.013	−.009
5+ persons	−.018	−.014	−.017	−.012	−.013	−.009
Nonwhite, age 65+						
1–2 persons	−.012	−.010	−.009	−.013	−.012	−.004
3+ persons	−.012	−.010	−.009	−.013	−.012	−.004

Table D.2. Gross price elasticity of demand for 0–1 bedroom unit in a small multi-apartment building in the lowest-quality neighborhood

Race and life cycle	Annual income					
	$0–2,999	$3,000–4,999	$5,000–6,999	$7,000–9,999	$10,000–14,999	$15,000+
White, age < 35						
1–2 persons	−2.05	−1.95	−2.11	−2.05	−1.23	−1.10
3+ persons	−2.05	−1.95	−2.11	−2.05	−1.23	−1.10
White, age 35–64						
1–2 persons	−1.54	−1.42	−2.11	−1.64	−1.44	−1.10
3 persons	−1.88	−1.80	−1.15	−1.84	−1.64	−1.54
4 persons	−2.22	−1.95	−1.54	−2.05	−2.46	−1.32
5+ persons	−2.39	−1.80	−2.50	−1.84	−1.64	−1.54
White, age 65+						
1–2 persons	−2.05	−1.80	−1.73	−2.67	−2.46	−0.88
3+ persons	−2.05	−1.80	−1.73	−2.67	−2.46	−0.88
Nonwhite, age < 35						
1–2 persons	−2.05	−1.87	−1.96	−1.88	−1.22	−1.10
3+ persons	−2.05	−1.87	−1.96	−1.88	−1.22	−1.32
Nonwhite, age 35–64						
1–2 persons	−2.22	−1.53	−1.42	−1.88	−2.03	−1.54
3 persons	−2.73	−2.04	−1.78	−2.44	−1.62	−1.10
4 persons	−3.08	−2.38	−3.03	−2.26	−2.64	−1.98
5+ persons	−3.08	−2.38	−3.03	−2.26	−2.64	−1.98
Nonwhite, age 65+						
1–2 persons	−2.05	−1.70	−1.60	−2.44	−2.44	−0.88
3+ persons	−2.05	−1.70	−1.60	−2.44	−2.44	−0.88

room unit in a small multi-apartment building in the lowest-quality neighborhood, for all ninety-six types of households included in the Demand Submodel. The gross price elasticities included in table D.2 are based on the average gross prices for all Chicago work zones and the probabilities of choice exhibited by demanders in 1970. As the estimates reveal, a 1 percent increase in gross price would cause a 1.5 percent decline in the probability that a low-income (less than $3,000), one- or two-person, white, middle-aged household would choose a zero- to one-bedroom unit in a small apartment building in the lowest-quality neighborhood. In contrast, the same probability for an otherwise identical household with an annual income of more than $15,000 in 1970 would decline by only 1.1 percent.

Calculation of Gross Prices

Before the submarket demand equations can predict the bundle choices of each sample household participating in the market this period, the Demand Submodel must first convert estimates of this period's gross monthly rents and interzonal travel costs into an array of gross prices. The first step in the calculation of gross price surfaces for each workplace, income class, and housing bundle is to estimate interzonal travel costs for primary workers employed at each workplace and the generalized accessibility cost for each residence zone.

Travel costs are based on estimates of travel time between each of twenty workplaces and fifty residence districts. In this calculation, the large number of residence zones has been combined into residence districts to summarize the matrix of interzonal travel time. Transportation costs between any workplace and the residence district include both out-of-pocket costs and the value of time spent by the primary wage earner in commuting between home and work. Out-of-pocket expenses, obtained from the Chicago Area Transportation Survey, are based on an average speed of 24 mph and vehicle operating costs of four cents per mile; the value of travel, assuming a forty-hour work week, is set at four-tenths of a pseudo hourly wage, derived from annual household income. We use household income to compute the pseudo hourly wage for lack of accurate measures of the primary worker's share in total income. Moreover, empirical tests indicate that secondary workers tend to work either near the primary worker's job location or near their residences, and thus the inclusion of their earnings is consistent with their effect on residence location.

The combined money and time costs of travel between each workplace zone and each residence district are calculated for two modes.

Assuming that these calculations fully reflect commuting costs and that consumers are rational, the tripmaker will use the cheaper mode and actual costs will equal the lowest combined expense. The travel cost matrix used in the Demand Submodel therefore incorporates an implicit determination of modal choice.

The actual travel costs arrary for each period, derived from equations D.9 and D.10, is precalculated and stored in an on-line disc file. The Demand Submodel simply reads in exogenously specified estimates of interzonal travel costs for each period.

$$(D.9) \quad \text{TCOSTX}(I, J, HY, M) = \text{OPC}(I, J, HY, M) + 0.4 \text{ WAGE}(HY)$$
$$* \text{ HRS}(I, J, M)$$

$$(D.10) \quad \text{TCOST}(I, J, HY) = \text{minimum over mode of}$$
$$\text{TCOSTX}(I, J, HY, M)$$

where $\text{TCOSTX}(I, J, HY, M)$ = Travel cost from residence zone I to workplace J for income class HY and mode M;

$\text{OPC}(I, J, HY, M)$ = Out-of-pocket costs for mode M;

$\text{WAGE}(HY)$ = Implicit wage rate of income class HY;

$\text{HRS}(I, J, M)$ = Interzonal travel time for mode M;

$\text{TCOST}(I, J, HY)$ = Minimum cost of travel assuming the cheapest mode is utilized.

The resulting matrix of travel costs from each of fifty residence districts to each of twenty work zones for six household income classes and two modes contains 12,000 elements; even after the higher cost mode for each origin/destination/income combination has been discarded, it still contains 6,000 elements.

The range in transportation costs by household income reflects how different incomes influence mode choice and the value of travel time. The assumptions that travel time is valued at four-tenths of the pseudo wage and that primary wage earners work a standard forty-hour week imply that primary workers belonging to households with an annual income of $15,000 value each minute of travel time at five cents but that primary workers belonging to families with an annual income of $6,000 value their commuting time at only two cents per minute. The further assumption that primary workers make one round trip per working day, or slightly less than twenty-one round trips per month, implies that each minute of travel time between home and work costs a household with a $15,000 annual income an estimated $2.08 per month. Similarly, for households with a $6,000 annual income, the cost of residing one minute further from work is approximately $0.83 more per month. Opportunity costs of this size provide strong incentives for households to locate as close to their workplace as preferences for structure type and neighborhood quality allow.

The cost of nonwork trips is accommodated into the current version of the model by a generalized accessibility measure. This index depends on the location of local retail and service employment, and on the assumption that shopping opportunities have the same geographic distribution as these industries. The spatial variation in local retail and service employment is thus used to proxy each zone's relative accessibility to shopping, commercial, and recreational centers.

The value of this general accessibility index depends on the frequency of nonwork trips and their costs. We assume that each household makes an average of one round trip per day and that the cost per trip depends on the density of secondary employment and shopping opportunities around the household's residence, as equation D.11 indicates.

$$(D.11) \qquad \text{GCOST}(I, HY) = \frac{\sum_J \text{TCOST}(I, J, HY) * \text{EMP}(J)}{\sum_J \text{EMP}(J)}$$

where $\quad$ GCOST(I, HY) = Generalized accessibility for each residence zone I for households with income of HY;

$\quad$ TCOST(I, J, HY) = As before;

$\quad$ EMP(J) = Number of employees in industries 8 – 11 (general wholesale and retail, general services, local retail, local government, and education).

The second component of gross prices is the gross monthly rent for each type of housing bundle in each residence zone, RENT(K, I). These rents are formulated by the Structure Rent Submodel using the adaptive expectations framework described in appendix G. For the CHIP simulations, the model maintains a four-year history of gross monthly rents for ten types of structures located in 182 residence zones. Since housing bundles are defined as combinations of structure and neighborhood type and since each residence zone belongs to one of five neighborhood types, it follows that the model includes a four-year history of rents for each of the fifty types of housing bundles by residence zone.

Calculation of the gross price surface by the Demand Submodel involves one further complication. It is well-documented that minority households do not have equal access to all portions of the metropolitan housing stock. Exclusion appears to result from both economic and noneconomic discrimination. Spatial variations in price discrimination explain part of the observed segregation patterns, but probably even more important are differential search costs, nonprice discrimination by white sellers and real estate agents, and black fear of white hostility. The CHIP simulations employ separate submarket demand equations for black and white households and use a series of zone-specific discrimination markups that apply to black families seeking housing in integrated or all-white areas. These discrimination markups are also employed in the Market Submodel; in both applications, we assume that the markups, DCOST(H, I), increase as the distance to the nearest area of concentrated black households increases, and decreases as the percentage of black households in the current zone decreases.

Lacking any formal econometric analyses of price and nonprice discrimination, we performed simulations of discrimination markups using a stand-alone version of the Market Submodel. From these simulations we were able to determine what markups, when applied to the 1970 sample of black and white households in Chicago, best reproduce the actual geographic distribution of black households. We must emphasize here that HUDS has tremendous potential value as a tool for analyzing the nature and effects of racial discrimination in urban housing markets, and high priority should be given to this area of research.

The last step in the computation of gross prices, shown in equation D.12, combines each of the cost elements described above to produce an estimate of the gross price surface.

$$
\text{(D.12)} \quad \text{GPX}(I, J, K, HY, HR) = \text{TCOST}(I, J, HY) + \text{GCOST}(I, HY) \\
+ \text{DCOST}(I, HR) + \text{RENT}(K, I)
$$

where $\text{GPX}(I, J, K, HY, HR)$ = Array of gross price surfaces over residence zones I for each workplace J, for housing bundle K, income class HY, and racial group HR;

$\text{TCOST}(I, J, HY)$ = Travel cost for the cheapest mode for trips from residence zone I to work zone J by income class HY;

$\text{GCOST}(I, HY)$ = Average travel cost for nonwork trips, for households of income class HY residing in residence zone I;

$$\text{DCOST}(I, HR) = \text{Discrimination markup for race}$$
$$HR \text{ in residence zone } I;$$
$$\text{RENT}(K, I) = \text{Monthly rent for housing bundle}$$
$$K \text{ in residence zone } I.$$

The gross price array for the Chicago simulations contains data for 198 residence zones, fifty bundle types (ten structure types times five neighborhood types), and for each of 276 discrete work zone, income, and racial categories. Since each residence zone is uniquely classified as a neighborhood type, the gross price matrix is implicitly dimensioned by neighborhood type as well. Fortunately, not all prices are relevant: although a household must first consider the entire gross price surface for each housing bundle, only the minimum gross price for each bundle enters into the submarket demand equations. The household's selection of its utility-maximizing housing bundle and location first involves a scan of the gross price surface for each bundle type to determine the least costly location in which to consume that particular bundle. Since each of the fifty bundle types are assumed to be homogeneous in all respects except location and monthly rent, and since gross prices include all costs associated with a bundle's consumption, we assume that households will consider only the minimum gross price of each bundle in choosing among housing bundles. Thus, as equation D.13 illustrates, only the minimum gross price for each bundle type appears in the submarket demand equation.

$$(D.13) \quad \text{MINGP}(J, K, HY, HR) = \text{Minimization over residence zone}$$
$$I \text{ of GPx}(I, J, K, HY, HR)$$

where $\text{MINGP}(J, K, HY, HR)$ = Minimum gross price for each housing bundle K, work zone J, household income HY, and race HR.

In addition to calculating the minimum gross price of each housing bundle for households of each income and racial category, employed at each of the twenty work zones, the Demand Submodel must also prepare estimates of the number of available vacant dwelling units for each type of housing bundle. These calculations are simply an aggregation of the available units provided by the Movers, New Construction, and Structure Conversion submodels.

After the matrixes of gross prices and available vacant units have been produced, the Demand Submodel evaluates equation D.7 for each household on the Demand List. The probability of choosing each bundle, calculated for each household on the list and converted to a cumulative probability function, is then compared with a random number between zero and one to determine which bundle should be assigned to the household. The procedure assures, subject to stochastic error, that the aggregate proportions of each bundle type chosen by each household type correspond to distributions obtained from the logit model.

With more than 2,000 distinct household types defined in terms of income, life cycle, work zone, and labor force status, choosing from fifty possible bundle types, the programming of the Demand Submodel proved quite difficult. Equation D.7 must be evaluated for each household on the Demand List, or about 12,000 model households in a simulation year. Careful programming and continued advances in high-speed computers, however, have made this task more than feasible, since the average cost of operating the Demand Submodel per simulation year is only about three dollars.

The Tenure Submodel

After the Demand Submodel has determined both the housing bundle and neighborhood choices of each moving household, the Tenure Submodel ascertains whether these households will own or rent their units. As equation D.14 indicates, a particular household's tenure assignment is made from a matrix of probabilities that depend on past tenure, current income, age and race of household head, and the type of housing bundle consumed previously.

$$(D.14) \quad \text{TENURE}(H, J, K) = \text{PROBTENURE}(HPT, K, HY, HA, HR)$$
$$* \text{HOU}(H, J, K)$$

where $\quad$ TENURE(H, J, K) = Tenure assigned to the household;

PROBTENURE(HPT, K, HY, HA, HR) = A matrix of probabilities by prior tenure (own, rent, or new household), bundle type, family income, and age and race of household head.

In earlier simulations prepared for evaluating housing allowance programs, the tenure choice was limited to owner-occupied single-family units, or owner-occupied small multi-family units. Recent increases in condominium conversions have focused attention on the household ownership of individual apartments in large multi-family structures. The current Basic List has room for inclusion of condominium ownership, but we have yet to calibrate this portion of the tenure choice equation. Experience gained in previous modeling efforts suggests that it would be desirable to make individual dwelling units, rather than structures, the sampling unit represented on the Basic List. Among other advantages, this change in model structure would enable us to increase the spatial disaggregation of the model and provide for the many forms of ownerhip currently available for individual dwelling units in large mutli-family structures.

In combination, the Tenure and Demand Submodels make two simplifying assumptions about housing choice. First, they assume that prior tenure has no effect on the type of bundle chosen by the household. Next, they assume that there is no relationship between prior and current tenure that is independent of bundle choice. In other words, households are not labeled "owners" and then assigned to units suitable for ownership; rather, bundle choice precedes tenure choice and is independent of prior tenure.

Although it may be useful in the future to consider modifications that would explicitly include these interactions, such as extension of the model is not currently warranted by empirical evidence on the relationships among prior tenure, current tenure, and bundle choice. As it is, the Demand Submodel involves the estimation of housing choice probabilities for fifty structure – neighborhood type combinations for each moving household defined in terms of thousands of socioeconomic characteristics; and the Tenure Submodel recognizes forty-eight individual classes of households and calculates over 2,000 separate homeownership probabilities.

APPENDIX E

The Supply Sector and the Role of Expectations

The Supply Sector of the HUDS model consists of five interrelated submodels that simulate the supply decisions of landlords, home-owners, and developers. Two of these submodels, Structure Conversion and Capital Improvements, simulate the decisions of property owners to maintain, improve, or otherwise alter the characteristics of existing residential structures. The quantities and characteristics of embodied capital strongly influence the costs of producing structure services. The provision of structure services is simulated by a third component of the Supply Sector, the Structure Services Submodel. A fourth submodel, New Construction, simulates decisions of developers to build new structures of various types at particular locations. Finally, the Expectations Submodel projects changes in neighborhood quality and rental income required for the profitability calculations carried out by the other supply submodels.

This appendix presents a brief description of the entire Supply Sector of the current model. We discuss the Expectations Submodel in detail, however, since important investment decisions represented in the model depend to some extent on the expectations of property owners about future rents, operating costs, interest rates, and property values.

An Overview of the Supply Sector

The Supply Sector represents housing services as a bundle of heterogeneous attributes that must be consumed jointly. HUDS explicitly recognizes four distinct types of housing bundle attributes: accessibility, neighborhood quality, structure type, and the quantity of structure services provided. The first dimension, accessibility of the housing bun-

198

dle to workplaces and other desirable destinations, depends solely on the parcel's location. Accessibility can be viewed in two ways. First, particular locations are more or less accessible to the destinations demanded by specific households. This aspect of accessibility is represented in the model by gross prices and it influences individual household demand for specific housing bundles and residence locations. Second, particular sites may be characterized by their overall accessibility to destinations demanded by households in general; this aspect of accessibility is reflected in the market rents for particular housing bundles at particular locations. Once a particular structure has been built, its accessibility and structural attributes are inextricably linked, since structures are seldom moved from one location to another.

Neighborhood quality, a characteristic of the residence zone in which a particular structure is located, is a composite of such factors as the socioeconomic and demographic characteristics of neighborhood residents, the condition and quality of the structures, and the level of local public services. The CHIP simulations employ a single index of neighborhood quality, defined by the average quantity of structure services provided by dwelling units located in each residence zone. Existing empirical knowledge about consumer preferences is insufficient to support a more sophisticated index.

The simulation model assumes that individual property owners have no discernible influence on overall neighborhood quality, or at least behave as though this were true. Instead, neighborhood quality depends on the aggregate effects of decisions made by hundreds or even thousands of individual housing suppliers; on the aggregate effects of location decisions made by an even larger number of individual households; and on the types and level of local public services.

Individual property owners can, however, alter the physical characteristics of their buildings and the quantity of structure services they supply. Changes in structure type and the quantity of structure services may involve one or more of the housing inputs over which the property owner exercises direct control. The current version of the model considers four categories of housing inputs: structure capital, construction type, maintenance capital, and operating inputs.

Structure capital is very durable and hard to modify; a change in the existing structure type can be effected only with considerable cost and difficulty. For example, although a bedroom can be added to many single-family homes quite easily by an incremental capital outlay at a cost that is not much greater than the incremental capital cost of a room of the same size in a new unit, most other changes in structure type require demolition of the existing structure and its replacement by an entirely new building. The more extensive types of conversion cannot be completed within the same year, and thus property owners who decide to change structure type must often forgo their rental income or consumption benefits during the construction period. These considerations help explain why structure conversions are relatively infrequent.

Construction type is an index of both the original quality of a structure and its degree of obsolescence. Changes in construction type are assumed to be more readily accomplished than structure conversions. Improvements that would upgrade a building's construction type include major renovations of kitchens and bathrooms; renewal of electrical, heating, and plumbing systems; and extensive rearrangement of interior space. In contrast to neighborhood quality and structure type, construction type does not appear in the submarket demand equations; it does, however, have a major effect on the cost of producing various quantities of structure services. In essence, we assume housing suppliers can compensate for the effects of inferior construction type by using more operating inputs and maintenance capital.

Maintenance capital, the final component of the structure's capital stock, is assumed to be much more easily augmented, and much less durable, than either structure type or construction type. Maintenance capital includes items such as lighting fixtures, carpeting, appliances, painting, and other minor and short-lived forms of capital improvements.

Operating inputs, the third category of inputs used to produce structure services, include labor inputs such as management, janitorial services, and security guards, as well as expenditures for fuel and other utilities. The form of the structure services production function used in the model assumes that the quantity of operating inputs can be quickly increased or decreased in response to shifts in demand or changes in input prices.

Thus the durability of inputs used to produce structure services varies greatly; it ranges from completely nondurable labor and operating inputs, through maintenance investments of low durability, to highly durable structure capital and construction type. Classifications of the various inputs used to produce structure services in terms of their service lives and substitutability must, however, be somewhat arbitrary. The use of three input categories in the Supply Sector represents a compromise between our interest in providing a rich and detailed representation of the housing production function and an equally strong need to devise a framework that is feasible in terms of modeling and econometric estimation. The three classes of inputs over which property owners individually have control allow a useful representation of available investment strategies. Presently available data do not allow finer distinctions to be made; indeed, they barely support the level of analysis included in the model. With this caveat in mind, the discussion turns to the Expectations Submodel.

The Expectations Submodel

Decisions to make highly durable capital investments, from major investments in existing structures to the construction of new buildings, depend strongly on the projections investors make about future costs, market rents, and the aggregate demand for each type of structure. These projections are produced in the current version of the model by the Expectations Submodel.

The Detroit Prototype of the NBER urban simulation model employed a simple adaptive expectations framework to estimate current-year market rents and used these estimates in simulating both housing consumer and supplier behavior. HUDS adopts the same method to estimate current-period market rents, form gross prices, and predict housing bundle choices by the Demand Submodel, but considers the use of only current-period rents insufficient for determining major investment decisions. The model's representation of the decision to build new structures or to undertake extensive rehabilitation relies on projections of rents for the property owner's planning period, which is five years in the CHIP simulations. Two kinds of information are required for these forecasts: a projection of future rents for each housing bundle in each residence zone, and a projection of future neighborhood quality.

For the CHIP simulations, neighborhood quality is defined as the mean quantity of structure services provided by the dwelling units located in each residence zone. For use in the Expectations Submodel, the continuous representation of neighborhood quality is divided into five levels, and each residence zone is characterized by one of these five levels. The several components of rent for each dwelling unit are then calculated and stored for each of the five neighborhood quality levels.

The Expectations Submodel maintains a history of neighborhood quality by residence zone, which is stored in an array AVQUAL(I,T) where T takes on values of -1 to -4 for the previous four years. The projected change in neighborhood quality for each residence zone is obtained from a simple extrapolation of trends for the previous four years, as depicted in figure E.1 for three hypothetical residence zones. Each zone in the example is assumed to have an average of 288 units of dwelling unit quality in 1960 and thus belong to neighborhood type II. Extrapolation of the 1956–1959 experience for these zones, however, yields

APPENDIX E

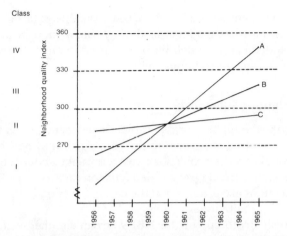

Figure E.1. Four-year history of neighborhood quality and projections of change over the planning period for three hypothetical residence zones in 1960

markedly different projections of average quality in 1965: while residence zone C continues at level II, residence zone B reaches level III, and residence zone A reaches level IV by the end of the planning period. As shown in the figure, the projected quality levels in 1965 are 348 for residence zone A, 318 for residence zone B, and 294 for neighborhood C.

The projected level of neighborhood quality for each zone determines the assignment of investor types to each structure. For the CHIP simulations each property owner is assigned to one of two investor classes in the initial year: investor type I consists of those property owners who expect the residence zone to remain at the same neighborhood quality level; investor type II, those who expect their residence zone to improve or deteriorate by one neighborhood quality level. This feature of the Expectations Submodel is calibrated so that the proportion of property owners in each residence zone assigned to each investor type depends on how far the projection of average dwelling unit quality for the residence zone is from the boundary of the initial quality class. For example, residence zone A in figure E.1, with a projected quality level of 348 in 1965, is well beyond the boundary of neighborhood quality level II. Indeed, its projected quality actually falls in the interval for level IV. Similarly, the level of neighborhood quality projected for zone B, 318, is well within the interval for level III. In contrast, the projected level of quality for zone C, 294, has not yet reached level III.

The Expectations Submodel, therefore, assigns to investor type II a larger fraction of zone B property owners than zone C owners, and a still larger fraction of zone A owners.

The specific proportion of property owners in each residence zone assigned to each investor class depends on how much the projected level exceeds the value that defines the boundary of the next quality level. Thus, for zone B in figure E.1, the projected neighborhood quality level of 318 is 18 units above the upper boundary of neighborhood type II, which is 300. This distance is divided by the width of the interval for quality level III (330 − 300), and the resulting ratio is compared to the function shown in figure E.2 to determine the proportion of property owners in zone B to be assigned to investor type II. As figure E.2 indicates, the ratio for zone B (18/30 = .6) determines that 56 percent of the property owners in zone B should be assigned to investor class II. Similar calculations for zones A and C result in the assignment of 92 and 18 percent, respectively, of property owners to investor class II. The remaining property owners in each zone are assigned to investor class I.

It should be emphasized that although the examples depicted in figures E.1 and E.2 relate to improving neighborhoods, the Expectations

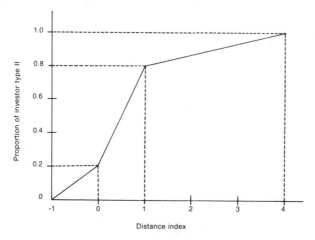

Figure E.2. Proportion of property owners who expect a change in neighborhood quality level

(Vertical axis is the proportion of property owners who expect the residence zone to change in neighborhood quality level. Horizontal axis is the distance of the projected neighborhood quality from the upper boundary of the current neighborhood type divided by the width of the interval of the projected neighborhood type.)

Submodel projects neighborhood decline as well. In cases of decline, the calculations all refer to the lower boundary of the neighborhood quality level.

The third task performed by the Expectations Submodel is to project rents for each housing bundle in each residence zone. Future rents depend on neighborhood type, structure type, and accessibility. Rents for structure services are projected in a different manner, as discussed in appendix H. Projections are based on rent histories by structure type and residence zone. The rent projections used in the CHIP simulations are based on simple extrapolations of four-year rent trends, with the constraint that rents at the end of the planning period cannot exceed 30 percent of the long-run supply price for a particular housing bundle type at a particular location. Simple trend projections of rents for a specific housing bundle type in two hypothetical residence zones are shown in figure E.3. Assuming that neighborhood quality remains unchanged, the rent expected at the end of the planning period, ERENT($I,K,T = 5$), is $105 for residence zone A and $140 for zone B. In the investment calculations, however, the rent at the end of the planning period is assumed to be $125, or 130 percent of the long-run supply cost. For the several investment analyses carried out by the Supply Sector, we assume that landlords base their decisions on simple trend projections like those depicted in figure E.3 and that they expect the rents projected for the end of the planning period to persist forever.

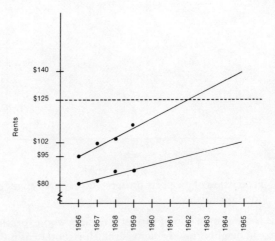

Figure E.3. Rental histories and projections of future rents for a hypothetical housing bundle and residence zone

These rents are converted to an annual net rental stream using equation E.1.

(E.1) $\text{NET}(K,I,T) = \text{ERENT}(K,I,T) - \text{OCOST}(K,I,T)$

where $\text{NET}(K,I,T)$ = Net rent received for housing bundle K in residence zone I in time period T;
$\text{ERENT}(K,I,T)$ = Expected rent for housing bundle K in residence zone I in time period T;
$\text{OCOST}(K,I,T)$ = Operating cost for housing bundle K in residence zone I in time period T.

Given the assumption that rents are expected to change during the planning period to some new level that will then persist forever, the calculation of the present value of the net rental stream can be divided into two portions, as indicated in equation E.2.

(E.2) $\text{PVNETR}(K,I) = \sum_{T=1}^{5} \frac{\text{NET}(K,I,T)}{(1+i)^T} + \frac{\text{NET}(K,I,T=6)}{i*(1+i)^6}$

where $\text{PVNETR}(K,I)$ = Present value of the net rental stream for housing bundle K in residence zone I;
i = Rate of time discount, set to .03 for the Pittsburgh and Chicago simulations;
$\text{NET}(K,I,T)$ = As defined in equation E.1.

Property owners who expect neighborhood quality to remain at the same level will use the simple extrapolation of future rents and income depicted by equation E.1 in making their investment decisions. In contrast, property owners who expect a change in neighborhood quality will instead consider the rents of comparable structures in other residence zones that exhibit the projected neighborhood quality and have equal accessibility.

The simple extrapolation of rents for each zone expected to change in quality, shown in figure E.3, combines the quasi-rents associated with each particular type of structure, neighborhood quality, and accessibility level. Since neighborhoods of various quality levels are typically unevenly distributed across the metropolitan area, location must be taken into account. As equation E.3 indicates, the Expectations Submodel makes these adjustments by subtracting an estimated locational premium from the composite rent projected for each bundle type in each residence zone.

(E.3) $\text{SRENT}(K,I,T) = \text{ERENT}(K,I,T) - \text{LRENT}(K,I)$

where   SRENT(K,I,T) = Structure rent for residence zone I,
bundle type K, and time period T;
LRENT(K,I) = Location rent for bundle type K in
residence zone I in the current period.

Then, as equation E.4 indicates, the Expectations Submodel classifies each zone by its current neighborhood type ($N = 1, 2, 3, 4,$ or 5), and calculates a stock weighted average of structure prices for the residence zones belonging to each of the five neighborhood quality levels.

$$(E.4) \qquad \text{NRENT}(K,I,T) = \frac{\sum_{I} \text{SRENT}(K,I,T) * \text{STOCK}(K,I)}{\sum_{I} \text{STOCK}(K,I)}$$

where   STOCK(K,I) = Number of dwelling units of type K in
residence zone I in the current period.

The estimated average rent for each structure type in each type of neighborhood provides an estimate of the expected rental premium applicable to each structure type if a neighborhood changes in quality.

The composite projections of rents for each residence zone and housing bundle at the end of the planning period, shown in equation E.5, then combine the location premium for each residence zone and structure type, LRENT(K,I), with the average rent for each neighborhood and structure type, NRENT(K,I,T).

$$(E.5) \qquad \text{FRENT}(K,I,T) = \text{LRENT}(K,I) + \text{NRENT}(K,I,T)$$

where   FRENT(K,I,T) = Projection of rents during the planning
period for bundle type K in each
residence zone I, for neighborhoods that
are projected to change to quality level
N by the end of the planning period.

If property owners expect a change in neighborhood quality, they will use equation E.6 rather than equation E.1 to calculate their expected net revenue. The only difference in the two equations is that FRENT(K,I,T) is used instead of ERENT$(K,I,T = 5)$ as the estimate of net rents during the planning period.

$$(E.6) \qquad \text{ENET}(K,I,T) = \text{FRENT}(K,I,T) - \text{OCOST}(K,I,T)$$

where   ENET(K,I,T) = The expected net rent received for
housing bundle K, residence zone I, and
time period T;

FRENT(K,I,T) = The forecast rent for housing bundle K,
residence zone I, and time period T,
which depends on both the current
period and forecast quality levels;

OCOST(K,I,T) = As before.

Equation E.7 then is identical to Equation E.2 except that ENET(K,I,T) rather than NET(K,I) is used to calculate the present value of net rental income.

$$(E.7) \qquad \text{PVNET}(K,I) = \sum_{T=1}^{5} \frac{\text{ENET}(K,I,T)}{(1+i)^T} + \frac{\text{ENET}(K,I,T=6)}{i*(1+i)^6}$$

Although the programming of the Expectations Submodel is quite complex, its operation is quite simple. Each structure is assigned an investor type, which determines the appropriate end-of-planning-period rent and operating cost projections to be used in comparing the profitability of alternative investments.

Demand Targets

The Expectations Submodel also forecasts the total number of dwelling units of each housing bundle type that consumers will demand at the projected rental levels. These quantity forecasts are summarized by a series of aggregate demand projections for each structure and neighborhood type combination. The demand targets represent the common information on marketwide conditions and on demographic, income, and cost trends that influence the investment decisions of developers.

In addition to simple extrapolations of rents for each type of housing bundle, the Expectations Submodel also considers current vacancy rates and historical trends in demand in determining final targets. Thus, the Expectations Submodel calculates the difference between current-period and desired vacancies for each type of housing bundle. Current-period vacancies are defined as the supply of available units — that is, units vacated this period by bundle type, as determined by the Movers Submodel. Desired vacancies are assumed to be 2.5 percent for all housing bundle types and include units in the process of being sold or rented, units temporarily taken off the market for repairs, and other vacancies required for a normally functioning housing market.

An initial estimate of target demand, BASIC(S,N), is defined by equation E.8.

$$(E.8) \qquad \text{BASIC}(S,N) = \text{DEMAND}(S,N) + \text{VAC}(S,N) - \text{AVAIL}(S,N)$$

where   BASIC(S,N) = Basic target demand for each housing bundle, that is, for each structure type S and neighborhood N;

           DEMAND(S,N) = Number of units of each housing bundle type demanded this period;

           AVAIL(S,N) = Number of available vacant units of bundle type S,N;

           VAC(S,N) = Number of dwelling units needed to satisfy the normal vacancy rate.

To make new construction activity more responsive to short-term fluctuations in demand the BASIC(S,N) demand targets are adjusted to reflect last-period changes in rental levels for each bundle type. In submarkets with rapidly increasing rents and values and low vacancy rates, builders will attempt to speed completions; similarly, even if basic demand targets indicate a strong long-term demand for additional units of a particular type, builders will slow down their completion rates if rents are falling and vacancies are high.

Equation E.9 illustrates how the Expectations Submodel uses data on the historical rate of change in market rents to adjust basic demand targets to obtain a final set of demand targets, TARGET(S,N).

(E.9)   TARGET(S,N) = BASIC(S,N) + PRDEL(S,N) * STOCK(S,N);
                  if TARGET(S,N) < 0, then TARGET = 0

where   TARGET(S,N) = Target for new construction or conversion activities for each bundle type;

          PREDEL(S,N) = Average rate of change in rents for each bundle type;

          BASIC(S,N) = As above.

A simple example may be helpful in clarifying the lengthy discussion presented above. Assume there are 1,000 units available on the market, and 985 households demand these units this period, leaving 15 vacant. The expected vacancy rate of .015 is less than the normal vacancy rate of .025. A comparison of these two rates reveals a 1 percentage point or 10-unit shortage of the bundle type in question. Whether the projected shortage is met this period depends on recent trends in rents: if there has been no significant change in average rents for the bundle type, next period's construction target will be 1 percent of the number of existing units of that type, or 10 units. If rents have been decreasing at 1 percent a year, the target will be lowered by 10 units and thus the target will be set at 0. If rents have been increasing at a rate of 1 percent, the final demand target will be raised by 10 units to a total of 20. Thus, bundle-specific demand targets calculated by the Expectations Submodel reflect past-period changes in rents and projections of excess supply and demand.

TARGET(S,N) provides information on expected demand by structure type and neighborhood. Since many individual residence zones will change neighborhood types over time, builders operating in a zone currently classified as one type must also be aware of excess demand and supply of specific structure types in other neighborhoods. To provide information on marketwide demand and supply patterns, the model sums the bundle targets to produce structure specific targets. Thus,

$$\text{STARG}(S) = \sum_N \text{TARGET}(S,N)$$

where   STARG(S) = Target for new combination or structure
conversion activities for structure type S.

For a particular structure type S, there could be marketwide excess demand, as revealed by STARG(S), yet excess supply in specific neighborhood types, as revealed by TARGET(S,N). In combination the two targets seek to guide construction activity toward structure types that are in short supply in the metropolitan area, at the same time providing a check against current-period shortages or surpluses present in any specific type of neighborhood.

APPENDIX F

New Construction and Structure Conversion

This appendix presents detailed descriptions of two Supply Sector submodels: New Construction and Structure Conversion. Both submodels initiate and in subsequent periods complete the production of the ten structure types included in the model. In determining whether to provide a particular type of structure in a particular residence zone, the New Construction and Structure Conversion submodels perform similar profitability calculations using projections of net rental income obtained from the Expectations Submodel. The principal difference in the two submodels is that the Structure Conversion Submodel uses existing structures as inputs rather than vacant land.

New Construction Submodel

The New Construction Submodel determines the profitability of building each type of structure in each residence zone, ranks these construction activities from most to least profitable, and initiates construction of successively less profitable activities of each type until next year's demand targets have been satisifed. The profitability calculations for new construction activities involve a comparison of the projected rents, obtained from the Expectations Submodel, with the projected costs of owning and operating the potential structure over its lifetime. Projected ownership costs are the annualized capital expenditures required to build a particular structure type, plus land costs; annual operating costs are the outlays necessary for the structure to produce the most profitable level of structure services.

Construction Costs

The construction costs used for the CHIP simulations are engineering cost estimates for each of the ten structure types used in the model, derived from data developed for each city using McGraw-Hill's Building Cost Calculator. For simplicity, the CHIP simulations aggregate the continuously variable number of dwelling units into three structure-size categories: one, three, or eight units. Similarly, the continuously variable single-family lot sizes are collapsed into two categories: small lot (less than 0.125 acres) and large lot (more than 0.125 acres). The estimated construction cost per structure and dwelling unit for Chicago in 1960 varies from a low of $11,744 for a zero- to two-bedroom unit to a high of $94,896 for a structure of eight units with three bedrooms in each. The cost per dwelling unit varies from a low of $10,148 for a zero- or one-bedroom unit in an eight-unit building to a high of $17,383 per unit for a single-family home with four or more bedrooms. Although both the cost per dwelling unit and the total cost per structure are given, the investment calculations performed by the current version of the model are based only on the total costs per structure, $\text{COST}(S)$.

Vacant Land Costs

Vacant land prices, the second major component of capital costs for each housing bundle, account for most of the geographic variation in development costs. The valuation of urban land is a poorly understood and exceedingly complicated phenomenon, and these portions of HUDS reflect the unsatisfactory state of empirical and theoretical knowledge of land market dynamics.

We assume that the value of undeveloped land depends entirely on its current and future demand for urban development, and that its current market value can be divided into three parts: a rent or premium for the parcel's accessibility; a second premium that is structure type – specific and reflects various nonmarket restrictions on its use, such as zoning and structure-specific parcel development costs; and a third premium that depends on neighborhood quality. For the CHIP simulations, the latter two premiums, though conceptually distinct, are combined into a single bundle-specific land value premium. Although a detailed discussion of how accessibility premiums are computed by the model is provided in appendix G, it is useful to provide a brief explanation of these issues at this point.

Land with no accessibility advantages generally has a value for some alternative use, typically agriculture or recreation. In addition, vacant land at the urban fringe will often be valued at more than its current worth for nonurban purposes because of anticipated returns from future urban growth. For the CHIP simulations the minimum land value in 1960 was estimated at $10,000 per acre. The accessibility premium for a Chicago residence zone in 1960, then, is defined as equal to the capitalized value of the zone's transport cost savings relative to undeveloped land at the periphery. As we will discuss in appendix G, the estimated transport savings for each type of housing bundle in each residence zone are obtained from a linear programming algorithm that minimizes total accessibility costs for each of the fifty submarkets. These linear programming solutions represent the spatial competition among households for residence locations within a metropolitan housing market.

Raw land prices are stored in terms of cost per acre; none of the ten model structure types, however, uses as much as an acre. The CHIP simulations assume that single-family homes are built on either one-eighth or three-eighths of an acre and that large multiple units require one-quarter of an acre. These lot sizes convert to net residential densities that vary from 2.5 units per acre for large-lot single-family homes to 32 units per acre for large multiples.

Our econometric research reveals that the demand for lot size is highly elastic with respect to income, and there is some evidence from earlier Pittsburgh and Chicago simulations that our use of only two lot sizes, particularly three-eighths of an acre for our largest lot, is somewhat unsatisfactory (Brown and Kain, 1972; Kain and Quigley, 1975). Since we are using the model to evaluate programs that principally affect central-city neighborhoods, we do not regard this problem as a serious one. (Even so, we plan to experiment with additional lot-size categories in the future.) The second component of land costs per dwelling unit is a premium that depends on structure type and lot size. There is ample evidence that the prices of developed lots are not proportional to their size and that the relationship between lot size and price per acre is a complex one that varies with location as well. The cost of developed lots incorporates a large number of factors that are a nonlinear function of lot size. For example, most costs for utilities, access streets, sewers, water, electricity, and telephones to single-family houses increase less than proportionally with lot size (Kain, 1967). Since these costs depend primarily on frontage, proportional increases in both frontage and depth not only double frontage but also cause disproportionate increases in area. In addition, lower development standards, such as narrower streets, may be used in lower-density neighborhoods without reducing quality. Finally, many development costs involve a basic charge per unit that is invariant, or nearly invariant, with lot size.

Zoning regulations may also cause the price per acre of different-sized lots to vary according to structure type. Minimum lot zoning for single-family homes and restrictions on the location and size of apartment structures fragment the land market. To the extent that zoning constraints are binding, they tend to produce separate land markets for lots used for building different types of structures. Zoning typically takes two forms that are especially pertinent to the present version of the model: it can prohibit certain types of structures, such as multi-family units, in certain neighborhoods, and it can prescribe minimum lot sizes for particular areas. The practical effect of these restrictions is often to increase the value of parcels zoned for multi-family development above the value of parcels where only single-family development is allowed, and to raise the price per square foot of smaller lots where these are permitted.

The third component of land value is related to neighborhood quality. Abundant evidence exists that structures and building lots located in high-quality neighborhoods have higher market values than otherwise identical ones located in low-quality neighborhoods. In the current model, neighborhood quality is represented by the average quality of dwelling units, which proxies the diversity of neighborhood attributes that people value in selecting a home. We assume that actual and potential rental payments for neighborhood quality are capitalized into land value.

Enjoyment of neighborhood amenities is to a large extent independent of the size of the parcel occupied by the household. Eight households living in a large apartment building on a quarter-acre of land have the same access to neighborhood services as households living in single-family units built on one-eighth-acre lots. This observation goes a long way toward explaining restrictive zoning practices that force residents to buy a minimum quantity of housing and thus discourage certain types of households from living in the community. It would be surprising if these nonmarket factors did not produce interactions between the structure type, amount of land used, and the land value premium of particular parcels.

Because of their complexity and the inadequacy of existing theoretical and empirical knowledge relating to their determination, the parcel development and neighborhood premiums are supplied exogenously for the CHIP simulations. The estimates of neighborhood and parcel development premiums are based on an unpublished econometric analysis by Roberton Williams of Pittsburgh rents and housing values carried out as part of the earlier housing allowance simulation study, on similar analyses for Chicago, and on numerous calibration runs of the model in both Chicago and Pittsburgh.

The objective of these analyses was to decompose rent and housing value payments into the four components represented in the current version of the HUDS model: (1) structure services; (2) quasi-rents for particular structures; (3) quasi-rents for neighborhood quality; and (4) accessibility. Although these data were far from ideal for this purpose, the findings are consistent with a priori expectations and with available descriptive accounts of vacant land prices in the developing parts of urban areas. There is no doubt, however, that the issues discussed in this section deserve far more attention than we have afforded them. In particular, there would be a great advantage in assembling and analyzing historical data on land values for the period covered by the baseline simulations. The behavior of land markets and the determinants of land values is only one of many areas of empirical research that would benefit the design and calibration of the HUDS model and enhance the model's capability as a policy analysis tool.

The structure type and neighborhood quality premiums used in the CHIP simulations change over time. At the start of the decade, the premiums applied to each housing bundle varied from a low of $1,579 for small single-family lots in the lowest-quality neighborhoods to a high of $68,208 for a quarter-acre lot zoned for large apartment structures in the highest-quality neighborhood. The premium per dwelling unit ranged from $17,368 for a large-lot single-family home in the best neighborhood to $790 for a unit in a large multiple structure in a low-quality neighborhood. Premiums per dwelling unit are consistently smaller for apartment structures than for single-family units, reflecting the smaller quantity of land required for multi-family units. It should be recognized that the land value premiums used in HUDS draw on specific features of each parcel that are too detailed to include in a model of this kind. It is hoped, however, that the parcel development, neighborhood, and accessibility premiums included in the current model capture the principal determinants of urban development patterns.

Equation F.1 illustrates how the New Construction Submodel combines the various elements of land values and construction costs to produce an estimate of the total supply cost for each housing bundle type in each residence zone.

(F.1) $\text{DEVCOST}(K, I) = \text{COST}(S) + \text{NSVALU}(K) + \text{AVALU}(K, I)$

where   DEVCOST(K,I) = Total development cost for housing
                  bundle K in residence zone I;
       COST(S) = Cost of building a new structure of type S;
    NSVALU(K) = Neighborhood- and structure type –
                  specific land value premiums for
                  housing bundle K;
    AVALU(K,I) = Capitalized location rent for each
                  bundle type K and residence zone I.

The composite construction costs define the total capital costs of building a particular type of structure in a particular residence zone. The New Construction Submodel computes these capital costs for each structure type in each residence zone, annualizes them, and adds the annual operating costs for each structure type; the sum is then compared to the projected annual net rents for each residence zone and structure type obtained from the Expectations Submodel.

Summarized in table F.1 are the total costs of supplying each of the fifty housing bundles represented in the CHIP simulations in 1960 for a hypothetical residence zone with a locational premium of $20,000. These estimates illustrate how the costs of acquiring different-sized lots

Table F.1. Construction costs in a residence zone with an accessibility premium of $20,000 per acre in 1960

Structure type	Neighborhood type				
	I	II	III	IV	V
Small-lot single-family					
0–2 bedrooms	$ 16,051	$ 20,788	$ 23,946	$ 27,104	$ 31,840
3 bedrooms	19,514	24,251	27,409	30,567	35,303
4+ bedrooms	21,801	26,538	29,696	32,854	37,590
Large-lot single-family					
0–2 bedrooms	26,288	31,025	34,182	37,340	42,077
3 bedrooms	29,751	34,488	37,645	40,803	45,540
4+ bedrooms	32,038	36,775	39,932	43,090	47,827
Three-family					
0–1 bedrooms	36,209	42,893	46,682	50,472	55,155
2+ bedrooms	42,176	48,860	52,649	56,439	61,122
Eight-family					
0–1 bedrooms	94,076	113,024	125,654	141,286	155,968
2+ bedrooms	108,060	127,008	139,638	152,270	169,952

in different quality neighborhoods for each of the ten model structure types affect the costs of supplying various housing bundles. Although the current version of the model could also incorporate differential risk premiums and tax payments by neighborhood, we have been unable to locate any systematic data on these potentially important variables (Schafer et al., 1975).

The estimated operating costs and carrying charges for each structure type can be combined to produce an estimate of the expected annual costs of break-even operation for each new structure. Break-even operation covers the depreciation of structure capital and allows for a normal return on investment, including a risk premium and property taxes. The resulting estimates are shown in table F.2 for hypothetical zones with a \$20,000 locational premium. As the estimates illustrate, if the projected monthly rent for a single-family, small-lot, two-bedroom house in the highest-quality neighborhood exceeds \$175 per month, the builder would expect to make more than a competitive rate of return on the project. The excess profit rate for the project is defined by equation F.2.

$$(F.2) \qquad \text{PROFIT}(K,I) = \frac{\text{PVNETR}(K,I)}{\text{DEVCOST}(K,I)}$$

where $\text{PVNETR}(K,I)$ = Present value of net rental income as defined in equation 6.2, where neighborhood type at the end of the planning period is that obtained from a trend projection of neighborhood quality;

$\text{DEVCOST}(K,I)$ = Projected development costs.

It should be noted that construction costs depend on projected as well as current neighborhood quality. The original neighborhood quality determines the development costs for the project and related carrying charges, while the projected neighborhood type affects the net rental income a builder or developer can expect. As a result, new construction will be most profitable in those zones where neighborhood quality is expected to improve.

All feasible projects — that is, projects expected to provide at least a competitive return — are placed on a New Construction List to be subsequently compared to potential structure conversions. After profitability calculations have been completed for both new construction and structure conversion activities, all projects are ranked by profitability

Table F.2. Break-even rent for a residence zone with a location premium of $20,000

Structure type	Neighborhood type				
	I	II	III	IV	V
Small-lot single-family					
0–2 bedrooms	$ 75	$ 90	$100	$100	$120
3 bedrooms	93	108	118	128	143
4+ bedrooms	104	119	129	139	154
Large-lot single-family					
0–2 bedrooms	110	125	135	145	160
3 bedrooms	128	143	153	163	178
4+ bedrooms	139	154	164	174	189
Three-family					
0–1 bedrooms	60	66	70	74	80
2+ bedrooms	70	76	80	84	90
Eight-family					
0–1 bedrooms	57	65	70	75	82
2+ bedrooms	66	73	78	83	91

and selected in order of decreasing profitability until the final demand targets for each housing bundle are satisified.

Many types of new construction and structure conversions require more than a year to complete. Thus, after these projects have been initiated, they are placed in the "in progress" file; this file is examined during each simulation period so that completed structures can be deleted and added to the Basic List. Large multiples are generally regarded as "in progress" for eighteen months, small multiples a year, and single-family homes less than a year.

The Structure Conversion Submodel

In contrast to the New Construction Submodel, the Structure Conversion Submodel uses existing dwelling units as inputs, which also entails the removal of occupants from the structure. Structure conversion costs, defined by equation F.3, depend on the cost of acquiring the input structure plus the cost of conversion, as shown in table F.3. The acquisition cost, provided by the Expectations Submodel, is the discounted present value of the net rental stream obtained by optimum operation of the structure. Net rents are gross rents minus operating costs.

Table F.3. Transformation costs by original structure type and new structure type

| | New structure type | | | | | | | | | |
| | Small-lot single-family | | | Large-lot single-family | | | Three-family | | Eight-family | |
Original structure type	0–2	3	4+	0–2	3	4+	0–1	2+	0–1	2+
Small-lot single-family										
0–2 bedrooms	—	$ 4,000	$ 8,000	$ 26,500	$ 29,500	$ 32,000	$41,000	$44,000	$ 96,000	$104,000
3 bedrooms	—	—	4,000	29,000	30,000	33,000	42,000	45,000	98,000	106,000
4+ bedrooms	—	—	—	34,000	35,000	36,000	44,000	47,000	102,000	110,000
Large-lot single-family										
0–2 bedrooms	—	—	—	—	4,000	8,000	35,667	38,667	84,000	92,000
3 bedrooms	—	—	—	—	—	4,000	36,000	39,000	84,500	92,500
4+ bedrooms	—	—	—	—	—	—	36,667	39,667	85,500	93,500
Three-family										
0–1 bedrooms	33,000	35,000	37,000	73,000	75,000	77,000	—	6,000	120,000	128,000
2+ bedrooms	38,000	40,000	42,000	88,000	90,000	92,000	—	—	130,000	138,000
Eight-family										
0–1 bedrooms	43,000	45,000	47,000	103,000	105,000	107,000	63,000	66,000	—	16,000
2+ bedrooms	45,500	47,500	49,500	110,500	112,500	114,500	65,500	68,500	—	—

(F.3) $\text{CONCOST}(K_m \rightarrow K_n, I) = \text{LANDPRICE}(K_m, I)$
$+ \text{TRANCOST}(K_m \rightarrow K_n, I)$

where $\text{CONCOST}(K_m \rightarrow K_n, I)$ = Cost of converting structure
type m to structure type n;
$\text{LANDPRICE}(K_m, I)$ = Land cost for structure type K_m
in residence zone I;
$\text{TRANCOST}(K_m \rightarrow K_n, I)$ = Transformation cost for
converting from structure type
K_m to structure type K_n.

At first glance it might appear that the total cost of converting one structure type to another would be obtained by adding the current market value of a particular structure in a particular residence zone to the areawide cost of conversion. As the discussion in the previous section indicates, however, the market value of undeveloped parcels includes a lot development premium resulting from zoning regulations, structure type–specific development costs, and similar factors, which apply to structure conversions as well. Thus, the land prices used in the Structure Conversion Submodel, shown in equation F.4, equal the current market value of a particular structure in a particular residence zone, $\text{MVALUE}(K_m, I)$, minus the development markup applicable to the existing structure, $\text{NSVALU}(K_m)$, plus the development markup applicable to the proposed structure type, $\text{NSVALU}(K_n)$.

(F.4) $\text{LANDPRICE}(K_n, I) = \text{MVALUE}(K_m, I) + \text{NSVALU}(K_n)$
$- \text{NSVALU}(K_m)$

where $\text{MVALUE}(K_m, I)$ = Current market value of bundle type K
in residence zone I;
$\text{NSVALU}(K_m)$ = Neighborhood- and structure type–
specific land value premiums.

The capital outlays are annualized by multiplying them by a composite normal rate of return, tax rate, and risk premium. They are then added to the annualized cost of acquiring the input structure to define the total expected cost of the conversion project.

The expected profitability of potential structure conversions, calculated in equation F.5, is derived in precisely the same way as that of new construction projects: the Structure Conversion Submodel subtracts the projected operating and maintenance costs from the projected rental income to form an estimate of the expected annual return over the planning period.

$$(F.5) \qquad \text{PROFCON}(K_m \rightarrow K_n, I) = \frac{\text{PVNETR}(K, I)}{\text{CONCOST}(K_m \rightarrow K_n, I)}$$

The projected net return is then divided by the total cost of the project to obtain an estimated speculative rate of return on invested capital.

To determine which structure conversions to allow, the Structure Conversion Submodel calculates the profitability for each possible conversion and compares the expected profit to that earned by the marginal supplier of the same housing bundle type in the previous period. If the expected profit earned from converting housing bundle type K_m to type K_n is greater than that of the marginal supplier minus 1 percentage point, the structure is placed on a potential conversions list to be compared finally with the list of profitable new construction activities. The most profitable projects are then selected from the combined list to satisfy demand targets created by the Expectations Submodel.

To prevent unrealistically large numbers of conversions in a single zone during a single period, only 10 percent of the potentially profitable conversions of a particular bundle type in the same residence zone are included in the combined conversions/new construction supply list. When the Basic List is processed during the next simulation period, the structures actually selected for conversion are placed on the project's "in progress" list, and their occupants are evicted by the Movers Submodel.

It should be noted that structure conversions as defined here are not a common activity because they involve changes in the most durable elements of a building—the number of bedrooms and the number of dwelling units. Activities that do not alter the basic elements of a structure are classified in HUDS as either maintenance investments or changes in construction type. Comparison of the conversion, renovation, and maintenance activities simulated in HUDS with available statistics on building and investment activities should therefore be made carefully to insure that consistent definitions are used.

Determination of Residence Location and Structure Rents

This appendix presents descriptions of two components of the Market Sector, the Market and Structure Rent submodels. Using the bundle type assignments from the Demand Submodel and the Available Units List compiled from the Movers, New Construction, and Structure Conversion submodels, the Market Submodel determines the residence zone locations of each household. In assigning households to particular residence zones, the Market Submodel treats each of the fifty housing bundles as a discrete submarket. The competition among households for available units within each submarket is represented by a linear programming assignment algorithm, which produces so-called shadow prices for each housing bundle in each residence zone. The Structure Rent Submodel then combines the shadow prices with the rents for each bundle in the marginal zone and with rents from previous periods to calculate market rents for each housing submarket and residence zone.

The Market and Structure Rent submodels included in HUDS employ a market clearing algorithm that is similar in approach to the one first developed for the Detroit Prototype, but the particulars differ in several important respects. First, HUDS explicitly considers the problems arising from the existence of noncompeting groups of demanders in a single housing submarket. In our simulations with the Detroit Prototype we failed to appreciate the problems caused by noncompeting groups within the same submarket; subsequent research, however, has demonstrated the need for careful treatment of these situations. Second, since HUDS uses a series of lists to store household and dwelling unit characteristics, the assignments of workplace and residence zones obtained from the Market Submodel must be matched to specific households on the Demand List. Finally, HUDS interprets the shadow prices somewhat differently than earlier versions and makes a somewhat different use of these data to calculate market rents for each housing bundle in each residence zone.

The Market Submodel

The Demand Submodel uses a series of multinomial logit demand equations to assign particular sample households from the Demand List to one of fifty distinct housing bundle types. At the same time that households on the Demand List are assigned a housing bundle type, they are summarized in a matrix, DEMAND(K,J,HR,HY), where K defines the bundle type assigned to the household; J refers to the workplace of the household's primary worker; and HR and HY are the race and income of the household. The demand matrix is one of the three basic inputs into the Market Submodel.

The second list used by the Market Submodel is the Available Units List, which consists of vacant units provided by the Movers, New Construction, and Structure Conversion submodels. Characteristics of dwelling units from the Available Units List relevant to the market clearing problem are tabulated in a second matrix, AVAILS(K,I), where K refers to the specific bundle type and I to the residence zone.

The Market Submodel also uses a matrix containing 1,000 pairs of workplace zone/residence district accessibility costs. The measures of interzonal accessibility costs are assumed to apply to every residence zone located in the same residence district. To calculate the interzonal accessibility cost matrix, the Market Submodel begins with a matrix of interzonal commuting costs TCOST(I,J,HY). This matrix, described briefly in the discussion of gross prices in appendix D, is an estimate of the time and money costs of commuting between each residence zone and workplace by the least-cost mode. Costs vary by income because higher-income households value the time spent in travel more, and because households at different income levels make different decisions about auto ownership and use.

Three residence zone–specific costs are added to the matrix of interzonal travel costs in calculating total accessibility costs. The first, GCOST(I,HY), is an estimate of the local accessibility costs associated with each residence zone. This cost, which is lower in high-density zones and in those well served by public transit, also varies by income. High-density zones and zones with high levels of transit service are assumed to enable low-income households to have much lower accessibility costs because they can more often avoid the high cost of auto ownership. The matrix DCOST(I,HR), which is subscripted by race and residence zone, contains the discrimination markups discussed in appendix D. These costs include both the higher housing prices black households must pay and the time, money, and psychological costs they incur in attempting to obtain housing outside of residence zones sanctioned for black occupancy. For the Chicago simulations the discrimination markup was calibrated using a stand-alone version of the Market Submodel; the markups increase as the proportion of black households in a residence zone decreases and as the distance from the ghetto increases.

The final element of accessibility costs, $\text{QCOST}(I,HY)$, provides information about the variation in average dwelling unit quality for residence zones of the same level of neighborhood quality. For the CHIP simulations $\text{QCOST}(I,HY)$ is calibrated to make zones of above-average dwelling unit quality, within the same neighborhood quality category, more attractive to higher-income than lower-income households.

The Market Submodel then uses the linear programming assignment algorithm described by equations G.1 – G.3 to match households in the demand matrix, $\text{DEMAND}(J,HY,HR,K)$, to dwelling units in the available units matrix, $\text{AVAILS}(K,I)$, in such a way that accessibility costs — that is, the matrix $\text{ACOST}(I,J,HY,HR)$ — are minimized for each housing submarket (housing bundle).

(G.1)
    Minimize $\text{ACOST}(I,J,HY,HR)$ for each housing bundle K subject to:

(G.2) $\displaystyle\sum_I \text{MARKET}(K,I,J,HR,HY) = \text{DEMAND}(J,HR,HY,K)$

(G.3) $\displaystyle\sum_{HY}\sum_{HR}\sum_{J} \text{MARKET}(K,I,J,HR,HY) = \text{AVAILS}(K,I)$

where $\text{ACOST}(I,J,HR,HY) = \text{TCOST}(I,J,HY) + \text{GCOST}(I,HR) + \text{QCOST}(I,HY)$

           $\text{QCOST}(I,HY) =$ Matrix of cost discounts, which depend on the relative level of neighborhood quality within a neighborhood quality interval and household income;

           $\text{TCOST}(I,J,HY) =$ Matrix of travel costs from workplace zone J to residence zone I;

      $\text{MARKET}(K,I,J,HR,HY) =$ Matrix of households by income class HY, race HR, work zone J, housing bundle K, and residence zone I;

$$\text{GCOST}(I,HY) = \text{The cost of nonwork trips originating in each residence zone } I;$$

$$\text{DCOST}(I,HR) = \text{The discrimination costs incurred by black households to obtain a unit in each residence zone } I.$$

Since each of the 198 Chicago residence zones in the simulation corresponds to one of five neighborhood types, between 20 and 60 residence zones are represented in the AVAILS matrix for each bundle type.

The Market Submodel assumes that each housing bundle type is a discrete housing submarket; that is, the Market Submodel must make the same bundle assignment as the Demand Submodel. The independence assumption implies that substitution among housing bundle types occurs solely in the Demand Submodel, which assigns households to housing bundles on the basis of relative gross prices. The Market Submodel treats all the dwelling units in a submarket as perfect substitutes, except for differences in gross price. This important restriction allows the residential location assignment task to be reduced to fifty smaller and more quickly solved problems. The resulting savings in computational cost are substantial since the cost of solving linear programming problems of the kind incorporated in the Market Submodel tends to increase as the cube of the number of rows and columns included in the problem. The maximum number of rows included in the programming problems solved by the Market Submodel, 240, is given by the number of work zones (twenty) times the number of income classes (six) times the number of races (two). The maximum number of columns is determined by the number of residence zones included in each neighborhood type. Of course, the actual number of rows and columns in the problems solved by the Market Submodel tends to be much smaller because not all rows and columns contain households or available units.

This absolute separation of residence zone and housing bundle choices is obviously unrealistic. It should be emphasized, however, that HUDS allows considerable interdependence between these two choices because the same accessibility costs determine the housing bundle assignments made by the Demand Submodel and the subsequent residence zone assignments made by the Market Submodel. As a result, the housing bundle assignments made by the Demand Submodel implicitly contain a great deal of information on the relative locational advantage of residence zones and on the geographic distribution of each housing bundle type. The Market Submodel thus makes explicit the locational choices entailed in selecting a particular housing bundle type.

The linear programming algorithm, which is an adaptation of the so-called transportation or Hitchcock problem, requires that the total number of households awaiting assignment exactly equal the total number of dwelling units available. HUDS, however, permits excess demands and supplies to exist in any period. To resolve this apparent inconsistency, we employ the following conventions. In submarkets characterized by excess supplies during each market period — that is, when more available units exist than households demanding them — pseudo-households are added until the number of households is exactly equal to the number of available units. Since pseudo-households are assumed to have zero travel costs to all residence zones, the Market Submodel matches them to those residence zones that are least preferred by actual households.

When a submarket is characterized by excess demand in a given period — that is, when the Demand Submodel has assigned more households to a particular housing bundle type than there are available units — pseudo-units are added as needed to make the supply of units of each bundle equal to the demand for them. Pseudo-units are assigned higher accessibility costs than any available unit, and may be interpreted as locations outside the metropolitan area or as expensive temporary quarters, such as hotel rooms or accommodations with relatives or friends. Households assigned to pseudo-units are returned to the Demand List next period, when they will be reassigned to a housing bundle by the Demand Submodel and then to a residence zone by the Market Submodel. Available units not assigned to sample households by the Market Submodel are treated as vacant and placed on the Available Units List for the next period.

Structure Rent Submodel

The Structure Rent Submodel uses the shadow prices, produced by the assignment algorithm in the Market Submodel, to calculate current period rents by housing bundle and residence zone. The shadow price for each housing bundle and residence zone is a measure of the savings in total accessibility costs that would result from adding one dwelling unit to each residence zone, on the assumption that the households are then reassigned in such a way that total accessibility costs are again minimized.

The Hitchcock-type programming algorithm used by the Market

Submodel is typically used for problems that are concerned solely with obtaining least-cost assignments among pairs of origins and destinations. A common application of the Hitchcock linear programming algorithm is the determination of a least-cost routing for the delivery of merchandise from a number of warehouses to consumers residing at a number of geographic locations. In addition to the least-cost assignments, however, the transportation algorithm also produces dual solutions, which indicate how much total costs would be reduced by the addition of one unit of capacity at each destination, taken one at a time, after a new minimum cost assignment has been produced. These so-called shadow prices contain valuable information largely ignored by analysts.

Because users of Hitchcock-type transportation problem algorithms have shown so little interest in shadow prices, the standard linear programming packages, including the one used in the Detroit Prototype, have serious shortcomings for our analysis. Despite their weaknesses we decided to modify these standard Hitchcock packages because they are much faster than other linear programming algorithms that deal more explicitly with shadow prices.

The dual solutions provided by standard packages have one degree of freedom, so an infinite number of shadow price surfaces that differ only by a constant term may be obtained without affecting the assignments. In the Structure Rent Submodel we resolve this indeterminacy by setting the shadow price for the residence zone with the least desirable location equal to zero, and by scaling the shadow prices for the remaining zones accordingly.

This convention, however, does not completely eliminate the problem created by noncompeting groups. On close examination, many of the linear programming problems solved by the Market Submodel represent situations where the market for a particular housing bundle may be divided into two or more independent groups of residence zones and households with nonoverlapping demands. As noted above, the linear programming solution for a single housing bundle may involve the assignment of as many as 240 types of households, consisting of six income classes and two racial groups, employed at as many as twenty different workplaces, to between twenty and sixty residence zones. Frequently all of the households belonging to one of the 240 demand categories are uniquely assigned to one residence zone or a subset of zones, creating a situation where the zone or subset of zones has only one type of household assigned to it. We can readily obtain an assignment that minimizes the objective function depicted by equation G.1, subject to constraints shown by equations G.2 and G.3. It is quite difficult with standard programming packages, however, to identify non-competing residence zones or to interpret their effect on the dual solutions obtained from the model. In essence, the presence of non-competing groups leads to a range of indeterminacy for each subset of zones, which is characterized by a range of shadow prices associated with an identical assignment.

While the mechanisms of the method used to resolve this indeterminacy problem in the Market Submodel are quite complex, the conceptual basis is quite simple. We merely extend the approach used to calculate shadow prices for the standard case: when noncompeting groups exist, we again set the shadow price of the least accessible residence zone to zero; in cases where a range of permissible shadow prices exist, we lower the shadows to the point where further reductions would change the original optimal assignments of households to residence zones. This procedure assumes that locational premiums are maintained only to the extent that a zone offers a marginally superior locational advantage over the zone with the next-best accessibility, and that locational premiums in excess of this amount will be competed away.

It should be clear from the preceding discussion that there are major problems in interpreting the shadow price information obtained from available linear programming algorithms. By limiting their attention to the assignment pattern, researchers avoided the problems of multiple solutions and noncompeting groups; interpreting the shadow prices as location rents, however, creates difficulties by producing multiple sets of shadow prices. The algorithm developed for the current version of the HUDS model tests for the presence of noncompeting groups and indeterminacy and selects that set of shadow prices where (1) the location rent for the least accessible zone is equal to zero, and (2) the location rent for each residence zone is as low as possible without changing the assignment solution.

Calculation of Market Rent

In calculating current-period rents for each housing bundle type in each residence zone, all vacant units belonging to the same submarket are assumed to be perfect substitutes except for their location. Where these conditions hold, the differences in location rents identified above produce corresponding differences in market rents among residence zones. Thus, the procedure used to calculate current-period rents, defined by equation G.4, is to derive a surface of location rent for each submarket $\text{SHDW}(K,I)$; the corresponding surface of current-period rents for each housing bundle is calculated by adding the location rent surface to the regionwide average quasi-rent appropriate to that structure and neighborhood type.

(G.4) $$\text{RENT}(K,I) = \text{SHDW}(K,I) + \text{QRENT}(K)$$

where $\text{RENT}(K,I) =$ The total current-period rent for bundle type K in residence zone I;

$\text{SHDW}(K,I) =$ The current-period shadow or locational premium for the bundle type K in residence zone I;

$\text{QRENT}(K) =$ The quasi-rent appropriate for the structure and neighborhood type combination forming bundle K.

The current-period quasi-rents for each structure and neighborhood type, which are also computed by the Structure Rent Submodel, are defined as the average rents earned during the period by each housing bundle, $\text{QRENT}(K)$. In a competitive housing market in long-run equilibrium, the rents for each structure type equal the annual cost of supplying that type of structure where the embodied capital earns a competitive return. The magnitudes of neighborhood quasi-rents in either the long or short run are more difficult to estimate since neighborhood quality is not produced by competitive firms (Kain and Quigley, 1975). In the short run, rents for structure type could differ from long-run equilibrium rents by amounts that depend on the extent of persistent excess supply or demand for each housing bundle type.

During each simulation period the quasi-rents for each housing bundle $\text{QRENT}(K,T)$ are adjusted to reflect the extent of excess supply or demand. In these calculations we consider the number of households who demand a particular bundle during the period and make an allowance for normal vacancy. The overall rental level for a particular housing bundle is assumed in the CHIP simulations to increase by 1 percent for each percentage point of excess demand, including the provision for normal vacancies. Conversely, the average rent is assumed to decrease by 1 percent for each percentage point of excess supply.

Since we know of no definite empirical analysis of the adjustment rate, we assume that the supplies of durable structures and neighborhood quality respond quite slowly to changes in market rents and that the technological and economic forces that determine location rents also change quite slowly. Results from the Chicago baseline simulations indicate that our qualitative views on these issues are broadly consistent with the experience of the two areas during the decade 1960–1970. The shadow prices obtained from the individual linear programming problems may, however, vary a great deal from one simulation period to the next because of temporary or random shift in the supply or demand of particular housing bundles. This is one of several reasons that we do not interpret the shadow prices obtained for a single period as market rents. As equation G.5 illustrates, the Structure Rent Submodel forms a current-period location rent surface for each housing bundle by computing a weighted average of last period's location rents for each residence zone and housing bundle, $\text{LRENT}(K,I,T-1)$, and this period's shadow prices for each housing bundle in each residence zone, $\text{SHDW}(K,I)$.

$$(\text{G.5}) \quad \text{LRENT}(K,I) = A * \text{LRENT}(K,I,T-1) + (1-A) * \text{SHDW}(K,I)$$

> where $\quad \text{LRENT}(K,I)$ = Location rents for bundle type K in zone I in time period T;
> A = Expectations coefficient, set to .75 for the current simulation;
> $\text{LRENT}(K,I,T-1)$ = Location rents for bundle type K in zone I in the previous simulation period, $T-1$;
> $\text{SHDW}(K,I)$ = A matrix of shadow prices obtained from the linear programming solution for bundle K.

Since each zone is a particular neighborhood type, equation G.5 incorporates both the neighborhood and structure type dimensions of housing bundles. In addition, the adaptive expectations framework embodied in equation G.5 reflects the view that housing rents and values change relatively slowly over time, and respond only to persistent indications of excess demand or supply.

The use of the adaptive expectations framework to calculate location rents follows procedures employed in the Detroit Prototype. The adaptive expectations framework represented by equation G.5 assigns decreasing weights to each previous year's rents in a regular manner; the relative weight assigned depends on the expectations coefficient A. The value of .75 that we used in the Chicago simulations places a rather heavy weight on current-period shadow prices. Rents earlier than the previous five or six years have little significant impact. Lowering the expectations parameter to .1, however, would cause shadow price information for ten or more periods to have an impact on current price rents. By altering the coefficient of expectations in future model simulations, it will be possible to test the impact of alternative assumptions concerning the rate at which the housing market responds to shadow price changes generated by competition among relocating households.

After both the location rent surface, LRENT(K,I), and the quasi-rents for each housing bundle, QRENT(K), have been computed, the Structure Rent Submodel combines these data, as shown by equation G.6, to provide an estimate of current-market rents for each housing bundle in each residence zone RENT(K,I).

(G.6) $$\text{RENT}(K,I) = \text{LRENT}(K,I) + \text{QRENT}(K)$$

where   RENT(K,I) = Current-period rents by bundle type K and residence zone I;

LRENT(K,I) = Location rents for bundle type K in residence zone I;

QRENT(K) = Quasi-rents for each bundle type K.

Land Value Determination

The determination of land values for each residence zone is the final calculation performed by the Structure Rent Submodel. It seems clear that the value of undeveloped land in each residence zone should reflect neighborhood quality and accessibility since both dimensions influence the market prices of existing structures. The problem is complicated, however, by the fact that the several structure types found in a single residence zone have different location rents, reflecting differences in the spatial distribution of demand for, and the supply of, each housing bundle.

Although it is clear that the location rents for the several housing bundles present in the zone are relevant, it is less obvious just how these data should be used to determine land values. For the CHIP simulations, we calculated the shadow prices applicable to each structure type SHDW(S,I) weighted by the total amount of land used for each structure type. Equation G.7 shows the weighting formula.

(G.7) $$\text{LANDSHDW}(I) = \frac{\sum_K \text{SHDW}(K,I) * \text{STOCK}(K,I) * \text{REQUIN}(K)}{\sum_K \text{STOCK}(K,I) * \text{REQUIN}(K)}$$

where   LANDSHDW(I) = This period's shadow price on land in zone I;

SHDW(K,I) = As defined in equation G.4;

STOCK(K,I) = Stock of structure type S in zone I;

REQUIN(K) = Acres required for a structure of type K.

Like the location rent calculations depicted by equation G.5, the shadow prices for each residence zone are incorporated into the adaptive expectations framework, shown in equation G.8. Current-period land rents were estimated using a .75 coefficient of expectations.

(G.8) $\text{LANRENT}(I,T) = A * \text{LANRENT}(I,T - 1) + (1 - A) * \text{LANDSHDW}(I)$

where
$\text{LANRENT}(I,T) =$ Current-period rent on undeveloped land in zone I;

$\text{LANRENT}(I,T - 1) =$ Last period's land rent for undeveloped land in zone I;

$\text{LANDSHDW}(I) =$ This period's composite shadow price on vacant land in zone I;

$A =$ Expectations coefficient, set to .75 for the current simulations.

The particular method used in the CHIP simulations to combine the bundle-specific shadow prices into land rents is somewhat arbitrary and represents only one of several plausible approaches. The most obvious alternative would be to use the highest shadow price obtained for each zone or to weight the shadows by last period's new construction of each structure type in each zone.

APPENDIX H

Provision of Structure Services and Determination of Rents

This appendix describes two components of the Market Sector, the Structure Services and Structure Services Rent submodels. The Structure Services Submodel has two functions: it derives a supply curve for each structure and dwelling unit, and determines the quantity of structure services that would be demanded by each occupant at each price per unit of structure services. The Structure Services Rent Submodel uses these dwelling unit – specific supply and demand curves to calculate the quantity of structure services actually supplied by each dwelling unit and to form current-period rents per unit of structure services. Both submodels operate on the Basic List as part of the Basic List Subroutine. Determination of the level of structures services, their rents, and capital improvements in existing structures, which are logically the final aspects of behavior simulated for the current period, are carried out by the Basic List Subroutine at the start of the next simulation period.

Structure services are flows of housing services provided by existing dwelling units. Property owners produce them by combining current operating inputs with the type and quantities of maintenance and structure capital embodied in their structures at the start of the simulation period. Capital outlays this period which increase the quantity of maintenance capital or improve construction type reduce the amount of operating inputs required to produce a given quantity of structure services during subsequent periods but have no effect on this period's production. Even so, property owners can increase the quantity of structure services they supply during the current period by using more operating inputs, although at an ever-increasing unit cost. Because no long-term commitment is involved, moreover, property owners' decisions about the quantity of structure services to supply are more

232

strongly influenced by recent changes in rents and current vacancies than are their decisions to make capital improvements.

The quantity and cost of structure services also depend on the specific characteristics of the household currently occupying the dwelling unit. The list method of data storage and processing enables us to represent the effects of structure, landlord, and tenant characteristics and their interactions on supply decisions in great detail. Much of the potential benefit of the list method to the modeling of these interrelationships is unrealized, however, because we lack systematic research on the effects of these variables on the cost of supplying structure services.

Structure Services Submodel

Because we assume that owners of multiple-unit structures consider the profitability of the entire building when they make investments and therefore have uniform policies for all their units, we assume that all dwelling units within a multi-unit building possess the same quantities of structure and maintenance capital. In addition, we assume that all units in a multi-unit building have the same size, configuration, and other physical characteristics. These assumptions greatly reduce the model's bookkeeping and do not exact a significant cost in terms of its capabilities for policy analysis. Moreover, some scope exists to vary the quantity and quality of services supplied within a multiple-unit structure, because the Structure Services Submodel considers each individual dwelling unit and the demand of each occupant for structure services in its calculation.

Both landlords and homeowners have considerable discretion over the quantity of structure services they produce during the year. The amount of operating inputs required to produce each level of output, however, depends on the nature and quantity of capital embodied in the structure at the beginning of the year. If the structure has too little capital or the wrong kind of capital, it may be very expensive to produce some quantities of structure services. The unit cost of providing structure services depends on the characteristics of the structure services production function and the available quantities and kinds of three inputs: maintenance capital, operating inputs, and structure capital.

Both maintenance capital and operating inputs are aggregations of diverse inputs. Maintenance capital consists of a variety of capital goods with relatively short service lives. Operating inputs include labor, fuel, utilities, and other nondurable inputs expended during the year to produce structure services. For obvious reasons, the quantities of these various elements are weighted by a price index so that operating inputs and maintenance capital may be represented in terms of dollars. The simulations assume that one unit of maintenance capital and of operating inputs can be purchased for $1.00 (all calculations are done in terms of 1970 dollars). The cost of maintenance capital is converted to an annual opportunity cost by multiplying the price of capital times the rate of depreciation plus the normal rate of return. Should future empirical work identify important changes in the relative price of capital and operating inputs, these changes can easily be accommodated in the model. In addition, the model could also be used to evaluate the effects of neighborhood differentials in factor prices, if such differences could be documented. Schafer et al. (1975) provide some evidence that such differentials exist.

For the simulation presented in this report, we assume that the structure services production function is the same for rental units and owner-occupied single-family units. It would be a simple matter to incorporate different production functions for the two kinds of units if future empirical research indicates that such differences exist. For that matter, different production functions could be employed for large and small structures and for buildings operated by resident and nonresident owners. Sternlieb's study (1966) of Newark and research by Schafer (1975) support the use of different production functions for different types of landlords.

The structure services production functions also assume that a minimum quantity of structure capital is required to produce structure services and that the level of structure services produced each period depends on the amount of maintenance capital embodied in the building at the start of the period, the amount of operating inputs used, and the building's construction type. Newer structures, or structures that were originally built at a higher construction type, are able to produce a given level of structure services with fewer operating inputs than older structures or those built at a lower original standard. The structure services production functions assume that a decline in construction type from type 1 to type 3 increases by 40 percent the quantities of maintenance capital and operating inputs required to produce a given quantity of structure services.

For the Chicago simulations we have assumed that structure services are produced by a Cobb-Douglas production function with constant returns to scale. Cobb-Douglas production functions allow substitution among inputs in the production of structure services, but the extent of substitution is limited. The nature of this substitution is illustrated by figure H.1, which graphs the relationship between the quantities of maintenance capital embodied in the structure, the level of operating

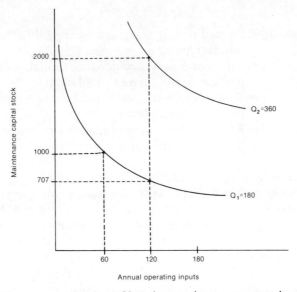

Figure H.1. The production of housing services: representative isoquants

inputs, and the amount of structure services produced. The curves shown, Q_1 and Q_2, referred to as isoquants, depict how maintenance capital and operating inputs may be substituted for one another in the production of structure services and what quantities of each input are required to produce a given level of structure services. Q_1 represents all the combinations of maintenance capital and operating inputs that would produce 180 units of structure services; Q_2 represents all combinations of these two inputs that would produce 360 units of structure services. For example, the isoquant Q_1 indicates that if the structure has 1,000 units of maintenance capital at the beginning of the period, an additional 60 units of operating inputs are necessary to produce 180 units of structure services.

If both maintenance capital and operating inputs are priced at $1.00 per unit, then 180 units of structure services can be produced with a stock of maintenance capital valued at $1,000 and an annual flow of operating inputs of $60. To convert these numbers to an estimate of the annual cost of producing structure services, a rental charge must be included for the stock of maintenance capital embodied in the structure. As shown in equation H.1, the cost of maintenance capital is equal to a real rate of return of 3 percent and a physical depreciation rate of 9 percent.

(H.1) $$R_K = P_K * (r + d)$$

where R_K = Annual rent on maintenance capital for housing
bundle type K;

P_K = Price per unit of maintenance capital, set to $1.00
per unit in the current simulation;

r = Real rate of return on capital, set to 3 percent in
the current simulations;

d = Rate of depreciation of maintenance capital, set to
9 percent in the current simulations.

Under these assumptions, $1,000 worth of maintenance capital has
an opportunity cost of $120 per year. Combining this charge with the
$60 annual cost of operating input produces a total cost of $180 for the
180 units of output represented by the first isoquant in figure H.1. The
input and output prices and quantities used in this example and in the
CHIP simulations are scaled so that one unit of structure services is
produced with $1.00 worth of inputs, assuming the dwelling unit has
the optimal quantity of maintenance capital to produce each quantity of
structure services and that input prices are expressed in 1970 dollars.
The annual price of maintenance capital is again assumed to be 12
percent of the stock of maintenance capital.

At any other point on the same isoquant — that is, if a different
combination of factor inputs is used — the cost of producing the 180
units of structure services is increased. For example, the same 180 units
of structure services could be produced with 120 units of operating
inputs and only 707 units of maintenance capital stock. The total cost of
producing 180 units of structure services in this case, however, would
be $205: $85 for the annual cost of maintenance capital and $120 for
the 120 units of operating inputs. The 180 units of structure services
produced in this example would cost $1.14 per unit to produce.

Isoquant Q_2 shows the quantities of maintenance capital and operating inputs required to produce 360 units of structure services. The
least-cost way to produce this quantity of structure services employs
2,000 units of maintenance capital. If this quantity of maintenance
capital is embodied in the unit at the start of the period, the annual cost
of producing the 360 units of structure services would be $360, or an
opportunity cost of maintenance capital of $240 plus an operating input
cost of $120.

Isoquants may also be used to illustrate how input prices affect the
quantities of each input a cost-minimizing property owner would use to
produce structure services. Figure H.2 replicates the isoquants shown

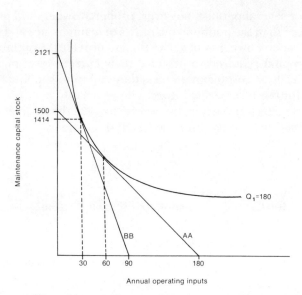

Figure H.2. Effect of input prices on the quantities of factor inputs used to produce structure services

in figure H.1 and adds two price lines, *AA* and *BB*. The line *AA* represents the input prices used in the preceding example, where both operating inputs and maintenance capital are priced at $1.00 per unit. This produces an annual opportunity cost of maintenance capital of $0.12 per unit. Changing the price of operating inputs to $2.00 and the price of maintenance capital to $0.70 produces line *BB*. In this instance, the point of tangency is at 30 units of operating inputs and 1,414 units of maintenance capital stock, and the total cost of producing 180 units of structure service remains at $180. As in the previous example, the cost of capital is $120 and the cost of operating inputs is $60, obtained by multiplying 1,414 times $0.085 and 30 times $2.00. One of the properties of the Cobb-Douglas production function employed in the CHIP simulations is that the relative expenditures for each input are not affected by changes in their relative prices. With constant returns to scale, the ratio $B/(1 - B)$ is equal to the ratio of the cost of capital to the cost of operating inputs when factors are paid their marginal products and production occurs at the most efficient point.

To produce a new level of structure services at minimum cost requires changes in the levels of both operating and capital inputs. Since maintenance capital inputs take time to provide and commit property owners for several periods, however, property owners will often have less or more than the optimum quantities of maintenance and structure capital. Property owners will not attempt to provide the optimum quantities of capital required to produce their current level of structure services in a least-cost manner unless they expect to supply at least that quantity for the foreseeable future.

Equations H.2 – H.5 depict the precise form of the structure services production functions used for the CHIP simulations.

(H.2) $\text{SERV}(K) = 1.2 * A * \text{MCAP}^B \text{OPER}^{1-B}$
$\quad$ for $CT = 1, \quad \text{SCAP}(K) > .8 \text{ STDDUR}(K)$

(H.3) $\text{SERV}(K) = A * \text{MCAP}^B \text{OPER}^{1-B}$
$\quad$ for $CT = 2, \quad .5 \text{ STDDUR}(K) < \text{SCAP}(K) \leq .8$
$\text{STDDUR}(K)$

(H.4) $\text{SERV}(K) = .8 * A * \text{MCAP}^B \text{OPER}^{1-B}$
$\quad$ for $CT = 3, \quad \text{MINSCAP}(K) < \text{SCAP}(K) \leq .5 \text{ STDDUR}(K)$

(H.5) $\text{SERV}(K) = 0 \quad$ for $CT = 1,2,3, \text{SCAP}(K) \leq \text{MINSCAP}(K)$

$\quad$ where $\quad \text{SERV}(K) =$ Level of structure services produced by housing bundle K;
$\quad\quad\quad \text{MCAP} =$ Stock of maintenance capital;
$\quad\quad\quad \text{OPER} =$ Operating inputs;
$\quad\quad\quad \text{CT} =$ Construction type;
$\quad\quad\quad \text{SCAP}(K) =$ Structure capital in housing bundle K;
$\quad\quad\quad \text{STDDUR}(K) =$ Good-as-new level of structure capital for housing bundle K;
$\quad\quad\quad \text{MINSCAP}(K) =$ Minimum structure capital required for operation;
$\quad\quad\quad A =$ Scaling parameter equal to .460;
$\quad\quad\quad B =$ Parameter equal to the share of rents for structure service which accrue to maintenance capital, set to .667 for the current simulations.

Derivation of Supply Curves

The structure services production functions and input prices for the current period provide all the information necessary for deriving short-run average and marginal cost curves for any two dwelling units A and B of a particular construction type. The short run is defined as the current simulation year, during which the property owner cannot change the

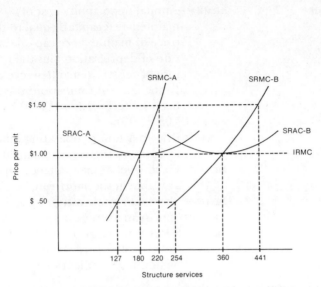

Figure H.3. Short-run average and marginal cost curves for two dwelling units of construction type 2

quantity of maintenance capital embodied in the unit or its construction type. The marginal cost curve, derived from the structure services production function, is defined by equation H.6 and shown in figure H.3 for two hypothetical dwelling units of construction type 2.

$$(\text{H.6}) \qquad \text{SRMC} = \frac{\text{PO} * \text{SERV}^{B/(1-B)}}{A^{1/(1-B)}\overline{\text{MCAP}}^{B/(1-B)}}$$

The two short-run marginal cost curves in figure H.3 reflect the different amounts of maintenance capital embodied in each of the two units at the start of the period. Figure H.3 also graphs the short-run average cost curve for the same two dwelling units and the long-run marginal and average costs of producing structure services. The short-run average and the total cost curves are defined by equations H.7 and H.8.

$$(\text{H.7}) \qquad \text{SRAC} = \frac{\text{RMK} * \overline{\text{MCAP}}}{\text{SERV}} + \frac{\text{PO} * \text{SERV}^{B(1-B)}}{A * \overline{\text{MCAP}}^{B}}$$

$$(\text{H.8}) \qquad \text{SRTC} = \text{RMK} * \overline{\text{MCAP}} + \frac{\text{PO} * \text{SERV}^{1/(1-B)}}{A * \overline{\text{MCAP}}^{B}}$$

where $\qquad$ RMK = Annual opportunity cost of maintenance capital, equal to the price of maintenance capital times the rate of depreciation plus the normal rate of return to maintenance capital. In the current simulations this has been set to $0.12, or $1.00 × (.03 + .09);

PO = Price per unit of operating inputs, set to $1.00 in the current simulations;

$\overline{\text{MCAP}}$ = Fixed level of maintenance capital available in the short run;

SRTC = Short-run total cost;

SRAC = Short-run average cost;

SRMC = Short-run marginal cost;

SERV(A), SERV(B) = Level of structure services produced by housing bundle A or B.

The minimum point of the short-run average cost curve for each dwelling unit represents the minimum cost of producing that quantity of structure services for construction type 2, assuming that the unit has the optimum quantity of maintenance capital to produce that level of structure services. As is evident from figure H.3, average and marginal costs are equal at the point where the average cost curve is at its minimum, as well as being equal to intermediate-run marginal costs at that point.

The marginal cost curve labeled SRMC-A in figure H.3 illustrates the marginal cost of producing structure services for a dwelling with 1,000 units of maintenance capital; curve SRMC-B, for a dwelling unit with 2,000 units of maintenance capital. Thus, the marginal cost of producing 180 units of structure services is $1.00 for the building depicted by the curve SRMC-A.

It is also evident from figure H.3 that the production function parameters used for the CHIP simulations imply a nonlinear short-run marginal cost curve. Since the B parameter has been set to .667, then $(B/1 - B)$ is equal to 2, and the marginal costs increase with the square of the quantity of structure services produced. This reflects the fact that with a fixed quantity of maintenance capital, larger quantities of operating inputs become increasingly less efficient in the production of structure services.

Each point on the marginal cost curve above average variable cost defines the quantity of structure services a property owner would be willing to supply at that price. Thus, if the market price per unit were $1.00, the owner of dwelling unit *A* would supply 180 units; 220 units at a price of $1.50; and 127 units at a price of $0.50. The owner of unit *A* would receive a normal return on his investment in maintenance capital at the price of $1.00, an excess profit at price $1.50, and less than a normal return on his investment at price $0.50. Nonetheless, he continues to supply structure services as long as his total rental income for the period at least covers his variable costs, that is, his expenditures for operating inputs. Assuming these same prices hold, the owner of dwelling *B* would supply the quantities 254, 360, or 441 units of structure services.

Demand for Structure Services

The marginal cost curve for each dwelling unit defines the quantities of structure services a profit-maximizing property owner would be willing to supply at each rental level, where rent is defined in terms of the cost per unit of structure services. The Structure Services Submodel calculates the appropriate marginal cost relationship for each structure type and combines this information with the occupant's demand for structure services to determine the quantity and price of structure services produced for a particular period.

Differences in household characteristics influence the demand for structure services. The Structure Services Submodel is calibrated so that household demand for structure services decreases with increases in the rent per unit of structure services, decreases in household income, or a change in tenure status from owner to renter. The relationships between demand for structure services, household income, and rents are familiar, but the influence of tenure requires further explanation.

A number of empirical studies have documented the fact that owner-occupants spend more for housing than otherwise identical renter occupants. Because many owners expect to remain in the same dwelling unit for significant periods of time, they are willing to make a variety of capital improvements that landlords find unprofitable to make for more mobile renters. For the CHIP simulations we account for at least part of observed differences by using separate structure services demand functions for owners and renters, shown in equation H.9.

(H.9) $$\text{DQ} = C(\text{HY}/\text{YBASE})^{\text{YELS(TEN)}}(\text{RQ}/\text{RQBASE})^{\text{PELS}}$$

242

APPENDIX H

where $\qquad$ DQ = Quantity of structure services demanded;
PELS = Price elasticity of demand for housing quality, set at -1 for the current simulations;
YELS(TEN) = Income elasticity of demand for housing as a function of tenure, set to .6 for renters and .7 for owners;
HY = Income of the household;
RQ = Renter per unit of structure services;
YBASE = Scaling factor, set to 3,000 for the current simulations;
RQBASE = Scaling factor, set to 1 for the current simulations;
C = Scaling factor, set to 150 for the current simulations.

The structure services demand function is characterized by constant income and price elasticities. For the CHIP simulations, the income elasticity of demand for structure services is assumed to be .6 for renters and .7 for owners, while the price elasticity of demand is assumed to be -1 for both groups.

A household with an annual income of $3,000 is used as the reference, and the intermediate-run marginal cost of producing one unit of structure services is set to $1.00. The demand function is calibrated so that a household with an annual income of $3,000 would demand 150 units of structure services at a unit price of $1.00; this represents an annual payment of $150 or a monthly payment of $12.50 for structure services. Figure H.4 illustrates the difference in demand curves of owner and renter households, where both have incomes of $7,000. The demand curve labeled DSS_R depicts the quantity of structure services a renter household would consume at various prices. At a price per unit of $1.00, this household will consume 250 units of structure services for a total expenditure of $250. Similarly, the demand curve DSS_O indicates that at a price per unit of structure service of $1.00 the owner household would consume 295 units.

The assumption that the price elasticity of demand for structure services of both owners and renters is -1 implies that increases or decreases in the price of structure services will be exactly offset by proportional and opposite changes in the quantities of structure services consumed. Consequently, a household's expenditures for structure services will be constant at all rent levels. For example, the renter household in figure H.4 would consume 250 units of structure services at a price of $1.00, for a total structure services expenditure of $250 per

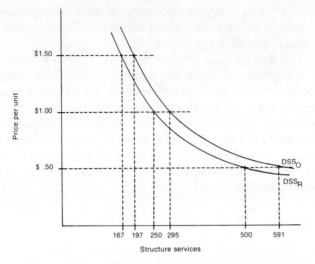

Figure H.4. Demand for structure services for two hypothetical owner and renter households with annual incomes of $7,000

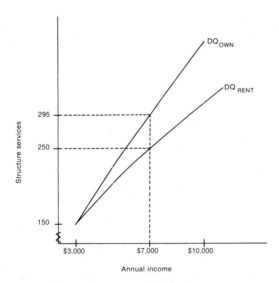

Figure H.5. Demand for structure services for owner and renter households, by income level

year. If the price of structure services were only $0.50, however, the same household would demand 500 units of structure services for the same annual expenditure of $250.

Figure H.5 depicts these demand relationships in a slightly different fashion. Specifically, it shows the quantity of structure services consumed by renter and owner households at each income level, again assuming that the price per unit of structure services is $1.00. As figure H.5 reveals, an owner household with an annual income of $7,000 would demand 295 units of housing services, while a renter household with the same annual income would demand only 250 units. This difference reflects owner-occupants' higher income elasticity of demand for structure services.

Structure Services Rent Submodel

The demand relationship assumed for equation H.9 and the marginal cost curve defined by equation H.6 are used by the Structure Services Rent Submodel to determine the quantity of structure services provided by each dwelling unit and the rent per unit of structure services for each of the four levels of structure services for each type of housing bundle in each residence zone.

Shown in figure H.6 are the short-run and intermediate-run marginal cost curves for a hypothetical housing supplier and the demand curve for the hypothetical household assigned to that unit. Curve IRMC represents the intermediate-run marginal cost of producing structure services using the optimal quantity of maintenance capital and construction type 2. In the long run it would be possible to change construction type as well, but such changes are expensive and difficult to accomplish; for example, a landlord then must evict tenants and lose rental income during the construction period. As a result, property owners behave as if construction type is fixed, at least in the short run. The quantity of structure services that would be supplied and consumed by a utility-maximizing owner-occupant, 220, is thus determined by the intersection of the household's short-run marginal cost and demand curves. The out-of-pocket cost per unit of structure services is $1.05, which is given by the level of the short-run average cost curve at the quantity 220. If the owner-occupant expects his demand to continue unchanged, he should undertake the investments required to reduce the costs of producing structure services to $1.00; at that time he would produce 330 units of structure services. The investment rules used to simulate the changes in construction type and maintenance capital that would cause the demand and intermediate-run marginal cost curves to inter-

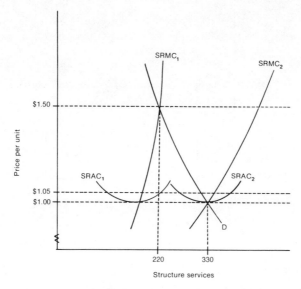

Figure H.6. Provision of structure services for a hypothetical owner-occupant

sect at $1.00 and 330 units are described in appendix I. For the CHIP simulations, however, we do not attempt to simulate the adjustment path followed by owner-occupants of single-family units in moving from the point $1.50/220 units to the point $1.00/330 units. Instead, for owner-occupied single-family units we operate the Structure Services Rent Submodel only at intervals of four years or when a new household occupies the structure. At that time, we assign the household the optimal quantity of structure services, 330, and make the capital improvements necessary to reach this point.

The analysis does involve one complication, however. If a change in construction type is required to achieve that quantity of structure services, the Capital Improvements Submodel first considers both current and projected neighborhood quality. If these suggest that the dwelling unit's location does not justify long-term investments, the construction type is not altered. This situation is depicted in figure H.7 by the intersection of the household's demand curve and intermediate-run marginal cost curve for a unit of construction type 2, where current and projected neighborhood quality do not justify the major capital outlays entailed in changing construction type. In this case we assume that the household consumes 330 rather than 412 units of structure services.

A more involved procedure is used to simulate the quantities of struc-

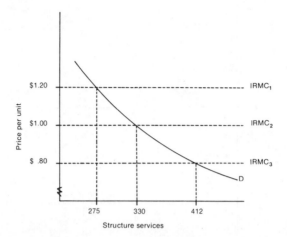

Figure H.7. Intermediate-run marginal cost curve with change in construction type allowed

ture services supplied by owners of rental structures, the quantities consumed by tenants, and the competition among landlords to obtain tenants. To determine rents and quantities for renter-occupants, the demand and supply curves for individual units must be aggregated to obtain market demand and supply curves for each type of structure in each zone. The market supply curve would be the envelope of the marginal cost curves of the individual suppliers. The determination of market rents and quantities for each housing bundle could then be simulated as a bidding process among households for available units. We considered using a miniature linear programming model to simulate the determination of rents for structure services, but concluded that it would be impractical to obtain market demand and supply curves for each residence zone, particularly since the demand for structure services supplied by a particular housing bundle in a particular residence zone depends on the price of structure services provided by competing structures in nearby residence zones.

The Structure Services Rent Submodel uses a simpler algorithm that exploits more general information about the likely characteristics of the market supply and demand curves for structure services in each residence zone. First, the structure services demand function is solved for each household in the Demand List using last period's market price for structure services for its assigned bundle type and residence zone. Then households are ordered by their expected demand for structure services and assigned to the available unit that is the most efficient producer of that particular quantity of structure services. The ranking of units by production efficiency depends on construction type and the amount of embodied maintenance capital; units of the highest construction type and those having the most maintenance capital are the most efficient producers of the largest quantities of structure services.

The ranking algorithm used to assign households to specific units within a bundle type and residence zone is depicted by figure H.8, which illustrates the assignment of three hypothetical households to three dwelling units. The intersection of the demand and marginal cost curves for the first dwelling unit household indicates a quantity of structure services q_1 and a price p_1 that is below the intermediate run marginal and average costs of producing structure services. This property owner will be earning less than a competitive return on his capital and will therefore allow some depreciation of maintenance capital to occur. In the second case, the occupant's demand curve intersects the unit's marginal cost curve at a price well above the intermediate-run marginal cost curve; this property owner will find it profitable to increase his stock of maintenance capital. In the third situation, the occupant's demand curve intersects the unit's marginal cost curve at the point where it is equal to the intermediate-run marginal cost; the quantity of maintenance capital embodied in this unit is exactly equal to the optimal amount. Since there is considerable uncertainty about demand and since property owners are assumed to be risk-averse, we assume that

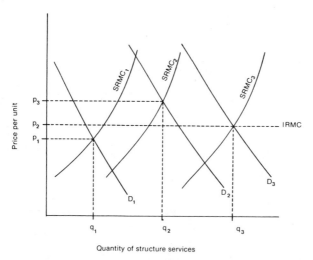

Figure H.8.   Assignment of three hypothetical households to dwelling units

property owners seek to satisfy only one-fourth of the gap between actual and optimal capital stock in each period.

Although the Structure Services Rent Submodel provides the rationale for assigning specific households to specific units within the same housing bundle type and residence zone, the Market Submodel actually matches households from the Demand List to specific dwelling units on the Available Units list. This assignment, of course, applies only to households on the Demand List and vacant units on the Available Units List. In making these assignments, the only distinction made between owners and renters of single-family units assigned to the same residence zone is that owners will demand more structure services and will thus be assigned to units of higher construction type with larger quantities of maintenance capital than renters of the same income. In the case of renters who were assigned to particular dwelling units in previous time periods, the construction type and quantity of maintenance capital embodied in their units depend on the quantities existing for their units at the same time they were assigned to their present units and any capital improvements made by the owners of their units in the interim.

Depreciation, Changes in Construction Type, and Investments in Maintenance Capital

This appendix describes how the Capital Improvements Submodel simulates the depreciation of structure and maintenance capital, investments in maintenance capital, and changes in construction type. As discussed previously, construction type depends on the quality of construction for new units, and on the quality of original construction and the extent of depreciation for existing units. Investments in maintenance capital and changes in construction type are influenced by both current and projected neighborhood quality. Like the Structure Services Submodel, the Capital Improvements Submodel performs its calculations for owner-occupied single-family units only when a new owner moves into the unit and every four years thereafter.

Depreciation

The current version of the model identifies two types of capital. Maintenance capital is a composite of a large number of structural elements that are of low durability and is assumed to depreciate at 9 percent a year. For the CHIP simulations we assumed that maintenance capital can be added incrementally in whatever quantities are desired and at a constant unit cost. Structure capital, which consists of the highly durable elements of the structure, depreciates at 4.5 percent a year. We assume that only two-thirds of annual depreciation can be offset by maintenance outlays. If the expenditures required for maintenance and structure capital are not made during a year, we assume that this neglect cannot be made up during subsequent periods; for this reason and because of its critical effect on the efficiency at which maintenance capital and operating inputs are used to produce structure services, the maintenance of structure capital has first claim on rental income after payment of fixed charges, such as mortgage payments and taxes, and this period's operating expenses.

As noted previously, structure capital has two dimensions. Structure type represents the initial quantity of structure capital required to provide each type of structure at the minimum quality level allowed or demanded. Construction type, in contrast, represents differences in the quality of original construction and obsolescence. The current model includes three construction types that correspond to different quantities of structure capital for each type of structure: construction type 1 has 125 percent as much structure capital as construction type 2 and 150 percent as much as construction type 3. Since one-third of structure capital depreciation cannot be offset by annual maintenance expenditures, a structure that was originally construction type 1 will depreciate to construction type 2 in fifteen years, even if the property owner pursues a good-as-new maintenance policy. In another fifteen years it will further depreciate to construction type 3. Of course, if no structure maintenance is performed, it will depreciate at three times the rate. A building that depreciates to construction type 2 or 3 can be upgraded to construction type 1 only at a cost significantly higher than the original difference in construction cost between the two types.

Improvements in Owner-Occupied Single-Family Units

The Capital Improvements Submodel applies a simpler set of rules for investment in maintenance and structure capital in the case of owner-occupied single-family units and carries out these calculations less frequently than for other kinds of units. Specifically, the Capital Improvements Submodel performs its calculations only when a new owner-occupant moves into the unit and every fourth year thereafter. The submodel operates after the Structure Services Submodel has determined the quantity of structure services demanded by the owner-occupant.

The Capital Improvements Submodel begins its investment calculations for owner-occupied single-family units by determining the optimal capital stock and construction type for the quantity of structure services that would be consumed by the current household at the long-run marginal cost of producing structure services. If these calculations indicate that a change in construction type is justified by the savings in maintenance capital and operating inputs for the quantity of structure services demanded by the household at the long-run marginal cost, the

Capital Improvements Submodel examines the current and projected levels of neighborhood quality.

The calculation used to assess changes in construction type discounts the savings in operating costs and maintenance capital over a ten-year period and compares the resulting estimate to the capital outlay required to upgrade the building's construction type; the cost of upgrading depends on the quantity of structure capital embodied in the structure and is always higher than the comparable new construction figure. If these calculations indicate that a change in construction type would be desirable, the Capital Improvements Submodel consults a matrix of construction type change probabilities, which depend on the current and projected demand for various quantities of structure services within the residence zone. If current and projected levels of neighborhood quality and the discounted savings in maintenance capital and operating cost justify the investment, the Capital Improvements Submodel changes construction type to a higher level.

If the Capital Improvements Submodel does change the construction type of the candidate structure, if recalculates the household's demand for structure services using the long-run marginal cost appropriate to that construction type, determines the optimal quantity of maintenance capital applicable to that level of structure services, and simply provides it. It should be noted that if the unit's construction type is not changed, the quantity of structure services provided will be less than the amount supplied if the current and projected level of neighborhood quality justified a change in construction type.

Improvements in Rental Buildings

The investment rules used to simulate changes in construction type and investments in maintenance capital are similar but considerably more complicated for rental buildings than for owner-occupied single-family units. To begin with, as noted above, the Capital Improvements Submodel performs annual calculations for all rental buildings. In the case of multi-family units, it must also take into account the demand for structure services by all occupants of the building. Finally, decisions to change construction type or to increase the quantity of maintenance capital embodied in the structure are subject to a number of constraints beyond those described for owner-occupied single-family units.

The Capital Improvements Submodel determines the quantity of maintenance capital investment for a particular rental structure by first evaluating the building's construction type. This evaluation process begins by assessing the annual savings in maintenance capital and operating inputs that would result from upgrading the construction type for the quantity of structure services currently being produced by the building; these calculations are performed on a per dwelling unit basis and then aggregated for the structure.

If these calculations indicate that the projected annual savings in operating costs are large enough to justify a change in construction type, the Capital Improvements Submodel examines several other constraints. The first consideration is whether the current and projected levels of neighborhood quality are high enough to warrant the investment necessary to change construction type, based on the same probability matrix that applied to owner-occupied single-family units. In the case of rental structures, however, it is assumed that only a fraction of property owners believe their residence zone will change quality levels; this fraction, which depends on the strength of the projected trends in neighborhood quality, is based on the investor type assigned by the Expectations Submodel to each building.

After the Capital Improvements Submodel has completed the calculations for upgrading construction type, it determines the optimal stock of maintenance capital to produce the quantity of structure services prescribed by the Structure Services Submodel. The quantity of maintenance capital at the start of the period is then subtracted from the estimated optimal capital stock to provide an investment target for the period. If the optimal quantity of maintenance capital is less than the quantity at the start of the period, the excess maintenance capital is simply allowed to depreciate up to a maximum rate of 9 percent for the period. If the optimal quantity of maintenance capital is more than the amount at the start of the period, and if the property owner expects his neighborhood quality to remain unchanged, the Capital Improvements Submodel provides up to one-third of the indicated amount. If the property owner expects his residence zone to decline to a lower quality level, however, he moderates his investment to only a fraction of this amount.

If a building passes the tests outlined above, it is further subject to a cash flow constraint to determine if the current rental income is sufficient to cover existing fixed obligations, current operating expenses, and the improvements. For the cash flow calculation the Capital Improvements Submodel begins with this period's rent for the building and makes a number of subtractions to estimate the amounts available to pay for the improvements in construction type. The calculation first subtracts the annual operating outlays; then an amount to pay the carrying costs on the capital value of the unit; then an amount equal to 3 percent of the structure capital stock to maintain the structure; and, finally, this period's maintenance investment. If the residual cash flow is large enough to pay for the investments in maintenance capital, the improvement is made.

The several investment rules used for the CHIP simulations could be easily adapted if further research indicates that they are inappropriate. Changes in the particular values — the 9 percent depreciation, the one-third of target investment, and the discount for neighborhood decline — require no reprogramming and thus can easily be subjected to sensitivity testing.

Demolition and Abandonment

Demolition and abandonment are the final decisions simulated by the Capital Improvements Submodel. The largest number of demolitions each year results from the destruction of units by fire, by public takings for highways, airports, and other municipal projects, and by other non-market forces. These demolitions are supplied exogenously for each structure type and residence zone. The model then demolishes units of the type indicated on a random basis. The current version of the model has the capability to simulate residential demolitions that result from industrial expansion as well, but their accurate representation requires highly specific geographic data, information on land use regulations, and other factors that are too detailed to include. As a result, these kinds of demolitions are also supplied exogenously for each zone during each simulated year.

A smaller number of demolitions results from market forces that are endogenous to the model. Since we assume that structure capital depreciates at 4.5 percent a year, a few years of neglect will make the building uninhabitable. For the CHIP simulations, if structure capital falls below 50 percent of the quantity embodied in a new building, the Capital Improvements Submodel removes the unit from production. Abandonment occurs when the rental income of a structure no longer covers the unavoidable costs of operating the building. These situations can arise even when the structure contains sufficient structure capital to continue the production of structure services.

Before it determines that a building should be abandoned, the Capital Improvements Submodel evaluates all possible investments in maintenance capital, structure conversions, and changes in construction type. In addition, it first seeks to minimize losses by cutting back to zero investments and expenditures to offset the depreciation of existing structure and maintenance capital. If these options provide a positive cash flow, the buildings will be kept in operation; if, however, the net rental income still remains negative after evaluating all possible investment and disinvestment options, the building will be withdrawn from production. For the CHIP simulations, we assume that such a withdrawal is followed by demolition of the building and the reversion of the site to vacant land. Although it would be possible to hold the vacant building for a period of time, the high level of vandalism and the high costs of securing a vacant building indicate that is is reasonably accurate to assume that abandoning operation is equivalent to permanently removing the building from the available stock.

Taken together, abandonment and demolition decisions complete a complex process in which initial investment is withdrawn from dwelling units in response to unforeseeable events or changes in the pattern of housing demand. The difficulty of removing structures from the market highlights the importance of accurately modeling the expectations of property owners as well as their decisions about conversion and capital improvements. Without a careful specification of each of these aspects of investment behavior, efforts to model the time path of urban development will continue to rest on weak foundations.

Bibliography

Adams, F. G., Grace Milgram, E. W. Green, and C. Mansfield. 1968. Underdeveloped land prices during urbanization: a micro-empirical study over time. *Review of Economics and Statistics,* 50(2):248–258.

Ahlbrant, Roger. 1975. *Preserving neighborhoods.* New York: Praeger.

Alonso, William. 1964. Location and land use. Cambridge, Mass.: Harvard University Press.

——— 1980. The population factor and urban structure. In Arthur P. Solomon, ed., *The prospective city,* pp. 32–51. Cambridge, Mass.: MIT Press.

Altman, James L. 1981. Analysis and comparison of the Mills-Muth urban residential land use simulation models. *Journal of Urban Economics,* 9(3):365–381.

Apgar, William, C., Jr. 1981. *Applications of Annual Housing Survey data in local policy planning.* U.S. Department of Housing and Urban Development, Office of Policy Development and Research.

——— 1984. *The demographic factor and urban decline.* Cambridge, Mass.: Joint Center for Urban Studies of Harvard and MIT, Working Paper W84-2.

Apgar, William C., Jr., and John F. Kain. 1974. Effects of a housing allowance on the Pittsburgh housing market. In John F. Kain, ed., *Progress report on the development of the NBER urban simulation model and interium analyses of housing allowances,* pp. 21–207. New York: National Bureau of Economic Research.

Arnott, Richard J., and James G. MacKinnon. 1977. The effects of the property tax: a general equilibrium analysis. *Journal of Urban Economics,* 4(4):389–407.

Bailey, Martin J. 1959. Notes on the economics of residential zoning and urban renewal. *Land Economics,* 35(3):288–292.

Ball, M. Y. 1973. Recent empirical work on the determinants of relative house prices. *Urban Studies,* 10:213–233.

Barnett, Lance. 1979. Expected and actual effects of housing allowances on housing prices. *American Real Estate and Urban Economics Journal,* 7(3): 277–297.

Batty, Michael. 1970. Some problems in calibrating the Lowry model. *Environment and Planning,* 2:625–636.

—— 1972. Recent developments in land use modelling: a review of British research. *Urban Studies,* 9:151–177.

—— 1979. Paradoxes of science in public policy: the baffling case of land use models. *Sistemi Urbani,* 1:89–123.

Birch, David, Reilly Atkinson, Sven Sandström, and Linda Stock. 1974. *The New Haven laboratory: a test bed for planning.* Lexington, Mass.: Lexington Books.

Birch, David, Eric S. Brown, Richard P. Coleman, Delores W. Da Lomba, William L. Parsons, Linda C. Sharpe, and Sheryll A. Weber. 1977a. *The community analysis model.* U.S. Department of Housing and Urban Development, Office of Policy Development and Research.

—— 1977b. *The behavioral foundations of neighborhood change.* U.S. Department of Housing and Urban Development, Office of Policy Development and Research.

Brewer, G. D. 1973. *Politicians, bureaucrats, and the consultant: a critique of urban problem solving.* New York: Basic Books.

Brown, H. James. 1975. Changes in workplace and residential location. *Journal of the American Institute of Planners,* 41(1):32–39.

Brown, H. James, and John F. Kain. 1972. The choice of housing types made by San Francisco households. In Gregory F. Ingram, John F. Kain, and J. Royce Ginn, *The Detroit prototype of the NBER urban simulation model,* Appendix B. New York: National Bureau of Economic Research.

Brown, H. James, J. Royce Ginn, Franklin J. James, John F. Kain, Mahlon R. Straszheim. 1972. *Empirical models of urban land use: suggestions on research objectives and organization.* New York: National Bureau of Economic Research.

Center for Real Estate and Urban Economics. 1968. *Jobs, people, and land (Bay Area Simulation Study).* Berkeley, Calif.: Center for Real Estate and Urban Economics.

Charles River Associates, Inc. 1972. *A disaggregated behavioral model of urban travel demand.* Cambridge, Mass.

Chicago Area Transportation Study. 1960. *Chicago area transportation study,* vol. 2, Data Projections.

Clay, Phillip L. 1979. *Neighborhood renewal.* Lexington, Mass.: Lexington Books.

Courant, Paul N. 1978. Racial prejudice in a search model of the urban housing market. *Journal of Urban Economics,* 5(3):329–345.

Crecine, J. P. 1964. *Tomm (time oriented metropolitan model).* Pittsburgh: Department of City Planning, CRP Technical Bulletin no. 6.

De Leeuw, Frank. 1971. The demand for housing—a review of the cross section evidence. *Review of Economics and Statistics,* 53(1):1–10.

——— 1973. Time lags in the rental housing market. *Urban Studies,* 10(1): 39–68.

De Leeuw, Frank, and Nkanta F. Ekenem. 1971. The supply of rental housing. *American Economic Review,* 61(5):806–818.

De Leeuw, Frank, and Raymond J. Struyk. 1975. *The web of urban housing: analyzing policy with a market simulation model.* Washington, D.C.: Urban Institute.

Dale-Johnson, David. 1982. An alternative approach to housing market segmentation using hedonic price data. *Journal of Urban Economics,* 2(3):311–332.

Dow building cost calculator and valuation guide. 1970. New York: McGraw-Hill, editions 58 and 161.

Downs, Anthony. 1981. *Neighborhoods and urban development.* Washington, D.C.: Brookings Institution.

Downs, Anthony, and Katharine L. Bradbury. 1980. *Do housing allowances work?* Washington, D.C.: Brookings Institution.

Ellickson, Bryon, Barry Rishman, and Peter Morrison. 1977. *Economic analysis of urban housing markets: a new approach.* Santa Monica, Calif.: RAND Corporation, R-2024-NSF.

Fleisher, Aaron. 1971. Review of *Urban Dynamics,* by Jay W. Forrester. *Journal of the American Institute of Planners,* 37(1):53–54.

Forrester, Jay W. 1969. *Urban dynamics.* Cambridge, Mass.: MIT Press.

Freeman, A. M., III. 1979. The hedonic approach to measuring demand for neighborhood characteristics. In David Segal, ed., *The economics of neighborhood,* pp. 191–217. New York: Academic Press.

Friedmen, Joseph, and Daniel H. Weinberg. 1981. The demand for rental housing: evidence from the housing allowance demand experiment. *Journal of Urban Economics,* 9(3):311–332.

Goldner, William. 1968. *Projective land use model (PLUM).* Berkeley, Calif.: Bay Area Transportation Study Commission, BATSC Technical Report 219.

——— 1971. The Lowry model heritage. *Journal of the American Institute of Planners,* 37(2):100–110.

Grether, D. M., and Peter Mieszkowski. 1978. Determinants of real estate values. *Journal of Urban Economics,* 5:471–484.

Hamburg, John, and Robert H. Sharkey. 1961. Land use forecast: Chicago. Chicago Area Transportation Study.

Hanushek, Eric A., and John M. Quigley. 1979. The dynamics of the housing market: a stock adjustment model of housing consumption. *Journal of Urban Economics,* 6(1):90–112.

Harris, Britton J. 1962a. *Basic assumptions for a simulation of the urban residential housing and land market.* Harrisburg: State Department of Highways, Penn-Jersey Transportation Study.

——— 1962b. *Linear programming and projection of land uses.* Harrisburg: State Department of Highways, Penn-Jersey Transportation Study.

——— 1966. *Research on the equilibrium model of metropolitan housing and locational choice: interim report.* Philadelphia: University of Pennsylvania.

Harrison, David, and John F. Kain. 1977. Cumulative urban growth and urban density functions. *Journal of Urban Economics,* 4(1):104–113.

Hartwick, John M., and Philip G. Hartwick. 1974. Efficient resource allocation in multinucleated city with intermediate goods. *Quarterly Journal of Economics,* 88:340–352.

Haugen, Robert A., and A. Jones Heins. 1969. A market separation theory of rent differentials in metropolitan areas. *Quarterly Journal of Economics,* 83(4):660–672.

Herbert, John, and Benjamin Stevens. 1960. A model for the distribution residential activity in urban areas. *Journal of Regional Science,* 2(2):21–36.

Hill, D. M. 1965. A growth allocation model for the Boston region. *Journal of the American Institute of Planners,* 31:111–120.

Hill, D. M., D. Brand, and W. B. Hansen. 1975. Prototype development of statistical land use predictions model for Greater Boston region. *Highway Research Record,* 114:51–70.

Housing Law Project Bulletin. 1978. HUD's role in the displacement of inner city low income residents.

Ingram, Gregory K. 1971. *A simulation model of an urban housing market.* Ph.D. diss., Harvard University, Cambridge, Mass.

——— 1979. Simulation and econometric approaches to modeling urban areas. In Peter Mieszkowski and Mahlon Straszheim, eds., *Current issues in urban economics,* pp. 130–164. Baltimore: Johns Hopkins University Press.

Ingram, Gregory K., and John F. Kain. 1973. A simple model of housing production and the abandonment problem. *American Real Estate and Urban Economics Association Journal,* 1:79–105.

Ingram, Gregory K., John F. Kain, and J. Royce Ginn. 1972. *The Detroit prototype of the NBER urban simulation model.* New York: National Bureau of Economic Research.

Ingram, Gregory K., Herman B. Leonard, and Robert Schafer. 1976. *Development of the supply sector of the NBER urban simulation model.* Report prepared for the U.S. Department of Housing and Urban Development.

Ingram, Gregory K., and Yitzhak Oron. 1974. A stand-alone supply model for dwelling unit quality. In John F. Kain, ed., *Progress Report,* pp. 296–324. New York: National Bureau of Economic Research.

——— 1977. The production of housing services from existing dwelling units. In Gregory K. Ingram, ed., *Residential location and urban housing markets,* pp. 273–315. Cambridge, Mass.: Ballinger Publishing Co.

James, Franklin. 1977. *Back to the city: an appraisal of housing reinvestment and population change in urban America.* Washington, D.C.: Urban Institute.

——— 1980. Private reinvestment in older housing and older neighborhoods. In Arthur P. Solomon, ed., *The prospective city.* Baltimore: Johns Hopkins University Press.

Kain, John F. 1962. The journey-to-work as a determinant of residential location. *Regional Science Association Papers and Proceedings,* 14.

——— 1967. *Urban sprawl and the costs of urban services.* Harvard University,

Kennedy School of Government, Program in City and Regional Planning, Discussion Paper no. 6.

———— 1968. Housing segregation, negro employment and metropolitan development. *Quarterly Journal of Economics,* 82(2):175–197.

———— ed. 1974. *Progress report on the development of the NBER urban simulation model and interim analyses of housing allowance programs.* New York: National Bureau of Economic Research.

———— 1975. *Essays on urban spatial structure.* Cambridge, Mass.: Ballinger.

———— 1976. Race, ethnicity, and residential location. In Ronald E. Grieson, ed., *Public and urban economics: essays in honor of William S. Vickery,* p. 267–293. Lexington, Mass.: Lexington Books.

———— 1980. A universal housing allowance program. In Anthony Downs and Katherine L. Bradbury, eds., *Do housing allowances work?* pp. 339–365. Washington, D.C.: Brookings Institution.

Kain, John F., and William C. Apgar, Jr. 1976. *Analysis of the market effects of housing allowances.* Harvard University, Kennedy School of Government, Program in City and Regional Planning, Discussion Paper D76-3.

———— 1977. *Simulation of market effects of housing allowances.* Vol. 2, *Baseline and policy simulations for Pittsburgh and Chicago.* Harvard University, Kennedy School of Government, Program in City and Regional Planning, Research Report R77-3.

———— 1979. Simulation of housing market dynamics. *American Real Estate and Urban Economics Association Journal,* 7(4):505–539.

———— 1980. *Some impacts of neighborhood improvement programs.* Harvard University, Kennedy School of Government, Program in City and Regional Planning, Research Report D80-13.

———— 1981. *Market responses to spatially concentrated housing and neighborhood improvement programs.* Harvard University, Kennedy School of Government, Research Report to the Department of Housing and Urban Development.

Kain, John F., William C. Apgar, Jr., and J. Royce Ginn. 1977. *Simulation of the market effects of housing allowances.* Vol. 1, *Description of the NBER urban simulation model.* Harvard University, Kennedy School of Government, Program in City and Regional Planning, Research Report R77-2.

Kain, John F., William C. Apgar, Jr., J. Royce Ginn, and Gregory K. Ingram. 1974. *First interim report on contract to improve the NBER urban simulation model and to use the improved model to analyze housing market abandonment.* New York: National Bureau of Economic Research.

Kain, John F., and John R. Meyer. 1961. *A first approximation to a RAND model for the study of urban transportation.* Santa Monica, Calif.: The RAND Corporation, Memorandum RM-2878-FF.

Kain, John F., and John R. Meyer, 1968. Computer simulations, physio-economic systems and intra-regional models. *American Economic Review,* 58(2):171–187.

Kain, John F., and John M. Quigley. 1972. Housing market discrimination, home ownership, and savings behavior. *American Economic Review*, 62:263 – 277.

———— 1975. *Housing markets and racial discrimination: a microeconomic analysis.* New York: National Bureau of Economic Research.

King, A. 1975. The demand for housing: integrating the roles of journey-to-work, neighborhood quality, and prices. In N. Terleckyj, ed., *Household production and consumption,* pp. 451 – 484. New York: National Bureau of Economic Research.

King, Thomas, and Peter Mieszkowski. 1973. Racial discrimination, segregation, and the price of housing. *Journal of Political Economy,* 81(3):590 – 606.

Lancaster, Kelvin J. 1966. A new approach to consumer theory. *Journal of Political Economy,* 74(April):132 – 157.

Lee, Douglas B. 1973. Requiem for large-scale models. *Journal of the American Institute of Planners,* 39:163 – 178.

Little, Arthur D. 1966. *Community renewal programming.* New York: Praeger.

Lowry, Ira S. 1964. *Model of a metropolis.* Santa Monica, Calif.: RAND Corporation, Memorandum RM-4036-RC.

———— 1967. *Seven models of urban development: a structural comparison.* Santa Monica, Calif.: RAND Corporation, P-3673.

McDonald, John F. 1981. Capital-land substitution in urban housing markets: a survey of empirical estimates. *Journal of Urban Economics,* 9(2):190 – 212.

McFadden, Daniel. 1968. *The revealed preferences of a government bureaucracy.* University of California, Berkeley, Institute of International Studies, Technical Report number 17, Project for Evaluation and Optimization of Economic Growth.

Marshall, Sue A. 1976. *The Urban Institute housing model: application to South Bend, Indiana.* Washington, D.C.: Urban Institute, Working Paper 216-26.

Mayo, Stephen K. 1981. Theory and estimation in the economics of housing demand. *Journal of Urban Economics.* 10(1):95 – 116.

Mills, Edwin S. 1970. Urban density functions. *Urban studies,* 7(1):5 – 20.

———— 1972. *Studies in the structure of the urban economy.* Baltimore: Johns Hopkins University Press.

———— 1978. *A critical evaluation of the community analysis model.* U.S. Department of Housing and Urban Development, Office of Policy Development and Research.

Mills, Edwin S., and J. MacKinnon. 1973. Notes on the new urban economics. *Bell Journal of Economics and Management,* 4(2):593 – 601.

Moffit, Robert. 1977. Metropolitan decentralization and city-suburb wage differentials. *International Regional Science Review,* 2(1):103 – 111.

Mooney, Joseph D. 1969. Housing segregation, Negro employment and metropolitan decentralization: an alternative perspective. *Quarterly Journal of Economics,* 83(2):299 – 311.

Muth, Richard F. 1969. *Cities and housing.* Chicago: University of Chicago Press.

———— 1973. A vintage model of housing stock. *Regional Science Association Papers,* 30:141 – 159.

———— 1974. Numerical solution of urban residential land use models. *Journal of Urban Economics*, 2(4):307–333.

Nelson, Susan C. 1977. Housing, discrimination and job search. In Gregory K. Ingram, ed., *Residential location and urban housing markets*, pp. 329–349. Cambridge, Mass.: Ballinger.

Ohls, James C., and Peter Hutchinson. 1974. Models in urban development. In *A guide to models in governmental planning and operations*, pp. 165–200. Washington, D.C.: Office of Research and Development, Environmental Protection Agency.

Olsen, Edgar. 1969. A competitive theory of the housing market. *American Economic Review*, 59(Sept.):612–622.

Orcutt, Guy. 1957. A new type of socioeconomic system. *Review of Economics and Statistics*, 58:773–797.

———— 1960. Simulation of economic systems. *American Economic Review*, 58:127–138.

Orcutt, Guy, Steven Caldwell, and Richard Wertheimer II. 1976. *Policy exploration through microanalytic simulation*. Washington, D.C.: Urban Institute.

Orcutt, Guy, Martin Greenberger, John Korbal, and Alice Rivlin. 1961. *Microanalysis of socioeconomic systems: a simulation study*. New York: Harper and Row.

Orcutt, Guy, H. W. Watts, and J. B. Edwards. 1968. Data aggregation and information loss. *American Economic Review*, 58:773–787.

Ozanne, Larry, and Raymond J. Struyk. 1976. *Housing from the existing stock: comparative economic analysis of owner-occupants and landlords*. Washington, D.C.: Urban Institute, Working Paper 221–10.

Peterson, George, Arthur P. Solomon, Hadi Madjid, and William C. Apgar, Jr. 1973. *Property taxes, housing and the cities*. Lexington, Mass.: Lexington Books.

Polinsky, A. Mitchell. 1977. The demand for housing: a study in specification and grouping. *Econometrica*, 45(2):447–461.

Polinsky, A. Mitchell, and Steven Shavell, 1978. Amenities and property values in a general equilibrium model of an urban area. *Journal of Public Economics*, 5:241–262.

Putman, Stephen H. 1980. *Integrated policy analysis of metropolitan transportation and location*. Report prepared for the U.S. Department of Transportation, DOT-P-30-80-32.

Quigley, John M. 1972. *The influence of workplaces and housing stocks upon residential choice: a crude test of the gross price hypothesis*. Paper presented at the Toronto meetings of the Econometric Society.

———— 1976. Housing demand in the short run: an analysis of polytomous choice. *Explorations in Economic Research*, 3:76–102.

———— 1979. What have we learned about urban housing markets? In Peter Meiszkowski and Mahlon Straszheim, eds., *Current issues in urban economics*, pp. 391–429. Baltimore: Johns Hopkins University Press.

Quigley, John M., and Daniel H. Weinberg. 1977. Intra-urban residential mobility: a review and synthesis. *International Regional Science Review*, 2(1): 41–66.

Rosen, Sherwin. 1974. Hedonic prices and implicit markets, *Journal of Political Economy*, 82(1):34–56.

Rydell, C. Peter. 1976. Measuring the supply response to housing allowances. *Regional Science Association Papers*, (37):31–53.

Schafer, Robert, William Holshouser, Keith Moore, and Robert Santner. 1975. *Spatial variations in the operating costs of rental housing*. Harvard University, Kennedy School of Government, Program in City and Regional Planning, Discussion Paper D75-4.

Schnare, Ann B., and Raymond J. Struyk. 1976. Segmentation in urban housing. *Journal of Urban Economics*, 3:146–166.

———— 1977. An analysis of ghetto housing prices over time. In Gregory K. Ingram, ed., *Residential location and urban housing markets*, pp. 95–135. Cambridge, Mass.: Ballinger.

Schelling, Thomas C. 1972. The process of residential segregation: neighborhood tipping. In Anthony H. Pascal, ed., *Racial discrimination and economic life*, pp. 157–184. Lexington, Mass.: Lexington Books.

Sepanik, Ronald J., Gary Hendricks, and John D. Heinberg. 1975. *Simulations of national housing allowances: an application of the TRIM model*. Washington, D.C.: Urban Institute, Working Paper no. 216-13.

Sherwin, Roger. 1974. Hedonic prices and implicit markets. *Journal of Political Economy*, 82(1):34–56.

Solow, Robert M. 1972. Congestion, density, and the use of land in transport. *Swedish Journal of Economics*, 1:161–173.

———— 1973. On equilibrium models of urban location. In M. Parkin, ed., *Essays in Modern Economics*, pp. 2–16. London: Longmans, Green.

Steger, William A. 1965. The Pittsburgh urban renewal simulation model. *Journal of the American Institute of Planners*, 31(May):144–150.

Sternlieb, George. 1966. *The tenant landlord*. Brunswick, N.J.: Rutgers University Press.

Straszheim, Mahlon R. 1973. Estimation of the demand for urban housing services from household interview data. *Review of Economics and Statistics*, 55(1):1–8.

———— 1974. Housing market discrimination and black housing consumption. *Quarterly Journal of Economics*, 88(1):19–43.

———— 1975. *An econometric analysis of the urban housing market*. New York: National Bureau of Economic Research.

———— 1980. Discrimination and the spatial characteristics of the urban labor market for black workers. *Journal of Urban Economics*, 7(1):119–140.

Struyk, Ramond J., Sue A. Marshall, and Larry J. Ozanne. 1978. *Housing policies for the urban poor*. Washington, D.C.: Urban Institute.

Sweeney, James L. 1974a. A commodity hierarchy model of the rental housing market. *Journal of Urban Economics*, 1(3):283–323.

———— 1974b. Housing unit maintenance and mode of tenure. *Journal of Economic Theory*, 8(2):111–138.

U.S. Bureau of Census. 1973. *1970 census of population and housing, metropolitan housing characteristics.* Washington, D.C.: U.S. Government Printing Office.

—— 1974. *1970 census of population and housing, components of inventory change.* Washington, D.C.: U.S. Government Printing Office.

Vandel, Kerry, and Bennett Harrison. 1976. *Racial transition in neighborhoods: a simulation model for incorporating institutional constraints.* Cambridge, Mass.: Joint Center for Urban Studies of MIT and Harvard University, Working Paper no. 39.

Vanski, Jan. 1976. The Urban Institute housing model: application to Green Bay, Wisconsin. Washington, D.C.: Urban Institute, Working Paper no. 216-27.

Weicher, John C. 1977. The affordability of new homes. *Journal of the American Real Estate and Urban Economic Association,* 5(Summer):209–241.

Weinberg, Daniel H. 1977. A simultaneous model of intra-urban household mobility. *Explorations in Economic Research,* 4(4):579–592.

Weinberg, Daniel H., Joseph Friedman, and Stephen K. Mayo. 1981. Intra-urban residential mobility: the role of transactions costs, market imperfections, and household disequilibrium. *Journal of Urban Economics,* 9(3):332–349.

Wheaton, William C. 1977. A bid rent approach to housing demands. *Journal of Urban Economics,* 4(2):200–217.

Williams, Roberton C., Jr. 1979. A logit model of demand for neighborhood. In David Segal, ed., *The economics of neighborhood,* pp. 19–41. New York: Academic Press.

Yinger, John. 1979. Prejudice and discrimination in the urban housing market. In Peter Mieszkowski and Mahlon Straszheim, eds., *Current issues in urban economics,* pp. 430–469. Baltimore: Johns Hopkins University Press.

Index

Abandonment: as displacement cause, 111; and CHIP subsidies, 116, 118, 129; NBER study of, 153; in Capital Improvements Submodel, 253–254

Accessibility, 198–199, 204; costs or premiums of, 211–212, 222–225

Ahlbrandt, Roger, 3

Allocation. *See* Targeting

Allowances, housing, 5, 159–162. *See also* EHAP

Alonso, William, 8, 10, 136, 137, 148

Apgar, William C., Jr., 7, 88, 93, 137, 157, 158, 159, 161, 162, 182, 184, 185

Available Units List, 25, 27, 172, 180, 222

Average housing quality, HUDS index of, 10

Ball, M. Y., 9

Barnett, Lance, 160, 161

Baseline: case studies' lack of, 5; and displacement assessment, 110, 130; simulations' lack of, 127

Baseline simulation: Chicago as site of, 29; for household characteristics, 31–34; for housing stock, 34–37; for components of inventory change, 37–41; for spatial distribution of households, 41–43; for neighborhood-quality changes, 43–47; for market rents, 47–48; and mobility, 111–114, 130; evaluation of, 134–135

Basic List, 19–20, 21, 162, 163, 164, 171

Basic List Subroutine, 172, 173, 232

Batty, Michael, 144

Bias, racial. *See* Discrimination markup; Racial discrimination and segregation

Birch, David, 7, 147, 148, 149

Black households: and discrimination, 11, 14–15; in Chicago population, 29, 34; spatial distribution of, 42–43; and housing allowances, 162; and employment, 179. *See also* Discrimination markup; Ghetto neighborhoods; Racial discrimination and segregation

Bradbury, Katharine L., 136, 161

Brand, D., 144

Brewer, G. D., 144, 145

Brown, H. James, 144, 152, 180, 212

Bundle rents, 15–18, 47

CAM (Community Analysis Model), 7, 147–150

Capital, housing: durability of, 4, 8–9, 12–13, 132; and housing services, 12–13; maintenance, 12–13, 25, 200, 233; structure, 12–13, 25–26, 200, 233. *See also* Maintenance capital; Structure capital

Capital grants, and housing market, 4

Capital Improvements Submodel, 25–26, 172, 198, 245, 249–254

Income: of Chicago households, 32–34; and HUDS model, 46, 137–138; effects of changes in, 67, 70, 91; CHIP-I impact on, 73, 75, 100, 124–126, 128, 129; CN/CS impact on, 97–100, 128; and CHIP-I displacement, 121–122; in CHIP simulations overall, 128

Ingram, Gregory K., 7, 150, 153, 158, 159

In-migrants: in New Households Submodel, 22, 182–183; and neighborhood quality, 65, 112; to nontarget neighborhoods, 71; in CHIP-I simulation, 91, 131. *See also* Mobility

Inner city. *See* Central city

Inputs, housing, 199–200. *See also* Construction type; Maintenance capital; Operating inputs; Structure capital

Inventory. *See* Components of inventory change

Investments: constraints on, 13; and CHIP, 63, 67–69, 70, 129, 253; and owners' expectations, 13–14, 66–67, 68; in CHIP-I simulation, 77, 97; in CN/CS simulation, 96–97, 102–103. *See also* Capital, housing

James, Franklin, 4, 136, 137

Job Change Submodel, 22, 138, 157, 172, 175–180, 183

Jobs. *See* Employment; Workplace location

Kain, John F., 4, 7, 8, 9, 14, 15, 17, 88, 93, 143, 150, 152, 154, 158, 159, 160, 161, 162, 179, 184, 185, 212, 228

King, A., 9

King, Thomas, 9

Labor market, and HUDS improvement, 137–138. *See also* Employment

Lancaster, Kelvin J., 8

Land use, and land value, 17

Land Use Submodel, 23–24, 169–170

Land values and prices, 17, 39, 140, 211–214, 230–231

Lee, Douglas B., 144, 145

Leonard, Herman B., 159

Little, Arthur D., 145

Location rents, 16, 17, 27, 227–229, 230

Lot size, 139, 140, 212

Low-income households, 75, 91–92, 122, 129–130. *See also* Displacement; Gentrification

Lowry, Ira S., 143, 144

McFadden, Daniel, 157, 184

Maintenance capital, 12–13, 200, 233; in Capital Improvements Submodel, 25, 26, 249–253; and structure services production function, 57–62, 141, 232, 234–241; and owners' expectations, 68–69; in CHIP-I simulation, 77, 85, 86; and optimal capital stock, 77, 247–248; in CN/CS simulation, 102–103; and efficiency, 247–248; depreciation of, 249

Market, housing: and housing stock, 3–4; and capital grants, 4; modeling of, 8–9, 132; and durability of housing capital, 12–13; submarkets in, 15, 16, 27, 221, 223–224

Market clearing: and quasi-rents, 15; algorithm for, 18, 158, 221; in HUDS and other models, 149

Market rents, 47–48, 140, 227–230, 246

Market Sector, 18, 19, 27–28. *See also specific submodels*

Market Submodel, 25, 27, 157, 194, 221, 222–225

Marshall, Sue A., 7, 145

Meyer, John R., 143, 150, 152

Mieszkowski, Peter, 9, 17

Mills, Edwin S., 149

Mobility, 65; costs of, 3; vs. attachment, 3, 132, 139; and displacement, 73, 75, 110–111, 112, 114; in CHIP-I baseline, 111–114, 130; and HUDS model, 114, 124; CHIP-I effect on, 119, 121–122, 122–124, 131; and HUDS improvement, 139–140. *See also* In-migrants

Moffitt, Robert, 138

Mooney, Joseph D., 179

Mosteller, Frederick, 149

Movers Submodel, 22, 31, 32, 157, 172, 173, 180–182, 186

Muth, Richard F., 8, 10, 15, 146, 148

NBER-HUDS history, 150, 151; phase I (development of Detroit prototype),